Symptom, Symbol, and the Other of Language

Every statement about language is also a statement by and about psyche. Guided by this primary assumption, and inspired by the works of Carl Jung, in *Symptom, Symbol, and the Other of Language*, Bret Alderman delves deep into the symbolic and symptomatic dimensions of a deconstructive postmodernism infatuated with semiotics and the workings of linguistic signs.

This book offers an important exploration of linguistic reference and representation through a Jungian understanding of symptom and symbol, using techniques including amplification, dream interpretation, and symbolic attitude. Focusing on Ferdinand de Saussure, Jacques Derrida, Michel Foucault, and Richard Rorty, Alderman examines the common belief that words and their meaning are grounded purely in language, instead envisioning a symptomatic expression of alienation and collective dissociation. Drawing upon the nascent field of ecopsychology, the modern disciplines of phenomenology and depth psychology, and the ancient knowledge of myth and animistic cosmologies, Alderman dares us to re-imagine some of the more sacrosanct concepts of the contemporary intellectual milieu informed by semiotics and the linguistic turn.

Symptom, Symbol, and the Other of Language is essential reading for academics and students engaged in the study of depth psychology. However, the interdisciplinary approach of the work ensures that it will also be of great interest to those researching and studying in the areas of ethology, ecopsychology, philosophy, linguistics, and mythology.

Bret Alderman graduated from the Pacifica Graduate Institute, Carpinteria, California, in 2013 with a PhD in Depth Psychology. He currently works as a professional freelance translator and editor. He also teaches courses on dreams and the roots of human behavior for the Summer Institute for the Gifted.

Research in Analytical Psychology and Jungian Studies Series

Series Advisor: Andrew Samuels, Professor of Analytical Psychology, Essex University, UK.

The *Research in Analytical Psychology and Jungian Studies* series features research-focused volumes involving qualitative and quantitative research, historical/archival research, theoretical developments, heuristic research, grounded theory, narrative approaches, collaborative research, practitioner-led research, and self-study. The series also includes focused works by clinical practitioners, and provides new research-informed explorations of the work of C. G. Jung that will appeal to researchers, academics, and scholars alike.

Books in this series:

Time and Timelessness
Temporality in the theory of Carl Jung
Angeliki Yiassemides

Apophatic Elements in the Theory and Practice of Psychoanalysis
Pseudo-Dionysius and C.G. Jung
David Henderson

C.G. Jung and Hans Urs von Balthasar
God and evil—a critical comparison
Les Oglesby

Bridges to Consciousness
Complexes and complexity
Nancy M. Krieger

The Alchemical Mercurius
Esoteric symbol of Jung's life and works
Mathew Mather

Archetypal Psychotherapy
The clinical legacy of James Hillman
Jason A. Butler

Jung's Theory of Personality
A modern reappraisal
Clare Crellin

Psychological, Archetypal and Phenomenological Perspectives on Soccer
David Huw Burston

Music as Image
Analytical psychology and music in film
Benjamin Nagari

Laws of Inheritance
A post-Jungian study of twins and the relationship between the first and other(s)
Elizabeth Brodersen

Jung and Levinas
An ethics of mediation
Frances Gray

Symptom, Symbol, and the Other of Language
A Jungian interpretation of the linguistic turn
Bret Alderman

Symptom, Symbol, and the Other of Language

A Jungian interpretation of the linguistic turn

Bret Alderman

Routledge
Taylor & Francis Group
LONDON AND NEW YORK

First published 2016 by Routledge

2 Park Square, Milton Park, Abingdon, Oxfordshire OX14 4RN
711 Third Avenue, New York, NY 10017

Routledge is an imprint of the Taylor & Francis Group, an informa business

First issued in paperback 2017

British Library Cataloguing in Publication Data
A catalogue record for this book is available from the British Library

Library of Congress Cataloging in Publication Data
Alderman, Bret, author.
Symptom, symbol and the other of language : a Jungian interpretation of the linguistic turn / Bret Alderman.
pages cm. — (Research in analytical psychology and jungian studies series)
1. Psycholinguistics. 2. Jungian psychology. I. Title.
BF458.A43 2016
401′.9—dc23
2015029579

ISBN: 978-1-138-92629-5 (hbk)
ISBN: 978-0-8153-5913-5 (pbk)

Typeset in Sabon
by Swales & Willis Ltd, Exeter, Devon, UK

Contents

Acknowledgments

I could not have written this book without the insight and encouragement of many people. I am especially grateful to Alexandra Fidyk, Susan Rowland, and Rinda West who closely supervised the doctoral dissertation from which this book has been prepared. Each, in her own way, engaged this project with both discernment and care. To Alex, in particular, I am deeply grateful. Early on in this years-long endeavor, she heard the murmurings of a nascent voice struggling to articulate itself and helped foster its fullest expression with healthy measures of enthusiasm and expertise. I would also like to extend my most genuine thanks to Chris Fiset, whose perceptive reading encouraged a boldness of expression that greatly benefited the work. I am likewise thankful to Karen Hyatt, whose careful attention significantly improved these pages, and whose friendship I truly cherish. My most genuine thanks go to the entire intellectual community of the Pacifica Graduate Institute, without which this work could not have come to fruition. The encouragement, warmth, and intelligence of both faculty and students have helped me through many crucial junctures in both my creative process and intellectual evolution. I would like to acknowledge, in particular, Robert Romanyshyn, Edward Casey, and Glen Slater. To Robert I feel especially indebted: Much of his genius enlivens this writing, and his enthusiastic reception of its initial conception greatly inspired me as the work progressed. Finally, I would like to acknowledge David Abram, Andy Fisher, and Paul Kugler, who all offered valuable feedback as this work began to emerge and whose voices have greatly informed it.

Introduction

This book is a work of mythopoetic imagination. Its intent is to manifest a symbolic attitude, or symbolic thinking. Such a form of thought arises from what Jung called a *spirit of the depths*, one that he contrasted with a *spirit of the times* (Jung & Shamdasani, 2012). The latter often alienates us from the former, making symbolic thinking seem strange and incomprehensible, irrational and aberrant. The spirit of the times seeks a solar clarity that would illuminate every crevice. It desires to split open everything that can be opened, from human bodies to atoms, and shed light upon what it finds. Yet in its passion for illumination, it can blind us with its light. This spirit, one of heroic mastery and ascent, desires to articulate with absolute rational lucidity all that it discerns, yet what it perceives is merely the outer surface of things. It is this spirit that must be sacrificed if symbolic thinking is to be embraced and we are to heed the beckoning call of the depths. What exactly this symbolic approach entails in relation to *the linguistic turn* will reveal itself as this work unfolds, but it is perhaps best to begin with a simple declaration of principle: *Statements about language, semiotics, and the workings of linguistic signs are also statements by and about psyche.* This is the primary assumption of the book that you are holding, or the text illuminating the screen before you. What it means is that, in the pages to follow, I will not merely address what a given set of theorists explicitly says, but also, more importantly, what their theoretical statements might express about the collective psyche of which they form a part.

Such an approach is not only Jungian, but also subtly subversive, insofar as it shamelessly reads between the lines and steadfastly refuses to take linguistic theories at face value. On the contrary, my intent is to address precisely what such theories not only do not say, but perhaps cannot say, by virtue of their own assumptions and methods, premises and postulates. It is my hope that an approach such as this, one deeply rooted in depth psychology, but also, more importantly, rooted in the depths of the imaginative psyche itself, might perceive the linguistic turn in a way that the linguistic turn itself cannot. If it does, in fact, manage to do this, it is by daring, as the late James Hillman (1975) would have it, to locate the discussion of ideas, not in the realm of thought, but in the realm of psyche. Relocating the discussion of language, semiotics, and linguistic signs within the realm of psyche recognizes that there are always complex symbolic, symptomatic, and mythic elements to this discussion. Complexes, symbols, symptoms, myths, and archetypes have a way of appearing in the most curious of guises. Of those guises, perhaps the least explored and most curious are those of epistemologies and their methods. Shared neuroses speak through symptom and symbol as they manifest in our ways of knowing, our approaches, and research orientations. The complex projection that is symptom, the symptomatic projection that is complex, and the complex symptom that is projection all speak a language of metaphors forgotten. In the words of Robert Romanyshyn (2007), "symptoms are unconscious metaphors. This is so for individuals, cultures, and epistemologies" (p. 213). To understand statements about language, semiotics, and the workings of linguistic signs as statements by and about psyche requires that we attend to images in ideas and symptomatic dimensions in abstractions. To return the discussion of ideas to the realm of psyche requires that we see myths in postulates and archetypes in arguments. Such a return of ideas to their psychic ground is important, and even necessary, because it allows their more fully human provenance to be acknowledged.

It is the nature of symbols that their meaning can never be exhausted (Jung & de Laszlo, 1993). Put differently, once a symbol has been thoroughly interpreted, if such a thing is even possible, it ceases to be a symbol. The well of symbolic meaning is bottomless, and there are always more images, metaphors, and similes to be drawn from it. The symbolic attitude, then, must always allow for an element of the unknown and the ambiguous, just as it allows for a plurality of meanings attaching themselves to a single image, motif, or idea. It is with such an understanding in mind that Jung construes the symbolic vis-à-vis theory: Because all theories contain hypotheses, they also designate something essentially unknown, and therefore have a symbolic element. In fact, every psychological phenomenon, "is a symbol when we are willing to assume that it purports or signifies something different and still greater, something therefore which is withheld from present knowledge" (Jung & de Laszlo, 1993, p. 344). Every psychological phenomenon—and this includes the realms of theories, hypotheses, and epistemologies—can be seen as a symbol, when it is understood to purport more than its ostensive meaning.

There is ample precedence for such a symbolic approach in Jung's psychology, in particular his work on medieval alchemy. For Jung, what the alchemist sees in matter was first and foremost qualities and meanings, the psychic nature of which he or she was entirely unaware (Jung, 1944/1968). Likewise, what the theorist of language sees in its workings, as ostensibly belonging to it, may be qualities and meanings of which he or she remains ignorant. What the semiotician believes to constitute the "data" of sign systems may, from another perspective, be seen as the "data" of something else entirely.

In approaching the linguistic turn in this way, with symbol and symptom in mind, my primary intent is not to articulate an argument for, or against, any particular theorist or school of thought. *Primary* is the key word here, for there is a philosophical intent to this book, yet it is not a sustained attempt to systematically dismantle or defend, undermine or champion, one linguistic theory over another through the establishment of premises and the extrapolation of logical conclusions. Such a work would not be properly depth psychological. Rather, what I am attempting is more akin to a dream analysis that musters what, in Jung's psychology, are the four primary modes of consciousness that humans possess: thinking, feeling, sensing, and intuiting (Hillman &Von Franz, 1986; Jung, 1921/1971). What I attempt in this book is a demonstration of method, a display of how a researcher might take a set of abstract ideas, amplifying and interpreting their denotations and connotations as if they were images in a dream. This is what Jung did. He used such dream interpretive techniques as *amplification* to decipher opaque religious manuscripts of the Orient, as well as Gnostic and alchemical tomes of centuries past (Clarke, 1994; Jung, 1960/1969, 1959/1969). Even scientific texts were not outside the purview of his symbolic mode of interpretation because he read them in the same way that he read dreams.

Imagine now a single affirmation in various guises: Words do not refer to things; language is completely self-referential; the transcendental signified is always absent. Such conceptions of linguistic reference have become widely accepted by many prominent post-structuralist, deconstructionist, and neo-pragmatist thinkers who form part of the linguistic turn, such as Michel Foucault (1973), Jacques Derrida (1976), and Richard Rorty (1979). A persistent image in their writings has been that of language as insular, self-enclosed, and divorced from, or only dubiously related to, its other—whether this 'other' is termed an extra-linguistic referent, a transcendental signified, or by any other nomenclature. It is this image of linguistic insularity, this question of linguistic reference that is the primary symbol of the dream interpreted in these pages. This book is an attempt to understand this image—and more broadly, a certain postmodern textualist focus—with symptom and symbol in mind, in the belief that, as a manifestation of psyche, it says much more than it intends.

It is here, upon the specific issue of reference, that this book revolves because it represents something analogous to what the great Russian actor and theatre director Constantin Stanislavski meant by a *through line*. A through line is needed for an actor's performance to cohere. It is the main purpose of his or her actions, their inner content, and the entirety of his or her performance—every nuance of expression, inflection of tone, pregnant pause, and expressive movement—should be subordinated to it. The through line is the profound organic tie that unites every thought, detail, and action of the actor's portrayal of his or her character (Moore, 1984). The question of reference is something like the through line of the linguistic turn. It is the organic tie that unites a great multiplicity of its adherents and a great multiplicity of the debates that it has inspired. This through line explains, as if by ellipsis, and with a maximal economy of expression, a good deal of the inner content of the turn which, in a very real sense, is subordinated to this question of how words relate to things, of how language relates to its other. This book interprets this through line, primarily, as it appears in four figures in particular: Ferdinand de Saussure, Michel Foucault, Jacques Derrida, and Richard Rorty. It does this in lieu of addressing the turn *in toto*, or a broad range of the thinkers that write under its auspices. Yet it does so in full knowledge that this same line, this same organic tie, can be recognized in multiple figures and configurations: It is there in Nietzsche's (Nietzsche & Ludovici, 1924) transvaluation of values, Lacan's (Lacan & Fink, 2006) reconfiguration of Freudian desire, Lyotard's (1983) notion of the *differend*, and even Butler's (2006) understanding of gender as performativity, to name but a few of its incarnations.

As actor upon the stage of twentieth and twenty-first-century thought, the linguistic turn has played a formidable dramatic role, and can rightly be described as a primary protagonist. Coined in 1953 by Gustav Bergmann, the phrase *the linguistic turn* was popularized by Rorty's publication in 1967 of an anthology by that same name (Neal, 2007). This coinage has come to allude to a pervasive shift in Western philosophy, humanities, and social sciences: Beginning in the early teens of the twentieth century, there was a growing acceptance of the idea that language, rather than merely *describing* or *reflecting* the world, *formed* it (Levenson, 2011). Influenced by the Nietzschean conception of language as an army of metaphors, the turn focused intently upon the heretofore neglected role of language in *constructing* our world and *creating* or *making* sense of it (Reason & Bradbury, 2006). The intellectual forefathers of this turn, however, pre-date Nietzsche, the first of them in the modern era being, arguably, the English philosopher John Locke (Losonsky, 2006). Yet its lineage can be traced further still, for Locke himself retained important links with the nominalist heritage of the medieval philosopher William of Occam (Stamos, 2003), a heritage that Jung was well aware of and addressed in his work *Psychological Types* (1921/1971).

Yet it was not until the early twentieth century, with such thinkers as Saussure, Wittgenstein, Heidegger, and others, that the focus on the formative power of language came to form a widely acknowledged 'turn' (Levenson, 2011). With growing influence, this focus has profoundly affected the entire intellectual milieu of a variety of disciplines, and many writers see it as being essential to, and, in part, generative of, the postmodern ethos, with its skeptical stance towards grand meta-narratives, and suspicion of essentialism and philosophical universals (Fairlamb, 1994; Gendlin & Kleinberg-Levin, 1997; Reason & Bradbury, 2006). Painted in the broadest of strokes and with primary colors, this ethos pictures a world in which language cannot reflect a reality outside of itself, but can only reflect the historical, cultural, and linguistic predispositions of the language user. Therefore, there are no criteria for knowing what phenomena are like, independent of the knowledge of how words are used, and there can be no way to evaluate the accuracy of descriptions (Rorty, 1979). Since our experience is always mediated by language, which is itself a product of our particular culture and moment in history, there are no truth claims that can be said to transcend this cultural, historical, and linguistic context (Brandom, 2000). What counts as true or valid is more a product of existing consensus-based habit than how any given claim might correspond to an actual state of affairs (Norris, 1996). Language, disengaged from a referent, cannot accurately represent anything: neither universal constants in nature, nor minute, intimate human particulars. The resultant worldview is a profoundly relativistic one in which no perspective can rightly claim more validity than any other (Dillon, 1995). Because we cannot view, from the outside as it were, our own sets of assumptions, or even the assumptions of others within our linguistic community, there is really little way to adjudicate among questions of truth. What goes by the name of truth, or regimes of truth, is the product of transient institutionalized power differentials (Foucault & Gordon, 1980). What appeared, in ages prior, to be the universal attributes of human nature, or even the nature of reality itself are, more properly speaking, constructs, *nomina*. We play language games, and although some may be more adept than others at such games, marshaling words with impressive rhetorical acumen, these words cannot speak to a truth beyond the very language from which they arose. They cannot be grounded in anything like *reality* or *phenomena*, *nature* or *essence* that transcends the descriptions themselves.

The question of reference, the question of how language relates to its other, is the lynchpin of the wheel upon which the aforementioned ideas turn. It is the node, or point of intersection, where they all meet. Such ideas still ripple throughout contemporary intellectual life and have far-ranging ethical, political, and epistemic implications. For this very reason, the question of reference contains the potential for radical disclosure. If we imagine the linguistic turn as a psychological complex and, as Jung (1983) thought, that each complex has at its very core an archetypal pattern—one that constitutes the nub of meaning and source of energy of that complex, as well as its curative potential—then reference is something like the archetypal core of the linguistic turn. Tending to this core, drawing parallels to it from myth, art, and philosophy, letting it play upon our imagination, amplifying its intuited sense, and fleshing out its perceived implications—in short, doing all that one would do to gain a better sense of the archetype hidden within the complex—we not only heal it, but allow it to heal us. Much has been made of the *crisis* of representation in the social sciences, a crisis intimately related to the linguistic turn (Flick, 2009; Reason & Bradbury, 2006; Richardson & St. Pierre, 2005). At the heart of this crisis is the doubt that social science researchers can in any way capture lived experience. Any linking of experience and text has been rendered problematic (Denzin & Lincoln, 2005). Construing linguistic reference in terms of symptom, symbol, complex, and archetype, while bringing to bear the insights of Jungian and post-Jungian psychology upon this crisis, can only serve to help resolve it and move beyond the impasse that it represents.

Like many disciplines in the social sciences and humanities, depth psychology has been profoundly influenced by the linguistic turn. To the extent that this is the case, within depth psychology there has been a concomitant recognition of the relativity of this discipline's own truth claims, with attention given to the social construction of knowledge, a suspicion of meta-narratives and universals, and a skepticism in regards to any description of human nature. Yet it would be hard to argue that depth psychologists, or more specifically, Jungians and post-Jungians, have formed an in-depth or substantive response *to* the linguistic turn. Writers like Paul Kugler (1982, 1997, 2005), Christopher Hauke (2000), and Michael Vannoy Adams (1992) have made important contributions in this area. These authors set Jungian and post-Jungian psychologies next to more postmodern, semiotically oriented approaches and elucidate important parallels and differences. But there is no extensive body of Jungian or post-Jungian literature that subjects the *thematic content* of the linguistic turn to an analysis that is specifically depth psychological, none that heeds the call of Hillman's entreaty to return ideas to their psychic ground. Such an analysis would involve understanding by way of *symbols*, *symptoms*, *complexes*, *archetypes*, and *archetypal images*, concepts that are the clear province of Jungian and post-Jungian thought. There is no such body of literature that asks what dream is being dreamt, or if there are any perennial psychological attitudes at play in the basic assumptions, ideas, and theoretical speculations of the turn. Nor is there a substantial body of literature that attempts to discern something of the turn's symbolic and symptomatic dimensions. Notable exceptions to this absence include the work of Susan Rowland (2005, 2006a, 2006b), and Stanton Marlan (2005). Their contributions are invaluable insofar as they seek to make intelligible something of the symbolic import of the turn. Susan Rowland offers a nuanced, complex, and provocative reading of post-structuralism and deconstruction, framing them in terms of sky-father and earth-mother mythologies. Stanton Marlan offers an imaginative and lucid reading of Derrida in terms of alchemical symbolism. Derrida, however, is not Marlan's primary focus, and relatively few pages of his work are dedicated to the man who coined the term *deconstruction*.

A Jungian interpretation of the linguistic turn is long overdue, one that arises from a spirit of the depths and manifests a symbolic mode of thought—one that is willing to find myth even in the rarefied air of ideas, and discern fantasy even in the most abstruse of theories. Such a symbolic attitude is grounded in the knowledge that it is the appearance of these ideas and theories in the psyche, "their significance as psychic events, their psychological effect and reality as experiences relevant for soul, that demand our attention as psychologists" (Hillman, 1975, p. 121).

References

Adams, M. V. (1992). Deconstructive philosophy and imaginal psychology: Comparative perspectives on Jacques Derrida and James Hillman. In *Jungian literary criticism* (pp. 231–48) Evanston, IL: Northwestern University Press.

Brandom, R. (2000). *Rorty and his critics*. Malden, MA: Blackwell Publishers.

Butler, J. (2006). *Gender trouble: Feminism and the subversion of identity*. New York, NY: Routledge.

Clarke, J. J. (1994). *Jung and Eastern thought: A dialogue with the Orient*. New York, NY: Routledge.

Denzin, N. K., & Lincoln, Y. S. (2005). Introduction and epilogue. In *The Sage handbook of qualitative research* (3rd ed., pp. 1–32, 1115–26). Thousand Oaks, CA: Sage.

Derrida, J. (1976). *Of grammatology*. Baltimore, MD: Johns Hopkins University Press.

Dillon, M. C. (1995). *Semiological reductionism: A critique of the deconstructionist movement in postmodern thought*. Albany, NY: State University of New York Press.

Fairlamb, H. L. (1994). *Critical condition: Postmodernity and the question of foundations*. Cambridge, England: Cambridge University Press.

Flick, U. (2009). *An introduction to qualitative research* (4th edn.). Los Angeles, CA: Sage Publications.

Foucault, M. (1973). *The order of things: An archaeology of the human sciences*. New York, NY: Vintage Books.

Foucault, M., & Gordon, C. (1980). *Power/knowledge: Selected interviews and other writings, 1972–1977*. Brighton, England: Harvester Press.

Gendlin, E. T., & Kleinberg-Levin, D. M. (1997). *Language beyond postmodernism: Saying and thinking in Gendlin's philosophy*. Evanston, IL: Northwestern University Press.

Hauke, C. (2000). *Jung and the postmodern: The interpretation of realities*. Philadelphia, PA: Routledge.

Hillman, J. (1975). *Re-visioning psychology*. New York, NY: Harper & Row.

Hillman, J. & Von Franz, M.-L. (1986). *Lectures on Jung's typology*. Dallas, TX: Spring.

Jung, C. G. (1921/1971). *Psychological types*. Princeton, NJ: Princeton University Press.

Jung, C. G. (1944/1968). *Psychology and alchemy* (2nd edn.). Princeton, NJ: Princeton University Press.

Jung, C. G. (1959/1969). Aion: Researches into the phenomenology of the self. In R. F. C. Hull (Trans.), *The collected works of C. G. Jung* (Vol. 9). Princeton, NJ: Princeton-Bollingen (original work published 1959).

Jung, C. G. (1960/1969). *The structure and dynamics of the psyche* (2nd ed.). Princeton, NJ: Princeton University Press (original work published 1960).

Jung, C. G. (1983). *The essential Jung* (A. Storr, Ed.). Princeton, NJ: Princeton University Press.

Jung, C. G., & De Laszlo, V. S. (1993). *The basic writings of C. G. Jung* (Modern Library edn.). New York, NY: Modern Library.

Jung, C. G., & Shamdasani, S. (2012). *The red book: A reader's edition*. New York, NY: W. W. Norton & Co.

Kugler, P. (1982). *The alchemy of discourse: An archetypal approach to language.* Lewisburg, PA: Bucknell University Press.

Kugler, P. (1997). Psychic imaging: A bridge between subject and object. In P. Young-Eisendrath & T. Dawson (Eds.), *The Cambridge companion to Jung* (pp. 71–85). New York: Cambridge University Press.

Kugler, P. (2005). *Raids on the unthinkable: Freudian and Jungian psychoanalyses.* New Orleans, LA: Spring Journal Books.

Lacan, J., & Fink, B. (2006). *Ecrits: The first complete edition in English.* New York, NY: W.W. Norton & Co.

Levenson, M. H. (2011). *The Cambridge companion to modernism.* New York, NY: Cambridge University Press.

Losonsky, M. (2006). *Linguistic turns in modern philosophy.* New York, NY: Cambridge University Press.

Lyotard, J. F. (1983). *Le différend.* Paris, France: Editions de Minuit.

Marlan, S. (2005). *The black sun: The alchemy and art of darkness.* College Station, TX: Texas A & M University Press.

Moore, S. (1984). *The Stanislavski system: The professional training of an actor : digested from the teachings of Konstantin S. Stanislavski* (2nd rev. edn.). New York, NY: Penguin Books.

Neal, A. (2007). *How skeptics do ethics: A brief history of the late modern linguistic turn.* Calgary, Canada: University of Calgary Press.

Nietzsche, F. W., & Ludovici, A. M. (1924). *The will to power, an attempted transvaluation of all values.* New York, NY: The Macmillan company.

Norris, C. (1996). *Reclaiming truth: Contribution to a critique of cultural relativism.* Durham, NC: Duke University Press.

Reason, P., & Bradbury, H. (Eds.). (2006). *Handbook of action research: Concise paperback edition.* Thousand Oaks, CA: Sage.

Richardson, L., & St. Pierre, E. A. (2005). Writing: A method of inquiry. In N. K. Denzin & V. S. Lincoln (Eds.), *The Sage handbook of qualitative research* (3rd edn., pp. 959–78). Thousand Oaks, CA: Sage.

Romanyshyn, R. (2007). *The wounded researcher: Research with soul in mind.* New Orleans, LA: Spring Journal Books.

Rorty, R. (1979). *Philosophy and the mirror of nature.* Princeton, NJ: Princeton University Press.

Rowland, S. (2005). *Jung as a writer.* New York, NY: Routledge.

Rowland, S. (2006a). Jung and Derrida: The numinous, deconstruction and myth. In A. Casement & D. J. Tacey (Eds.), *The idea of the numinous: Contemporary Jungian and psychoanalytic perspectives* (pp. 98–116). New York, NY: Routledge.

Rowland, S. (2006b). Nature writing: Jung's eco-logic in the coniunctio of comedy and tragedy. *Spring: A Journal of Archetype and Culture: Psyche and Nature, 75*, 275–97.

Stamos, D. N. (2003). *The species problem: Biological species, ontology, and the metaphysics of biology.* Lanham, MD: Lexington Books.

Chapter 1

Anatomical bodies

Fleshing out the image of linguistic reference

Of linear perspective vision and two types of bodies

Imagine this: A young Flemish anatomist, Andreas Vesalius, gently slices into a female cadaver. His incision reveals a tripartite sternum, thereby disproving the classical Greek belief that the sternum was composed of seven separate, yet connected, bones. It is 1543, the year that Copernicus died, after having sent the earth in motion around the sun. Vesalius is one of very few people in centuries to cut into human flesh in this way (Ball, 1910). Before this incision upon a female breast, dead bodies were not dissected, but commemorated, not de-membered, but re-membered. But with Vesalius, a scalpel cuts into human ligament and bone, tendon and cartilage, fibrous tissue and blood vessel, and with every carving motion of his incisive blade, the bodies of the deceased acquire a different meaning: Cadavers, as objects of study, no longer bear any relation to the souls of the departed. The corpse is invented—whereas before dead human bodies memorialized these souls, and the living related with empathy and respect to the stilled bodies of the dead, refraining, even criminalizing, incisions made upon them, with Vesalius the dead become inert material to be displayed and dissected, mapped and measured. They become *anatomical* bodies, the objects of a new science of human structure (Romanyshyn, 2004).

In this year, Vesalius will publish the first edition of his classic work *Fabrica*. Less than a century later, Descartes is to write his seminal *Meditations on First Philosophy* (Descartes & Tweyman, 2002). The former inaugurated the age of modern anatomy, of which he is widely considered to be the father. The latter birthed modern philosophy and one of its more trenchant dualisms, that of *res cogitas* and *res extensa*, or mind cleaved from matter.

In *Technology as Symptom and Dream* (2004), Robert Romanyshyn describes the invention of the corpse, the birth of the anatomical body, as part of a much larger process of cultural evolution involving a new, modern sense of self as detached spectator, and the body as spectacle and specimen. Born of the Renaissance, and having come of age in the Enlightenment, this new anatomical conception of the body arose from a zeitgeist of scientific rationality that finds full expression today in the technical expertise of the specialist, as well as the technological innovations that surround us—from smart phones to infrared scanners, nuclear bombs to nanobots, microchips to MRIs. It is an understanding of the body as an object to be opened, manipulated, diagramed, dissected, and explained. It differs greatly from the medieval understanding of the body that was revered even in death, a sacralized body, the postmortem evisceration of which could only be understood as irreverent and profane. The profanation lay in the fact, or belief, that even dead human bodies were imbued of soul, imbued of *anima*. Cutting into them, therefore, could only be a desecration and violation.

Now, another image: The year is 1911—well over three hundred years after the founding of modern anatomy. The place is a lecture hall at the University of Geneva. Ferdinand de Saussure is giving one of his now-celebrated lectures on linguistic structure, lectures that, once collected and reassembled from the notes of his students, will be published as the *Course in General Linguistics*. This work will not only revolutionize Saussure's own field, but will form the primary impetus for structuralism, an intellectual movement that exerts a formidable influence on the humanities and social sciences to this day. Copernican in its implications, Saussure's linguistics in many ways represents as radical a change in modern thought as the shift from a geocentric to a heliocentric cosmology. Just as Vesalius, Copernicus, and Descartes serve as historical signposts indicating the advent of a new zeitgeist, so does Saussure—his work helped form the ideological foundations for many postmodern modes of inquiry, including deconstruction and post-structuralism, but also, beyond this, it helped set the foundations for a more general postmodern ethos and sensibility.

A blackboard stands behind the middle-aged Swiss professor whose thick dark mustache virtually covers his entire mouth. On the blackboard is an oval traced in chalk with the French word for *sign* written above it. The oval itself is divided into two halves by a horizontal line. Above the line is the word *concept*, and below it, *sound pattern*. The distinguished gentlemen states in a ponderous yet emphatic tone, that "a science which studies linguistic structure is not only able to dispense with other elements of language, but is possible only if those other elements are kept separate" (Saussure, Bally, Sechehaye, & Riedinger, 1986, p. 14).

The two images, that of the sixteenth-century anatomist, and that of the twentieth-century linguist, appear to share little in common. Yet to an imagination imbued of symbolic vision, they have much more in common than what might first be supposed. Both form part of the same process of cultural evolution involving a new, modern sense of self as detached spectator, and the body as spectacle and specimen. A similar sense of self has been described in terms of a Cartesian split—the aforementioned dualism that divides the world into a *res cogitas* or mind and a *res extensa* or matter, including the body (Bordo, 1987). Many writers from a variety of disciplines (Berman, 1981; Brooke, 1991; Johnstone, 1992; Kleinberg-Levin, 1988; Spretnak, 1999) have told similar stories of estrangement in which a mind observes an object-body while a more viscerally felt body is implicitly omitted, or pejoratively reduced to something merely subjective. All tell tales of a mind purged of body and a body purged of blood.

The images of Vesalius and Saussure form chapters in this same overarching story of estrangement, in all of its various iterations, an estrangement brought about by a growing distance between two types of bodies: the anatomical body and the animate, ensouled body. Saussure's role as protagonist of this story is particularly relevant here because, in the years since his lectures were delivered, they have also become a seminal influence upon a variant of postmodern thought that undermines the referential aspect of language, the sense in which words might refer to, and reveal, things and phenomena. In so doing, this new school of thought calls into question the very possibility that the language we speak and write can be used to accurately portray any reality beyond itself (Alexander, 1995; Norris, 1990). Understood as such, Saussure's work represents a significant step in the severing of language from its other—a process by which many have come to understand human communication as taking place within a self-enclosed system of signs that has little or no relation to anything beyond, that is to say, anything transcendent to itself.

Let these two images play upon your imagination as you read the pages to follow: that of Vesalius standing before a corpse to inaugurate a science of human structure, and Saussure standing before a chalkboard to inaugurate a science of human signs. By way of these images, I intend to interpret a dream, one that is also a cultural-historical-psychological disposition within which we still very much find ourselves today as heirs to Vesalius, Descartes, Copernicus, and the scientific-technological rationalism that they helped create. The two images form both primary associations of this dream, and attempts to amplify its meaning.

Amplification and *association* are means by which Jung practiced a symbolic attitude that balances reason with imagination. Amplification is a more rational (though by no means comprehensive) description of the meaning of a dream image. Association is useful, in turn, when one is too bound to rational thought, when a person's fantasy has been stifled by a scrutinizing intellect that will not allow for the spontaneous associations that appeal to our felt, intuitive sense of a situation (Whitmont, 1969). Both amplification and association are needed to adequately apprehend symbols. Both are needed to have a symbolic attitude. In these pages, I attempt to write with this symbolic attitude, that is to say, to weave the intuitive development of image with the rational argument of idea.

To this end, I want to flesh out (pun intended) these two bodies—the anatomical and the ensouled. The German language is blessed with a terminological distinction lacking in English that may help us in this regard: The word *körper* refers to the physical, material body, extended in space and visible to the eye. *Leib*, in turn, is something a bit more subtle and elusive. It is most often translated into English as the *lived* or *living* body (Aho & Aho, 2008). It is not an object, but an experiential subject. The cold cadaver beneath Vesalius' scalpel is not a living body, not *leib*. It is *körper*. It is an anatomical body, one of technical function, an object, an epithelial container of an interior space filled with organs. The difference between this body and the animate or ensouled body is perhaps most clearly and poignantly brought to the fore by way of a kiss, or, more precisely, by an exploration of two very different ways of understanding kisses. When the body as technical function kisses another such body, "a rush of neurochemical processes initiated by pressure contact between two pairs of mucous membranes" occurs (Romanyshyn, 2004, p. 9). Your average Don Juan, doting mother, or celibate cenobite knows nothing of such a kiss; there is no insatiate eroticism, no lavish affection, no chaste longing by which each, in turn, might identify their own sense of what a kiss is. Such coupling of mucous membranes communicates little of the *lived experience* of any kiss, or any kisser. Yet the description is accurate. Kisses do, in fact, involve neurological processes and the meeting of mucous membranes, regardless of whether they are tentative and fleeting, decisively plucked, or coyly granted. The description is *technically* (or one might even say technologically) accurate, which is to say that it is accurate according to a particular style of vision, and a particular understanding of what is real and relevant. Within a given frame, the statement could not be more true.

I am not choosing the metaphor of a *frame* gratuitously. Framing, by way of the mathematical coordinates of linear perspective, is *the* cultural habit of mind that makes possible such an anatomical vision of the body. This artistic technique that sees by way of a geometric grid has become the cultural vision, the epistemology, that has come to form our contemporary technological world (Romanyshyn, 2004). Unknown before the fifteenth century, such a technique often involved the setting up of a frame between the painter and the object to be portrayed. The frame was divided by threads into small squares so that a grid was formed, through which the artist viewed a geometrically divided scene. This technique created a certain geometric sense of space: The establishment of vanishing points and horizon lines, the drawing of squares to be divided and subdivided, and the determination of a fixed vantage point, produced the illusion of a level plane that disappears in the distance. This plane was measurable and quantifiable. In the space that it created, we humans of the present era now live. We have come to see by way of this geometrically sectioned framing, and we have come to live by seeing.

The consequences of such a framing are formidable. Every procedure and condition involved in the creation of linear perspective has its implications: The establishment of a vanishing point necessitates the creation of a window which separates the subject as spectator from the object as spectacle. This separation eclipses the living, animate body insofar as it de-emphasizes the senses of hearing, touch, taste, and smell in favor of the sense of sight. The world, held at a distance made evident by the separating frame, becomes a mere matter of optics (Brooke, 1991; 2000). The location of a vanishing point—no higher than any figure to be depicted in the painting—creates the sense that all objects lie on a single uniform plane, implying a certain "erasure of differences so that things, like angels and demons, which belong to other levels of existence, become a subjective matter" (Romanyshyn, 2004, p. 54).

Pinpointed and focused, this style of vision stares straight ahead at the world and seeks to penetrate the depths *out there*. The creation of a fixed distance point, intended to be the viewpoint of the spectator, implies the static, almost inert, character of this spectator. In being placed directly opposite the vanishing point, it also creates an ideal space of potentially infinite vision. These procedures and conditions, in their attention to the world as a question of optics, create a vision that measures by way of quantifiable distances, spatial proportions, angles, and configurations. In ages prior, or in any form of painting that does not share this particular sensibility, the size of figures might be determined by their relative significance; an important personage like the Virgin Mary might appear to be three or four times larger than any other human figure in her surroundings. This was not intended to communicate that the mother of God suffered from gigantism, had hormonal issues, or lived amidst dwarves. Her measure upon the canvas was simply not metric. Her size could be perceived by the eye, but was not solely determined by it. She did not belong to a geometric space. Her measure was of importance or value. It sprang from an imagination informed by something more than the eye. Her size upon the canvas was brought forth by a more fully human engagement with her image that includes those other "levels of existence" that have become merely a subjective matter, according to the logic of linear perspective and scientific-technological rationality. In linear perspective vision, the size of a figure is determined solely by what the eye can see. It is the eye's perception alone that matters. Seeing in this way, we come to discount the "living relation between our flesh and the flesh of the world, and both size and distance as indices of value are eclipsed by size and distance as measured functions" (Romanyshyn, 2004, p. 56).

Through this vision, the corpse is conceived, for the anatomical body is a spectacle *out there*. This body is to be seen but not listened to, not tasted, not smelled, and touched only as needed. It is not the body *through* which one sees, but it is something that can be looked at. It does not feel. It cannot dream or desire. Because it is without sentience, it is not a *somebody*. It is *nobody* and *no one*. No person is there, no life, no self. This body is perceived by way of distance, even when it is one's own. Thus, Descartes writes, "the first thought to come to mind was that I had a face, hands, arms and the whole mechanical structure of limbs which can be seen in a corpse, and which I called the body" (Descartes, cited by Johnstone, 1992, p. 23). Such a mechanical structure of limbs is one whose depth can be penetrated and pierced by the eye. The Cartesian body is perceived by sight; it is first and foremost an object to be seen, a visual spectacle (Johnstone, 1992). To the extent that we now live in this visual, geometrized space that cuts the whole into parts, the space that forms the very sense of ourselves as mechanical structures of limbs, the corpse is the body that is real to us (Romanyshyn, 2004). The anatomical body is the real one—the living, animate body is not. Kisses have become merely the meeting of mucous membranes, and our own felt experience of a kiss has receded into the illusory realm of the subjective. We have succumbed to a disembodied understanding of what is real and what constitutes real knowledge.

What happens to the living, animate body when I perceive the world and myself through linear perspective vision? What happens when this way of perceiving becomes my own habit of mind? For this vision, the inner space that is filled with organs, tissues, and viscera is considered real, whereas the fantasies, longings, fears, dreams, and joys that I live daily are relatively illusory. The condition this provokes is one of radical estrangement:

> Today we know quite well this experience of estrangement, for the distance which separates our knowledge of the world from our experience of it has only increased. Between my body, which I know in living my life with others, and the body of medical knowledge, or between the atomic structure of matter and the things of the world, which I sense with my body, there lies an immeasurable distance, and in most respects each of us remains a stranger to these constructed realities. We *know*, often in fine detail, the world we have imagined and dreamed, the world we have created, but cannot *experience* it. No matter how hard I may try, for example, to experience my sight of a beautiful sunrise as the impact of electromagnetic radiation upon the retinas of my eyeballs where complex electrochemical reactions take place transforming physical stimuli into physiological events, I am doomed to fail. (Romanyshyn, 2004, p. 68)

The experiential, ensouled body is marginalized when the world and oneself are perceived through linear perspective vision. A critical estrangement arises between what is known and understood as real, on the one hand, and what is intimately experienced, on the other. This estrangement, this distance between the ensouled body and the geometric space that creates the anatomical corpse, results from a cultural habit of mind, the habit that believes the measure of the world is optical, and little more. If you doubt the centrality of such a form of vision for the present era, direct your attention to the near-ubiquitous experience of watching television, surfing the Internet, playing video games, or any other form of inhabiting virtual realities. Humans have become transfixed by screens, the contemporary iterations of Renaissance frames. We slouch before them, curving our necks toward apparatus alit with flattened images. Such a habitual way of perceiving, like most habits, functions without any real awareness on the part of the person, or culture, that has come under its sway. Without consciously knowing it, we have come to see the world as if our eyes were camera lenses.

One way of becoming aware of such habits is to search for the special and specific procedures and conditions that make such perceptions possible. I have already given a cursory sketch of such procedures and conditions as regards linear perspective vision. In addition to these, and implicit to them all, is some form of disruption; in order to see my own body as an anatomical object, I must be cut, wounded, or broken open in some way. Indeed, the very term *anatomy* is rooted in the Greek and Latin words for *cut* and *dissect*. For Vesalius to conceive of such an anatomical object of study, he had to acquire dead bodies to be incised with a scalpel or other such cutting instrument. Such a vision of the body is made possible by the specific and special condition of the living body's severance from the world, and this severance is later raised to the level of method. But the invention of the corpse, grounded on this "specific condition of disruption does even more: it transforms this condition into an epistemology, into a way of knowing which defines what is real" (Romanyshyn, 2004, p. 132). The knowledge conditioned on disruption is transformed into a habitual mode of construing what is real, relevant, and true. Stated in even starker terms, "the anatomized body . . . is the living body in its severed relation with the world. It is that moment in the living human body's history which is selected, isolated, and emphasized in the anatomical gaze" (p. 132). And it is this moment, a moment in which the body has been set aside, construed as an object bereft of context, and reduced to what can be perceived of it *from the outside*, that has been privileged. It is only this moment, according to a particular style of vision, that indicates what the human body "really" is.

Saussure's anatomy of language

"A science which studies linguistic structure," said Saussure, "is not only able to dispense with other elements of language, but is possible only if those other elements are kept separate" (Saussure et al., 1986, p. 14). With this phrase and many others, he founded what I will call here the *anatomy of language*. As with the anatomy founded by Vesalius, it required a certain severance of the living body's relation to the world, a certain separation of elements. As such, it forms another chapter in the story of estrangement brought about by a growing distance between the anatomical body and the lived, ensouled body. This is also the distance between the kiss as a meeting of mucous membranes, and the perfunctory peck of a resented formality, the slow smooch of a lazy afternoon, or your first taste of a secret pleasure. Just as the anatomized body is that moment in the living body's history which is partitioned off, set aside, and called attention to in the anatomical gaze, Saussure's anatomized language is that moment that is likewise selected, isolated, and emphasized. As with the anatomized body, anatomized language is brought about by a disruption, a severed relationship between the language user and the experiential field he or she inhabits.

Just as the world created by, and seen through, the artistic technique of linear perspective requires a set of special procedures and conditions to make it possible, so too with Saussure's understanding of language as structure. In this regard, he is conscientious, explicit, and methodical. He restates on numerous occasions that his intent to understand language *qua* system and structure requires that he set aside certain factors, characteristics, and attributes while focusing with singular intent on others. His methodology, in its quest to understand language as structure, for example, required a certain disregard for the external in favor of the internal. Thus, he states that "our definition of a language assumes that we disregard everything which does not belong to its structure as a system; in short everything that is designated by the term 'external linguistics'" (Saussure et al., 1986, p. 21). He goes on to enumerate these disregarded externalities, and includes within them questions of ethnology—the relation between the history of a language and the history of a civilization. Then, he adds to the list political history and colonization. Thereafter follow political relations, such as those between any given tongue and an institution, like the Catholic church. Then, also to be disregarded are the geographical extension of a language, as well as how it splits off into various dialects. All of these he recognizes as important subject matter for linguistics, but not for his own project. For Saussure's concern, and what made his approach so innovative and fecund, was to understand language as a self-enclosed system. This was what he called giving linguistic structure pride of place. In more contemporary parlance, this might be expressed as a *privileging* of structure over all other characteristics. The father of structuralism was explicit both in the fact of this privileging, as well as its motivation. His intent was to found a truly new approach to understanding language, a new science of signs, a semiology.

His disregard for everything that does not belong to the structure of language was purposeful and explicit. For him, linguistic structure is revealed only when a certain order of facts is considered to the exclusion of others. His project, then, required the foregrounding of certain elements, allowing others to form the background, and yet others to be left out of the frame entirely. Just as an artist learning the technique of linear perspective must disregard certain characteristics in determining the size of a given image upon the canvas (for example, the feeling value of the object or person portrayed), and must, on the contrary, focus solely on what his or her eye perceives, so too the linguist whose primary concern is structure and system must disregard characteristics that do not pertain to a particular technique. Put differently, just as certain procedures and conditions must be fulfilled to paint with a realism of the eye, a sensibility that understands the world as a matter of optics, so must certain procedures and conditions be fulfilled to comprehend language as structure and system.

The zeitgeist brought forth by the framing of linear perspective vision, in geometrizing space, cuts the whole into parts. It sees everything as divisible, and divides in order to understand. This cultural habit of mind atomizes as it anatomizes, splitting the world into ever smaller elements. The technological mindset of Descartes, Bacon, Copernicus, and Vesalius proceeds by an atomistic method; its underlying conviction is that knowing is a matter of subdividing everything into the smallest components possible (Berman, 1981). Understanding Saussure in terms of this vision, it should come as no surprise that what is most essential to his science is a very small thing indeed, nearly the smallest of divisible units: the linguistic sign. The sign is a twofold component of language—a word, suffix, prefix, radical, or more complex linguistic formation—composed of, on the one hand, a sound pattern or signifier, and, on the other, a concept or signified that is elicited by that sound pattern. What I hear when an individual speaks a sentence is a series of signifiers. The concepts these signifiers elicit within me are signifieds. The word *libro* in Spanish is a signifier or sound pattern that, for those who know the language, designates the signified or concept *book*.

Saussure described the sign as being arbitrary. The arbitrariness of the sign resides in the fact that the sound pattern or signifier half of the sign has no special relationship to the signified, other than that which is established by convention. Once agreed upon and accepted in general usage, any set of sounds can be made to signify any other concept. In English, we use the signifier *sea* to speak of the same signified that in Spanish is spoken of with the signifier *mar*. In French, German, Swahili, Farsi, and other languages, yet other signifiers, with remarkably different sound patterns, are used to speak of essentially the same concept. "The language we use is a convention," said structuralism's originator, "and it makes no difference what exactly the nature of the agreed sign is" (Saussure et al., 1986, p. 10). Although the rare cases of seemingly onomatopoetic words such as the "woof" of a dog, or the "meow" of a cat may suggest a relationship between signifier and signified that is not arbitrary but phonic, such words are the exceptions that prove the rule and are often less truly onomatopoetic than they appear. This twofold and arbitrary nature of the sign does not mean that in practice I can pronounce any random series of sounds and have them evoke in a listener a particular desired concept or signified. In other words, the signifier does not depend on the free choice of the speaker. The arbitrariness of the sign is relatively fixed at any given moment in time by the conventions of a particular linguistic community.

Saussure's insistence, however, on the arbitrariness of the sign is by no means uncontroversial. For David Abram (1996), signs are not as arbitrary as they may seem; Saussure minimized the gestural and echoic significance of spoken sounds. His very method served to hide the subtle and mutual attraction between signifieds and sound patterns, between the meanings of words and their phonetic qualities. His was a tin ear to a subtle form of ever-present onomatopoeia at work within language. Jungian analyst Paul Kugler (1982) also disputes the absolute arbitrariness of the sign, though in a different way. Rather than calling into question the arbitrariness of the signifier-signified relationship, he contends that there is a non-arbitrary aspect to signs that resides in the sound-to-sound relationship rather than the sound-to-meaning relationship. There are acoustic family resemblances or phonetic similarities between words that seem to group themselves around certain archetypal or symbolic themes. Yet Saussure's very method, his intentional, systematic disregard for everything which does not belong to language as structure and system, predisposed him to not seeing these non-arbitrary relationships.

This focus on units of language called signs, and the further division of the sign into signifier and signified may seem entirely natural to anyone initiated into the seemingly occult science of semiotics (or semiology, to use Saussure's term), or perhaps even to a layperson unfamiliar with his thought. It is not too difficult to conceive of language as being divided into discrete units such as words, suffixes, and prefixes, each arbitrarily associated with a given meaning or concept. To suggest, then, that such a focus stems from a cultural habit of mind that geometrizes the world, cuts the whole into parts, and atomizes as it anatomizes may seem strained. Yet the strain lessens if you consider ways in which other cultures and other times have conceived what is essential, primary, or of most importance as regards language. For the Navajo, the essential and important was a question of wind. Abram (1996), elucidating the work of James Kale McNeley (1981), tells us that the Navajo believed that of the four winds of their cosmology:

> two Little Winds linger within the spiraling folds of our two ears, and it is from there that they offer guidance to us, alerting us to near and distant difficulties, helping us to plan and to make choices. When a Navajo person finds himself thinking in words, this is said to be the voice of one or both of these two Little Winds speaking into his ears. Of course . . . these are simply little currents or vortices within the vast body of nilch'i—the Holy Wind—which exists everywhere . . . inseparable from the swirling body of air in which we are thoroughly immersed. (p. 234)

To conceive of words as Holy Wind may sound odd to you or I, as compared to the familiarity of considering words as divisible units called signs. That these units can be further subdivided like lines on a canvas sounds plausible because we already live in the space created by that canvas.

Significantly, structuralism's progenitor does not directly address the relationship that the signifier, the signified, or the sign as a whole, might have with the world of concrete referents. On the contrary, although Saussure explains in detail the signifier-to-signified relationship and gives a great deal of emphasis to the relationship between signs, he does not address what relationship signs may have with the world of objects. We learn that the sound pattern *book* has a conventional, though arbitrary (not intrinsic) relationship to the concept *book*, but how these two aspects of the sign relate to the bounded rectangular objects found in libraries is not explicitly addressed. In setting aside this relationship through his abstraction of signs and signifiers from a world of discernible palpable objects, Saussure methodically dispossesses an entire experiential realm, leaving it utterly bereft.

Although this approach—a quite conscientious and pragmatic delimitation of an area of study—has a certain theoretical justification, it implicitly calls into question what relationship, if any, the system of signs might have with the world within which it is spoken and written. Saussure's exclusion of the referential dimension of language was a question of methodological convenience, a heuristic device used to describe the structural economy of sign systems. It served to delineate, at the level of signifier and signified, a network of relationships and differences (Norris, 1990). It was not intended as a point of dogma as to the absolute dissociability of language in relation to a world to which it ostensibly refers. It was, on the contrary, a careful setting aside of one particular characteristic of language, and its living relationship to the world, for the explicit purpose of giving linguistic structure "pride of place." However, on this question there is some ambiguity. It may have been that Saussure simply did not assiduously distinguish between the signified and an object of reference. The arbitrariness of the sign may refer to the signified in its relation to the signifier or, on the other hand, it may refer "to the linguistic sign being arbitrarily related to the referents. It is generally assumed that Saussure was referring to the relationship between signifier and signified" (Kugler, 1982). On either reading—understood as methodological convenience, or as a fundamental ambiguity—the lack of any clear, discernible explication of the relation between signs and referents is perhaps the most important procedure or condition necessary for adopting Saussure's understanding of language as system or structure. It is, in a sense, *the* vanishing point established upon the canvas of his linear perspective vision.

Reference as vanishing point upon a canvas is not merely a convenient metaphor. The vanishing point, as its name clearly indicates, informs both artist and spectator as to the place where objects disappear from view. Although it may grant the illusion of the eye's near-infinite grasp, it also establishes the boundaries of vision. Reference is a vanishing point for Saussure because this is where his project meets its own self-imposed horizon, the frontier that, by virtue of its own spatial logic, cannot be traversed. The establishment of reference as vanishing point is a primary procedure that makes his particular vision of language possible. This vanishing point of reference also happens to circumscribe the limitations of post-structuralist and deconstructionist thought inspired by Saussurean linguistics. These limitations, following M. C. Dillon (1995) in his trenchant critique of Jacques Derrida, I will call here *semiological reductionism*.

The circumscription that this vanishing point represents makes more intelligible another primary feature of structuralism: The value of a sign is inseparable from its relationship to yet other signs. Upon this particular horizon, no word has value but for its relationship to other words within a language. When I open a dictionary to find a term, I am referred to yet more terms, more words, more signs (signifiers coupled to signifieds), which in turn will lead me to yet more signs, *ad infinitum*. To say that no sign has value in itself is much like making the quite valid point that a dictionary with only one word in it would be a meaningless document. Signs have value only in relation to a larger linguistic web, system, context, or structure. True to his method, and dedicated to his professed project of elucidating linguistic structure, Saussure does not address to what extent the value of a sign, or the sign system to which it belongs, might be determined by, or related to, non-linguistic elements. Such elements exist beyond the vanishing point of his vision. Though his thinking does address how a word, say *pain*, might accrue value by virtue of its relationship to other words, he does not address how its value might be influenced by the experience of a lacerated thigh, the end of a marriage, or the death of one's child. Such questions are simply outside the purview of his stated desire to explicate language *qua* structure.

Insofar as the project inspired by this desire can be understood as an anatomy of language, such a setting-aside of questions participates in the severance of the body from its lived context, and each individual's lived experience. The severance that makes possible the anatomic body is the one that makes possible the understanding of language as system or structure. Disrupting the relationship between sign systems and virtually everything that is their other is required to conceive of linguistic structure in Saussure's sense of the term. His suspension of (extra-linguistic) reference is a methodological necessity for a particular understanding of the *corpus* of language, just as Vesalius's suspension of the living body is a methodological necessity for a particular understanding of the body *qua* anatomical. As with the anatomized body, this corpus is brought about by a dissection that severs the relationship between language user and the experiential world he or she inhabits. As such, it amounts to a disembodied account of meaning.

Neither suspension invalidates the understanding of either body, not the human body as anatomical, or the linguistic corpus as structure and system. On the contrary, each suspension is what makes these understandings possible. Each suspension allows for a heretofore hidden dimension of both body and language to be revealed. Each suspension, as habit or a priori assumption, also conceals something. In addition to being methodological necessities with a certain theoretical justification, such suspensions may also be understood as symptomatic, that is to say, symbolically rich material that simultaneously conceals and reveals collective pathologies. All of the fundamental dynamics that Freud (1901/1981, 1905/1990, 1912/1958) laid bare: repression, condensation, displacement, compromise formation, conversion, repetition compulsion, and so on, are based upon this fundamental sense that *symptoms involve a complex amalgamation of concealment and revelation.*

The methodological suspension of reference, in its symptomatic guise, severs the relationship between the language user and the experiential world he or she inhabits. It is to structuralist epistemology what symptoms are to individuals, and in "their epistemological guise, methods as symptoms are shared neuroses, expressions of a collective, cultural unconscious" (Romanyshyn, 2007, p. 213). In the primary symbol and symptom that I have been asking you to imagine and think through—that of the suspension of linguistic reference—can be seen the estrangement that is the distance between the ensouled body and the geometric space that creates the corpse.

For Saussure, linguistic structure is most clearly seen when focusing on the *synchronic* as opposed to the *diachronic* aspect of language. The word "diachronic" refers to the temporal aspect of language, the way in which it evolves through time, how it got to be the way it is. A diachronic approach might, for example, focus on how one set of linguistic conventions, meanings, or habits established themselves and then vanished, or evolved into yet other conventions, meanings, or habits. It might delve into etymological and philological investigations and track the shifts that have taken place in Chaucer's English to make it into the twenty-first-century English of the worldwide Web. A synchronic approach looks at a language as it exists and functions in the present, setting aside historical causes that have contributed to its formation, so as to better focus on its present state. "The linguist who wishes to understand this state," said Saussure, "must rule out of consideration everything which brought that state about, and pay no attention to diachrony. Only by suppressing the past can he enter into the state of mind of the language user" (Saussure et al., 1986, p. 81).

Such a linguist seeks to paint a still life, the rendering of a static figure. He or she desires to present an image of an *inanimate* object; *animate* objects move through space, and this movement implies a temporal dimension, the dimension that is the diachrony to be ignored. A temporal context must be carefully eliminated, for the linguist seeks the realism of a photo that captures a moment suspended in time. Thus, Saussure compares his favored principle of synchrony to "the projection of a three-dimensional object on a two-dimensional plan" (Saussure et al., 1986, p. 87). This, too, has its parallel in linear perspective vision which, in addition to attempting to capture a three-dimensional optic reality within the two dimensions offered by the canvas, requires both a fixed vantage point and a fixed vanishing point. This, in turn, implies the omission of the temporal dimension of bodies in movement, bodies that shift from one perspective to another, animated bodies that engage a palpable world.

In speaking of animate bodies I am not alluding merely to their movement. Animate bodies are bodies with *anima*, bodies with soul. *Anima* is a key term in Jung's (1959/1969) psychology, one that he often pointed out is the Latin word for "soul," while its masculine cognate *animus* is frequently translated as "spirit." He notes that ancient views "held that the soul was essentially the life of the body, the life-breath, or a kind of life force which assumed spatial and corporeal form" (Jung, 1960/1969, p. 345 [*CW* 8 pt. 5 para. 662]). In speaking of inanimate bodies, I do so with these connotations in mind; I want to speak not only of bodies without movement, but also bodies without soul, without spirit, without the élan vital that distinguishes live bodies from dead ones. What differentiates the anatomical body from the experiential or lived body is anima: soul. What differentiates the anatomical body of language from language as I experience it, as I live it, is soul too.

In his quest for formal, structural understanding, Saussure set aside the question of content. Put differently, he looked at *how* a sentence means as opposed to *what* it means. His synchronic understanding of essentially arbitrary linguistic signs functioning as a self-enclosed system certainly may help one better comprehend how the sentence "The building is on fire" actually works. It will not help anyone, however, to know when it is time to head for the fire extinguisher or the nearest exit. Nor can it speak to the considerable difference in feeling tone inspired by one sign in comparison with another; both *table* and *murder* are signifiers that work within a seemingly infinite linguistic matrix governed by certain rules and habits, but the remarkable difference in how each signifier might make one feel is simply outside the purview of Saussure's thinking. The structuralist project that he initiated bleeds the linguistic body of all content, and the post-structuralism that it inspired, as will be addressed further on, does so even more: "To exalt the signified at the expense of the referent, and the signifier at the expense of the signified, is always to dismantle the still positive something that had survived until then" (Girard & Doran, 2008, p. 211). This emphasis on formal, structural elements is perhaps best described in Saussure's own words: "Language itself is a form, not a substance" (Saussure et al., 1986, p. 120).

No discussion of Saussurean linguistics would be complete without mention of his distinction between language (*langue*) and speech (*parole*). The latter is the execution of sound patterns, much like the playing of a musical instrument. It is what I do with my throat, tongue, mouth, and diaphragm. Language, in turn, is what makes those sounds make sense. It is a set of social conventions, relations, and distinctions that I draw upon in my speech. I can draw upon these as I choose, forming utterances according to what I desire to communicate. Language, in this sense, is necessary for speech to be intelligible. If you and I do not share a language, then my speech will not be meaningful to you. The distinction between language and speech is much like the distinction between code and message (Kugler, 1982). The code makes the message possible. I draw upon the code in forming a message. A message may be mine, or yours, or hers, or theirs. The code is not. A message is sent and received at a given moment. The code exists, in a sense, independent of any moment. If I talk now, and then grow silent, my speech is no longer, but the language I speak endures.

The distinction between language and speech; the division of the former into signs; the further splitting of signs into signifiers and signifieds; the privileging of synchrony over diachrony; the setting-aside of questions of political history, geography, and ethnology; the omission of the referential aspect of language—the way in which it might relate to a tangible world, and the concomitant sense that words have value only by virtue of their intralinguistic relations: these all represent procedures and conditions necessary for adopting Saussure's very specific sense of what is meant by "language." *What is procured by such procedures is to the language you are reading now what the anatomical body is to the living, ensouled body*; severed from its relation to the world and those who articulate it with tongue, throat and breath, such a corpus exists only on the condition of a disruption. This disruption sets aside a more fully human engagement with language that includes the other "levels of existence" that, by way of linear perspective and scientific-technological rationality, have become merely a subjective matter.

Sign systems, à la Saussure, are to the language of experience what the explanation of a kiss as the meeting of mucous membranes is to the experience of any kiss. Co-opting Romanyshyn's (2004, p. 115) words, and altering them only slightly, one can say that Saussure's vision involves a specific way of looking at the linguistic corpus that, in focusing on it as spectacle for observation, *isolates it from its living context or situation and fragments what it sees*. That vision which isolates and fragments, that vision out of which the corpse is generated, is the anatomical gaze. Such a vision requires distance from the phenomena to be understood, laying it before oneself, splaying it open for inspection to understand it as a relation of intracorporeal parts, the boundary of which is the dermis of the signifier, but not, as a matter of procedure, an entire phenomenal world which this body of language engages. As with the anatomical body of Vesalius, one might say that this linguistic corpus is one that has been set aside, construed as an object bereft of context, and reduced to what can be perceived of it *from the outside*.

Michel Foucault (1973) is a keen chronicler of a process akin to the very anatomization of language that I have portrayed here, for he describes a process in which language becomes an object of study beginning at the end of the Renaissance, at the birth of a modernity that will loosen words from their moorings in the things of the world: "[L]anguage as the spontaneous tabula, the primary grid of things, as an indispensable link between representation and things, is eclipsed" (p. xxiii). His portrayal of Saussure as rediscovering the project of a general semiology, a science of signs, begun in the age of Descartes, as well as the rediscovery of the binary nature of the sign, is congruent with my own reading of an affinity between Saussure and a Vesalian/Cartesian conception of the body. This anatomization, this splitting-off of language from its other, is perhaps most clearly stated by Foucault in the following lines:

> The profound kinship of language with the world was thus dissolved. The primacy of the written word went into abeyance. And that uniform layer, in which the seen and the read, the visible and the expressible, were endlessly interwoven, vanished too. Things and words were to be separated from one another. The eye was thenceforth destined to see and only to see, the ear to hear and only to hear. Discourse was still to have the task of speaking that which is, but it was no longer to be anything more than what is said. (1973, p. 43)

Foucault articulates the dissolution of a profound kinship, that of words and things. They no longer commingle with, and correspond to, one another. A disruption has occurred. An estrangement has come about, and with it, the senses have been cleaved from the language that might lend them voice. Words may still speak, but only of that which is spoken, and that which is spoken is taken to be all that is.

The linguistic body as conceived by Saussure was inherited, modified, and distorted by post-structuralism and deconstructionism in many important and complex ways. Post-structuralists, for example, accepted Saussure's sense of meaning as arising from the social conventions that are linguistic signs, and the sense that these signs hold meaning only by way of their intra-linguistic relations and differences; no sign has a meaning in and of itself (MacNaughton, 2005). Deconstructionists adopted much of Saussure's work as their theoretical framework, in particular his liberation of the sign from its object in the world, with which he originated the concept of the arbitrariness of signification (Taylor & Winquist, 2001). They took this sense of arbitrariness and applied it to such diverse fields as literary and cultural criticism, history, anthropology, gender studies, and others. Derrida saw in Saussure's writing an opportunity to shake the very foundations of Western metaphysics and expose its prejudices. He radicalized this Saussurean sense of differences between signs and transformed it into *différance*. In this way, he placed the corpus of language at an even greater remove from its experiential ground. Foucault adopted Saussure's structural linguistics and applied it to areas far outside the realm of its original intent, extending it to the analysis of the social and human sciences. Yet in the wake of Saussure's formidable influence, a methodological crisis ensued, one whose genesis can be traced back directly to his seminal work (Ricœur, 1977).

Broadly speaking, Saussure's oeuvre informed the ethos of a deconstructive postmodernism that understands and implicitly reduces all meaning to the signification of signs (Dillon, 1995). The conclusions that have been drawn from this belief are far-reaching: The language we speak and write no longer merely reflects a pre-existing reality—in many important ways, it constitutes it (Zalewski, 2000). Language no longer echoes something beyond itself, coming after and repeating what is. It is no longer understood to be "founded on the phenomena of the mirror, ego-alter ego, or of the echo, in other words, of a carnal generality" (Merleau-Ponty, 1973, p. 20 *n*). If meaning is a function of arbitrary social constructs, then what once seemed to have an existence independent of the sign system that names it, now appears to be merely the illusory result of that system. Through an evolution and transformation of Saussure's semiology, meaning itself has been upended, radically reconceptualized, and rendered problematic.

Logos, mythos, and the symbolic attitude

In these pages, I am attempting to bring a symbolic attitude to bear upon the seeming facts of Saussure's structural linguistics. This attitude understands that statements about language, semiotics, and sign systems are also statements by and about psyche. To a consciousness imbued with a sense of the symbolic, such linguistic facts allude to psychic facts, facts that can be described with words like *distance*, *division*, *dissection*, *detachment*, and *disembodiment*. Words such as these form an associative cluster of meaning much like you or I might arrive at through a careful engagement with a dream image, as we note all of the feelings, sensations, thoughts, and intuitions that arise in relation to it. Such words have been arrived at by way of a certain rationality of argument, one that draws parallels between procedures of linear perspective, on the one hand, and a particular conceptualization of linguistic structure, on the other.

Yet they have also sprung forth through a reverie that is willing to temporarily suspend judgment, as well as a willingness to be guided by fantasy without interference from the discriminating intellect. In its most essential elements, this is the process that Jung (1983) called "active imagination," a process that encourages the entwining of imaginative perception with threads of argument and reason. The symbolic attitude is one of respectful receptivity to psychic images (Brooke, 1991). Fantasies are to be tended to with the understanding that they contain psychological truths. For Jung, the careful meditation upon fantasy images is not merely a therapeutic endeavor but an epistemological one. A symbolic attitude is not merely a means by which individuals might heal their neuroses. It is also a means of knowing, and, in some essential sense, it is *the* way of knowing that undergirds all others, for there is no cleaving fantasy from understanding. Fantasy itself is inextricably bound to the four primary modes of apprehending the world that humans possess. As such, fantasy is "just as much feeling as thinking; as much intuition as sensation" (Jung, 1921/1971, p. 52 [*CW* 6 pt. 1 para. 78]). Feeling, thinking, intuition, and sensation are, of course, the four basic psychological functions of Jung's theory of psychological types, four primary modes of understanding and orienting ourselves in the world.

It is through such reverie and fantasy that I have come to a felt sense of consanguinity between the vision that isolates and separates the body as object, and the vision that isolates and separates language as object. So I have let voices creep in almost surreptitiously that tell of corpses and kisses, frames constructed, vanishing points, winds that speak, smart phones, splayed sternums, and eyes of near-infinite grasp. Strange images have arisen by way of drawing parallels, making associations, playing with images, and attempting to see beyond the face value of theories involving the division of linguistic systems into signs, the bifurcation of signs into signifiers and signifieds, the privileging of synchrony over diachrony, and so forth. Amplifying the images, I have arrived at statements fitting to the irrational logic of the oneiric: Saussure's language as structure is to the language I live, and that you are reading here, what the corpse is to the body that I live; in the space between sign and referent a soulless carcass lies; the animate, experiential body is shadowed by twins—the anatomical body and the corpus of anatomized language.

What Jung called a "symbolic attitude" was an attempt to integrate both rationality and imagination, or logos and mythos (literally "narrative" or "invented" story). In his writing and his psychology, it can also be seen in his understanding of two primary types of thinking: One is characterized by a wide-eyed, directed thinking that requires a certain rigor of rational and clarity of discernment. It works by way of logical propositions, reasoned argument, and linguistic formulations. This mode of thought Jung contrasts with one that is akin to dreaming, the thinking of reverie unchained from the bonds of strict causality. Such thought lingers in the image, swims effortlessly in the waters of fantasy, and does so with eyes closed, if not literally, then metaphorically (Jung & De Laszlo, 1993). Rational knowledge, reason, literal truth, and expression through conscious activity belong to logos, whereas mythos is the realm of mysticism, intuitive knowledge, imagination, metaphorical truth, and expression through manifestations of the unconscious (Shelburne, 1988).

For Jung, whether something "is a symbol or not depends chiefly on the *attitude* (q.v.) of the observing consciousness; for instance, on whether it regards a given fact not merely as such but also as an expression for something unknown" (Jung, 1921/1971, p. 475 [CW 6 pt.11 para. 818], original emphasis). This *symbolic attitude*, as he termed it, glimpses the deeper meaning of things and can view even something as unambiguous and unequivocal as a mathematical term, as a symbol for a heretofore unknown psychic fact. Because of this attitude, it is possible for one person to "establish a fact which does not appear in the least symbolic to himself, but is profoundly so to another consciousness" (Jung, 1921/1971, p. 475 [CW 6 pt.11 para. 818]). He contrasted this symbolic attitude with one that accentuated the factual while subordinating meaning to it.

One manner by which Jung put to practice this symbolic attitude was in the way he wrote. His written works proceed not merely by way of logical arguments that address ideas at face value, although they do resort to these. His writings also proceed by way of an imaginative storytelling that speaks to more than just the intellect of the reader. Rather than amassing evidence and relying upon purely logical methods to prove a thesis, he sought to persuade through analogy and metaphor (Rowland, 2010). He appealed to something more than the conceptual mind of his readers, knowing that this represented only a small portion of their faculties of perception and understanding. Insofar as he wrote in this way, he enacted the psyche that he purported to describe. The form of his writing corresponded to its content.

Jung's psychology is a grand dialogue between these two types of thinking, a dialectic between logos and mythos, a conversation between rationality and imagination (Rowland, 2010). The truth of the reasoning mind, the truth of concepts and theory, is, for Jung, not enough. Abstract, conceptual logos dissociated from imaginative, associative mythos is not sufficient to communicate truth. On its own, it can speak to only very limited truths. A narrative, imaginative, dreamlike form of thought is necessary as well, for only mythos "is able to invoke the unknown energies of the soul" (p. 22). The two forms of thought are needed to understand by way of a symbolic attitude.

This book attempts to understand the symbol, then, with neither the intensely focused and wide-eyed gaze of directed thought, nor with eyes blanketed cozily by the lids of slumber, but, rather, with eyes only half-closed. Towards the end of his autobiography, *Memories, Dreams, Reflections* (1961), Jung evokes this same imagery to speak of how one might "see and hear the form and voice of being" (p. 237). This voice, and this form, are only to be taken in "with half-closed eyes and somewhat closed ears" (p. 237). "If our impressions are too distinct," he warns the reader, "we are held to the hour and minute of the present and have no way of knowing how our ancestral psyches listen to and understand the present—in other words, how our unconscious is responding to it" (p. 237). Then, we are truly beholden to the spirit of the times. There is no overstating Jung's fidelity to fantasy as a way of knowing, for it is fantasy that bridges the "irreconcilable claims of subject and object" (Jung, 1921/1971, p. 52 [*CW* 6 pt. 1 para. 78]). It is fantasy that heals the estrangement of subjective mind from objective matter, the Cartesian split of *res cogitas* and *res extensa*.

With half-covered ears, and with an attention open to impressions that are not too distinct, but come, as dreams do, distorted by the baffle of sleep, hear this echo. It is the sound of two bodies reverberating through history, the anatomical body of Vesalius, and Saussure's anatomical body of language. They are not entirely dissimilar bodies, insofar as they are bodies born of a vision of distance and separation, estrangement and fragmentation. Their echo can be heard in the works of Foucault, the great historian of the body.

The echo of two bodies

In Judith Butler's essay "Foucault and the Paradox of Bodily Inscriptions" (1999), this dual echo goes by the name of a paradox. Two contradictory senses of the body underpin this paradox: *body as construction*, and *body as site of inscription*. The position that the body is in some sense constructed, she notes, is widely associated with Foucault. His notion of a constructed body, on Butler's account, resides in that he appears to argue that bodies do not, in fact cannot, exist outside the terms of their cultural inscription. This particular understanding of the body appears to deny it any ontic status independent of the cultural significations, the language, that ostensibly constructs it. The body cannot truly *be* anywhere other than within the meanings imparted by culture. It is but a term in a semiotic, or perhaps the complex effect of many terms. Bodies are born, not of the wombs of women, but of the wombs of discourse, matrixes of meaning, webs of signification. The body is a cultural artifact, the net result of a semiosis: the interpretation and production of signs. Thus, in a work not cited in Butler's essay, Foucault makes a similar point regarding *man*:

> One thing in any case is certain: man is neither the oldest nor the most constant problem that has been posed for human knowledge. Taking a relatively short chronological sample within a restricted geographical area—European culture since the sixteenth century—one can be certain that man is a recent invention within it . . . As the archeology of our thought easily shows, man is an invention of recent date. And one perhaps nearing its end. (Foucault, 1973, p. 386)

According to this understanding, man, like the body, is the effect of a culture within a discernible, restricted, geographical area, and does not exist outside the terms of his cultural inscription. It is conceivable, perhaps even desirable, that if a fundamentally different culture were to arise, one with a radically dissimilar semiotic, neither man, nor body, would exist. It is comforting, a relief in fact, to suppose that "man is only a recent invention, a figure not yet two centuries old, a new wrinkle in our knowledge, and that he will disappear again as soon as that knowledge has discovered a new form" (p. xxiii). Then, as in the final image left to the reader of *The Order of Things* (1973), "man would be erased, like a face drawn in sand at the edge of the sea" (p. 387).

The image is fecund, complex, and full of poetic irony. By way of the simile *man is like a face drawn in the sand*, there is an equation and conflation of human beings with their self-representations. A sense is given that when the representation disappears, so does that which it represents. This conflation is, granted, attenuated through simile; the statement is not that *man is a face drawn in the sand*, but merely that he is *like* that. Foucault's antiquated use of the gendered noun *man* to refer to the human species as a whole, subtly lends credence to the case that all conceptions of what is human are always being washed away by the tide of the times. That conception, the construct *man*, which seemed to be an unquestionable given in ages prior, now proves to be as ephemeral as stick drawings upon the beach. This reading is congruent with Foucault's general approach as an historian of ideas. *The Order of Things* (Foucault, 1973), and numerous other works (Foucault, 1977;

Foucault & Gordon, 1980; Foucault & Rabinow, 1984) constantly draw the reader's attention to the ever-changing sense of what is considered unchanging, the shifting order of what is considered the natural, un-shifting order.

Yet the image of the face, as well as the notion of *man as a recent invention*, is provocative, in part, because the somewhat outdated sense of the word, denoting human beings in general, is still intact. Because of this, the question cannot help but arise as to who, or what, invented these human beings, and an unavoidable suggestion is planted in the reader's consciousness: Like that pictograph upon the shore, humans may simply cease to be. Foucault plays upon differing senses of the word *man*, one of which conceives *it* as the fleeting product of a discernible history. Yet another sense of the word relies upon the reader's understanding of *man* as a species that she or he presumably identifies with. The reader who lets the word *man* resonate with this latter meaning is left with an apocalyptic and genocidal image: humans reduced to archeological rubble, or detritus as diminutive as grains of sand. The future may be post-human, and Foucault's work readily sets the stage for this future insofar as it construes man as an event within a knowledge that transcends 'his' temporal dimensions. He is, after all, merely a new wrinkle within that knowledge.

These dual senses of the word *man*, are also congruent with Butler's reading of Foucault's paradoxical writings on the body as both *construction* and *site of inscription*. The latter conception construes the body as a tablet upon which history, discourse, and power/knowledge inscribe themselves; cultural values result from inscriptions upon a body that is understood to be a medium, clay upon which forms can be engraved, or "a blank page, an unusual one, to be sure, for it appears to bleed and suffer under the pressure of a writing instrument" (Butler, 1999, p. 309). The body, here, is not a fragment of discourse, not a cultural artifact, not the effect of history. It is the site upon which discourse, culture, and history play themselves out. It is the tablet, and not the words written upon it. It is the blank screen, and not the text that illuminates the screen. The body is not a construct, but the place of construction. Speaking in this way cannot but suggest that there is one body that is, in some way, given, pre-existing, and available to become the place upon which its own supposed construction will occur. And therein lies the rub. For if the body is "the object or surface on which construction occurs [then, it] is itself prior to construction" (p. 307) and cannot, therefore, be the result of construction. There is, then, in Foucault's work, a simultaneous appeal to both the material fact of the body and the linguistically constructed idea of it, without an acknowledgement of the space in between. Put another way, it is as if in his writing there is a simultaneous and unresolved appeal to both Vesalius' anatomized body and Saussure's anatomized language. The former provides a site of inscription, and as such, is pre-given—it exists prior to, or independent of, the terms to be inscribed upon it. The latter understands body as merely *body*, as an ephemeral sign, the genealogy of which can be traced by the astute historian of ideas. This latter conception also understands man as an invention of culture, rather than, as some might suppose, being the inventor of it.

The reading I am developing here suggests that in the gap between the anatomized body and anatomized language, in the *aporia* between the *body as site of inscription* and the *body as construction*, lies the living, animate body. A wide range of critics from diverse fields lends credence to this claim in their portrayal of Foucault, and post-structuralism in general, as fostering a disembodied account of meaning (Fisher, 2002; Gendlin, 1992, 1997; Lakoff & Johnson, 1999; Spretnak, 1991, 1999). Such an account is anatomical insofar as it relies on a series of procedures that sever both language and body from their living relation to the world. It can portray the ways in which the body is inscribed and written upon like a fleshy page or screen, but is mute as to how language "is *of* the order of experiencing, and not simply a stamp *on* it" (Fisher, 2002, p. 63, original emphasis). For Foucault, the body is little more than a surface upon which history inscribes itself, little more than a docile receptacle or tablet upon which political power makes its mark. This docile receptacle is, of course, another way of speaking of the body as site of inscription. Those who share such a view, despite sometimes having the term *postmodern* associated with them, are still very much in line with modern thought; they not only resist incarnation, but "continue to side against nature, in favor of a free-floating language and all-ruling culture; they still seek to obtain release from the world by transforming it and themselves into a text" (p. 63).

The body as docile receptacle, and the transformation of oneself (one's body) into a text, are resonant with Butler's reading of Foucault's paradoxical sense of the body as *site of inscription* and as *construction*. The former is a physical mass *out there*, a palpable, material object; the latter is more akin to the epiphenomenon of sentences, words, phrases, paragraphs, prefixes, suffixes, phonemes, morphemes, signs, and signifiers. It is a textual body. What is lacking in these two bodies, what exists in the gap between them, is the living, animate body:

> What these thinkers assume is that our experiencing is wholly determined by the symbolic order, which is itself limited to cultural-historical-linguistic forms. *What they do not recognize is an organic, bodily felt, responding moment within this experiencing.* In other words they do not allow for how symbolic forms and experiencing *interact in a life process*. One of the consequences of this is a tendency to locate meaning only in language, rather than in a broader process of bodily living-in-the-world that *includes* language. (Fisher, 2002, p. 63, original emphasis).

To have a greater sense of what Fisher is getting at here, a sense of how your experiential body interacts with symbolic forms in a life process that cannot be reduced to these forms, consider the following sentence: *You are not reading these words*. Let the experience of reading those words resonate through you and note the felt sense produced by those words. Again, *You are not reading these words, nor are you reading this additional clause that follows. You are not reading this last sentence either*. I imagine that there is an organic, bodily felt moment in the experience of reading such phrases that provokes in you a sense of irony, disbelief, or chagrin. You have come to understand the words as having a certain meaning, and this meaning does not correspond to the existential context of reading them. I can tell you that you are not reading these words, but your experience tells you otherwise. You can viscerally sense the lie, or the fictional pretense. Your body can feel the counterfactual sense of the words. Such a profound disturbance, or even the chagrin (perhaps) provoked by the exercise above, are simple, rudimentary examples of what Fisher sees being left out of the post-structuralist account of meaning.

Now, to get a sense of what things look like when that 'something left out' *is* left out, imagine a frame upon which has been stretched a translucent veil divided into square sections by dark threads, so that a grid is formed. Such a frame was sometimes used by Renaissance painters for works of linear perspective technique. Now, envision the two following sentences placed just on the other side of that frame so that they are seen through the grid: *You are reading these words. You are not reading these words*. Because these sentences are on the other side of the separating frame, they do not apply to you. You are not the *you* referred to. The word's true reference is unknown, and there is no need to imagine yourself as that someone to whom these annunciations are intended. You are cut off from these statements in much the same way that a television viewer is cut off from the spectacle she or he views, yet even more so, for you feel no desire or compunction to participate in any unfolding drama. You understand these two sentences, but they are severed from your living context. You are able to recognize both sentences as equally valid uses of English. Both cohere, and follow accepted rules of grammar. The two sentences are structured differently, but in such a way that you can understand their working parts, and perhaps even diagram them, as in grammar school, marking subjects, predicates, direct objects, and the like. Yet doing all this, managing to see the two statements this way, relies upon a disrupted relation between these words and your experiential, animate body. Such a disrupted relation is necessary to understand the two sentences as pure structure, that is to say anatomically, in a way that allows for their dissection, or, better yet, their deconstruction. This disruption divorces the statements from any referential context, the broader process of bodily living-in-the-world that Fisher refers to above.

Fisher's concern, which I share, is that without an acknowledgement of our bodily living-in-the-world, without an acknowledgement of how our language is informed by a body imbued of anima and animus, of soul and spirit, we are left with a radical linguistic relativism that tacitly or otherwise assumes the absence of any organic basis to human life and, simultaneously, presumes that nature can make no claim upon us. The postmodern location of meaning in an ever-changing procession of shifting cultural-historical-linguistic forms obscures more general, transhistorical needs and behavioral patterns that belong to us as embodied, mortal beings; it obscures our own human nature, reducing it to mere *nomina*. It robs words of their referential value. If nature can make no felt claims upon us, if we are without an organic basis, the meaning we give life is arbitrary, as arbitrary as the relation between sign and signifier as envisioned by Saussure, if not more so. There being no intrinsic relation between our constructs and anything that is not merely the historically contingent, culturally bound world from which those constructs arise, it is, arguably, difficult to escape a nihilistic view; life is senseless and there is no firm ground for any meaning or truth.

Yet eschewing the exclusive location of meaning in language does not mean that one must embrace an opposite extreme that would deny words their due. Our felt sense of meaning is imbued with words, and can at least partially be described by them, if not reduced to them. We cannot understand the world in the particular way that we do without all the background meanings that have been given to us by the language, or languages, we speak; "*On the other hand*, our experience is also *thicker*, more 'intricate' than any words, concepts, theories, or existing forms; these do not, in other words, wholly *encompass* our experience (Fisher, 2002, p. 64, original emphasis). On this reading, we are not, nor ever could be, in the prison-house of language (Jameson, 1972). It is more truthful to say, along with Merleau-Ponty (1973), that language is sedimented in the body. Words are of the flesh and speak to the flesh.

Such a statement could almost serve as a pithy summation of George Lakoff and Mark Johnson's *Philosophy in the Flesh: The Embodied Mind and its Challenge to Western Thought* (1999). This linguist-philosopher collaborative duo, although coming from markedly different orientations than that of the ecopsychologist Fisher, nevertheless, voices a similar critique: Much of the critical thrust of their argument revolves around their understanding of metaphor, which they see as indispensable for humans to make sense of their experience. Far from being merely a poetic flourish, or simply an inherited meme, metaphor is at the very heart of our understanding of ourselves and the world. None of our thinking would be possible without it, for even the most abstract of philosophical systems, even those which deplore the use of metaphor, are inevitably rooted in it. Many of the metaphors we use are what they call *primary*. Far from being merely arbitrary social constructs, they are shaped by the nature of our bodies and brains and the realities of our daily interactions. Because of such basic shared human experiences as moving through space, carrying and moving objects, turning around, seeing objects appear and disappear, and getting lost, the meaning expressed in metaphors grounded in such experiences cannot be entirely arbitrary. Thus, the *grounding* metaphor used in the last sentence cannot be utterly arbitrary because of the universal human experience of being supported by the ground. If you take a moment to stand up and sense your weight as it presses through your feet into the earth or floor, a moment to sense yourself subtly drifting forward, backward, and side to side upon your firmly planted feet, you will have a greater sense of what I mean by grounding. Knowing what it feels like to have the earth firmly beneath you, to be supported by something solid and reliable, informs the metaphor that, in this case, speaks to having one's ideas based on a foundation that feels equally solid.

One type of common primary metaphor is what they call the *difficulties are impediments* metaphor, which can be subdivided into categories such as the *difficulties are blockages*, *difficulties are features of the terrain*, *difficulties are burdens*, and others. I am using a *difficulties are burdens* metaphor when I say that my research is weighing on me, that a certain relationship is a cross I have to bear, or that I carry the wounds of previous generations. Each one of these examples reflect idiosyncratic, culturally specific references resulting from social, cultural conditions that change over time. Yet they also arise from the trans-cultural, embodied experience of the difficulty of carrying a heavy object. Without this shared human experience, the *difficulties are burdens* metaphor would not be meaningful. Because Lakoff and Johnson view post-structuralism as having ignored the role of the embodiment of meaning, they contend that it has been likewise ignorant of the way in which metaphors are grounded in the body, being both constrained and informed by our embodied experience.

Yet Saussurean linguistics, in locating meaning exclusively in the arbitrary and timely sign, offered post-structuralists a view of meaning that avoided entirely this recognition of sedimentation within a living, feeling body. What post-structuralists have correctly perceived is the protean and polyformal nature of conceptual systems. They change over time, differing markedly from era to era and place to place. Yet they assumed that meaning, not being utterly timeless and universal, must be utterly arbitrary and changing (Lakoff and Johnson, 1999). Having seemingly seen through the pretense of the timeless and universal, they embraced the apparently arbitrary and ever-mutable aspects of language. What they did not embrace, however, in their appropriation and elaboration of structuralism, was the flesh. They disregarded the living, animate body as locus of meaning. Lakoff and Johnson, like Fisher, understand the absolute arbitrariness of signifiers as precluding the possibility of language being in any way rooted in experience. On their view, the resulting image of a radically decentered person for whom all meaning is arbitrary, entirely relative, fully contingent upon history, and in no way determined by the living body is an impossibility.

In *The Meaning of the Body: Aesthetics of Human Understanding* (2007) Johnson advocates a position that "thinking is not something humans 'bring' to their experience from the outside; rather, it is in and of experience—an embodied dimension of those experiences in which abstraction is occurring" (p. 92). In these words, he virtually parallels Fisher's above-cited contention that language is of the order of experiencing, and not merely a stamp on it. What Lakoff, Johnson, and Fisher, each in their own way, draw our attention to is a broader experiential realm without which our words and thought would not be meaningful or possible. In saying this, my desire is to paint a suggestive picture. To paint this picture, I ask: If bodies of thought have shadows, just as human bodies do, then what might be the shadows cast by Saussure and Foucault? The tentative response to this question is that what is left in the dark is the coupling of language to a broader experiential realm, without which words would be bereft of meaning.

What Lakoff, Johnson, and Fisher do is remind us that bodies are not merely sites of inscription, not merely anatomical objects *out there* upon which meaning is grafted. They remind us that a dead body upon a coroner's table is only the human body in a very particular sense, and the detached corpus of language as structure is only language in a particular sense. Yet because our words are always already in and of the flesh, always already meaning themselves *through* us as incarnate, mortal beings, it is mistaken to construe them as merely imposed systems of arbitrary distinctions. To view them as such relies upon a de-animation of the human body and a de-animation of the corpus of language. Such a vision relies upon the absence of anima, that is to say, the absence of soul. Or, put differently, to view words as merely imposed systems of arbitrary distinctions is to forget that something lies beyond the vanishing point of the linear perspective vision fostered by Saussure, then furthered in post-structuralism.

Philosopher and psychotherapist Eugene Gendlin (1992) takes issue with this vision that construes linguistic forms as being imposed upon bodies, as if from the outside. The reason that relativism (and nihilism) is so widely spread today in the West is because of the assumption that all experience is "derivative from forms, that these forms are given by history, and that they are therefore utterly relative" (p. 196). It stems from unidirectional interpretive approaches that move from cultural practices, to people, to bodies. The movement described by Gendlin *from* interpretation and culture *to* people and bodies implies a *view* of bodies (from the outside) rather than an *immediate experience* of them, through them, by them. The guiding assumption is that the corporeal is secondary, derivative. What is primary and originary are cultural and linguistic forms.

Gendlin mounts a frontal attack on the view that would claim that humans are but the repositories of cultural artifacts, or sites of inscription, as if language, history, and culture existed only on the outside of such creatures and were imposed upon them. He contrasts this view by ceaselessly reminding his reader that humans can speak from something more than conceptual patterns. And not only can we speak from this excess, this *more*; what we say with our words speaks to something that is greater than the words themselves. What language *says* always exceeds the patterns and distinctions that it brings. This excess, which Gendlin terms, variously, as *the more*, *experience*, *practice*, *situations*, *situatedness*, *wisdom*, *the body*, *thickness*, and *the open*, is akin to what Fisher refers to as a broader process of bodily living-in-the-world. Both thinkers draw their readers' attention to what, on their view, is othered by a current of thought that circumscribes everything within the confines of a reductive linguisticism. Both attempt, in their own way, to point to a space that exists outside the parameters dictated by the spatial logic of a linear perspective vision that sees language as all-determinative. Or, perhaps, it is truer to say that they shake the bodies of those who are transfixed before such a canvas, enamored of the view.

For Gendlin, the problem with a linguistically reductive postmodernism lies precisely in the ways in which it leaves the living, experiential body behind: "In the current postmodern impasse there are calls for some new way to philosophize from experience" (Gendlin & Kleinberg-Levin, 1997, p. 3). Yet, because it is always compromised by conceptual forms and distinctions already implicit within it, postmodernism discounts the role of experience, then, in turn, even discounts these conceptual forms and distinctions because, having an experiential aspect, they can never be purely logical.

Author Charlene Spretnak sees in deconstructive postmodernism the latest chapter in the patriarchal quest for autonomy and power. Gendlin's assertion that through this particular intellectual approach "we are elevated to be [the world's] 'constructors,' disembodied, floating beside the universe" (Gendlin & Kleinberg-Levin, 1997, p. 15) parallels Spretnak's understanding. For her, its underlying dynamics bespeak "patriarchal culture's brutal and self-destructive divorce from the body—the Earthbody, the female body, the body of the mother" (Spretnak, 1991, p. 260). On her view, the deconstructive ethos is more akin to a cultural neurosis than an enlightening emancipation. Like others before and after her (see Berman, 1981; Johnstone, 1992; Kleinberg-Levin, 1988; Bordo, 1987), she portrays a modernity that marginalized the knowing body, and in its place put a mechanical one. From her perspective, deconstructive postmodernism is a paroxysmal exacerbation of modernity's symptomatic alienation from the body. It is a continuation of the patriarchal project that distrusts and devalues the body, construing it as little more than a dumb receptacle of power-laden contents, regarding it as an unreliable and treacherous collaborator. The postmodern, then, is *most* modern.

Spretnak's plea is that our narratives, situated in particular cultural constructions, should be understood in a broader, fuller context that includes body, nature, and place. In its emphasis on the "constructed" nature of narratives, postmodernism implicitly undermines any sense of there being a reality that can be accurately, if not comprehensively, described: For deconstruction, there is no "real." There is only the omnipresent "social construction" of language and concepts that permeate all of human experience. What has been othered by the variant of postmodernism that reduces all to texts, narratives, and constructs—whether it be called deconstructionism, post-structuralism, neo-pragmatism, or by any other moniker—is a sense of the real. Yet, thankfully, "the knowing body, the creative cosmos, the complex sense of place—all these are asserting their true nature as we increase our abilities to see beyond the boundaries of the modern worldview" (Spretnak, 1999, p. 35).

Central to the critiques of Gendlin, Spretnak, Fisher, Lakoff, and Johnson are two key elements central to Jung's understanding of neurosis: meaning and experience. Broadly speaking, each writer takes issue with the understanding of meaning as put forth by a reductive linguisticism. Gendlin, Spretnak, and Fisher speak directly to the question of nihilism, the absence of any given, innate, or transhistorical meaning or truth that, on their view, arises from a decoupling of language from its other. Lakoff and Johnson (2003), in turn, share the view that the dominant ways of construing meaning in Western philosophy and linguistics are inadequate and that the post-structuralist account of meaning is particularly problematic. All of these writers, each in their own way, account for this problematic relation to, or lack of, meaning by speaking of a problematic relation to experience: Lakoff and Johnson appeal to an understanding of metaphor grounded in the body, and construe their own work as an experientialist alternative. Fisher draws attention to a bodily living-in-the-world that undermines the accounts of meaning (or lack thereof) offered by post-structuralism and deconstructionism. Spretnak (1991) speaks of the need to "come to our senses" (p. 149), through a re-encounter with our experiential bodies, as a medicine for the postmodern malaise. Gendlin (1992, 1997), both in his writing and in the awareness technique known as "Focusing" that he originated, calls his readers and students to return to their immediate felt experience as a way of recovering meaning that is not always immediately available in language.

The image of the grid revisited: Foucault's archeology of knowledge

The image of the grid, as discussed previously, is not merely a convenient way to speak of a disruption between statements and their referential context, an expedient metaphor for describing a particular view of language in terms of a distance from the living, ensouled body. Nor is it merely a way to reintroduce the idea of reference as vanishing point of postmodernism's linear perspective. The grid is, in fact, an image favored by Foucault. It appears and reappears throughout *The Order of Things* (1973). And it is language, conceived as a system of signs, that forms the grid. Such a grid is presented as something to be seen through. It is a representative lattice by which, and through which, humans perceive and articulate their world. It is the linguistic grid that establishes what humans discern:

> When we establish a considered classification, when we say that a cat and a dog resemble each other less than two greyhounds do, even if both are tame or embalmed, even if both are frenzied, even if both have just

> broken the water pitcher, what is the ground on which we are able to establish the validity of the classification with complete certainty? On what 'table', according to what grid of identities, similitudes, analogies, have we become accustomed to sort out so many different and similar things? What is this coherence – which, as is immediately apparent, is neither determined by an *a priori* and necessary concatenation, nor imposed on us by immediately perceptible contents? (p. xix).

The ground that might serve to determine the validity of any taxonomy, tellingly, Foucault looks for in the very grid or table that is used to express these taxonomical, classificatory distinctions. The grid of identities, similitudes, and analogies, for him, can not be determined by an a priori, by something that comes before the grid, either temporally, or spatially. Nor is the grid imposed by anything that is immediately perceptible. Perception does not determine what is considered identical, similar, or analogous, "in fact, there is no similitude and no distinction . . . that is not the result of a precise operation and of the application of a preliminary criterion" (Foucault, 1973, p. xx). An individual perceives similarities and differences based on the criteria she or he already possesses. A person's sense of order, for Foucault, has no existence except in the grid that is created by language, the grid that *is* language. Yet, paradoxically, Foucault acknowledges that order is also "at one and the same time, that which is given in things as their inner law" (p. xx). Some form of order in its pure primary state plays a critical role in the formation and reformation of a culture's grid. Its linguistic codes and conventions of perception and practice can be critiqued and invalidated by virtue of an order that is not that of the grid of primary identities, similarities, and differences created by language.

Foucault refers to such codes as the episteme of an age; they determine what is considered valid or certain knowledge. The grid of language that is imposed upon the world determines what, and how, an age knows. Conceptual-linguistic grids from one age can be described and compared with those of another, much like an archeologist might compare unearthed artifacts from different eras, or cultures. Thus, for example, he describes the episteme of the sixteenth century as an analogical cosmography with a propensity for finding meaningful links by way of resemblance. Such a cosmography drew parallels between tempests and apoplectic attacks; the furrows upon one's palm and the intricate meanderings of one's life path; the folded form of walnuts enclosed within a protective shell, and the pleated tissue of the brain within the skull. It was resemblance, he tells the reader, that guided interpretation. The following century, however, had a different grid, one that would not see a meaningful correlation between the form of walnuts and the tissue of the brain. The central, overriding concern and argument of *The Order of Things* (1973) lies in this historical process of one episteme, one grid, being replaced by another, and then another, in a seemingly endless procession. The coroner of epistemes past, Foucault conducts autopsies upon linguistic bodies.

In an exercise of comparative anatomy, he catalogues these epistemes with a quasi-positivist zeal. In his comparative study of epistemes, one can detect an echo of the two bodies, two bodies with a paradoxical or problematic relation to one another. The constructed body is a point upon a linguistic grid. Just as, in Butler's phrasing, it "does not exist outside the terms of its cultural inscription" (1999, p. 308), it belongs, in Foucault's phrasing, to an order that "has no existence except in the grid created by a glance, an examination, a language" (1973, p. xx). Yet, it would seem, another body, one that serves as a site of inscription, one that belongs to order in its pure primary state, also exists. This is the body that is, in some way, given, pre-existing, and available to become the site of its own supposed construction. It belongs to that pure primary state to which Foucault alludes. The problem here is not that a distinction is being made between an object and its representation—between bodies, on the one hand, and a culture's conceptions of them, on the other. The relationship between the two bodies is problematic because the body that has no existence except in the linguistic grid, the body that is mere *nomina*, cannot simultaneously be the body that does in fact exist prior to, or independent of, the grid. Likewise, to say that man is an invention, appeals to the sense that *man* is but a feature of a particular grid, a figure not even two centuries old, and raises the question of who or what, then, created the grid; who or what is responsible for said invention?

You may have rightly noted that Romanyshyn also shares this same sense of the body as an invention, a cultural artifact of sorts, a point upon the grid. It is not so much a given, a fact, a matter of nature. It is a human cultural invention. He concedes that "only in the most minimal sense can we consign the human body to a realm of pure nature divorced from history and culture" (Romanyshyn, 2004, p. 110). Here, Romanyshyn's vision is congruent with Foucault's sense of a constructed body, a body that bears a family resemblance, and was perhaps even born of, Saussure's anatomized language. Such a constructed body, as both Foucault and Romanyshyn skillfully demonstrate, results from the historical process of one episteme, one grid, being replaced by another, and then another. What the body is depends upon the history, culture, and language that creates it. Yet Romanyshyn, as with Foucault, acknowledges another more material body, one that offers a site of inscription, a Vesalian, material body. There is, then, in both authors' work, a simultaneous appeal to both the material fact of the body and the linguistically mediated idea of it.

However there is yet another body to which Romanyshyn alludes, one that, I believe, shares much in common with Spretnak's knowing body, Fisher's and Gendlin's felt, experiential body, and Lakoff and Johnson's body as ground of meaning and metaphor. This body is neither pure construct, nor a mere mass *out there*. Rather, it is a subtle, pantomimic, lived, gestural and erotic body—not merely matter, not merely idea—but an animated body that cannot be reduced to an anatomical object or a linguistic invention. It is, perhaps, in between these two bodies, yet encompasses them both. This animate flesh is neither the body that does not exist outside the terms of its cultural construction, nor merely a site of inscription. In describing this notion of a gestural or subtle body, which Romanyshyn (2000, 2001, 2004) has developed in several works, he alludes repeatedly to a space that exists between the empiricism of facts and the rationalism of ideas. It is a place that exists between things and thoughts. Into that betwixt space, "into that void between matter and mind, the feminine soul as animate flesh disappears" (2000, p. 33). And this disappearance coincides with "a de-animation of the flesh which transforms the vital, gestural body into a mechanism, and with a broken connection between the ensouled sensuous body and the sense-able world" (p. 37).

Jung acutely sensed the disappearance of the soul and animate flesh. He knew of the experiential, animate body that can be reduced to neither matter nor mind, neither Vesalian corpse nor linguistically mediated idea, neither material fact nor ephemeral sign. He knew of the two bodies of which I have endeavored to speak. Paul Kugler, in his seminal essay "Psychic Imaging: A Bridge Between Subject and Object" (1997) portrays Jung's entire psychology as a mediating third position between the ideological extremes that these two bodies represent. In this far-reaching text, Kugler describes the Western philosophical tradition's approach to the image and a concomitant ideological split between realists and nominalists. He traces the medieval debates between these two groups, drawing upon Jung's own exploration of this theme in *Psychological Types* (1921/1971), and updates them, drawing parallels between the present-day postmodern constructionist vs. universalist debate; the former pole of the antinomy, he notes, appeals to "the sociological, the historical, or the inter-subjective" (Kugler, 1997, p. 83) in its critique of universals, although it implicitly universalizes its root metaphors. This pole corresponds to what, in the current inquiry, I have called the body as construction, the linguistic body, the body that cannot exist outside the terms of its cultural inscription. The latter pole allies itself more closely with the body as material object, a body that possesses an ontic status, or true being, independent of the cultural significations, the language, that ostensibly constructs it.

The ideological extremes that these two bodies represent manifest themselves in the debate between nominalism and realism. Nominalists argue that there is no connection between words and their referents. Realists understand language as speaking to a reality beyond itself. This debate is a very old one, yet it has "reemerged as a result of the post-structural critique of referentiality in language" (Kugler 1997, p. 83) and is expressed today in 'constructionist vs. universalist' terms. Those of a postmodern or deconstructionist frame of mind advocate a variety of nominalism and "typically appeal to the sociological, the historical, or the inter-subjective categories to demonstrate that universal attributes are constructed through language in time, rather than given as metaphysical realities" (Kugler, 1997, p. 83). Thus, the old debate rages on, and what may have appeared to be merely a struggle of contemporary sensibilities, shows itself to have roots in times gone by. Those who in the past doubted the relation between words and things continue in opposition to those who trust that language can speak to a reality beyond its own.

It is important to note that this historical analysis by which Jung situates himself takes place in the context of a psychological typology. Jung places epistemological questions within a psychological context. This is the case not only regarding the question of nominalism versus realism, but also rationalism versus empiricism, intellectualism versus sensationalism, idealism versus materialism, dogmatism versus skepticism, etc. He locates the discussion of ideas, not in the realm of thought, but in the realm of psyche.

Jung's opus is an attempt to integrate and transcend these extreme dispositions through an understanding of their complementarity and an invocation of a third element that unites and transcends the two. The transcendent third that Jung bases his psychology upon goes by the name of *anima*. Jung, in contrasting nominalist and realist arguments notes that what is needed is not yet another argument. Rather,

> a third, mediating standpoint is needed. *Esse in intellectu* lacks tangible reality, *esse in re* lacks mind. Idea and thing come together, however, in the human psyche, which holds the balance between them. What would the idea amount to if the psyche did not provide its living value? What would the thing be worth if the psyche withheld from it the determining force of the sense-impression? What indeed is reality if it is not a reality in ourselves, an *esse in anima*? Living reality is the product neither of the actual objective behavior of things nor of the formulated idea exclusively, but rather of the combination of both in the living psychological process, through *esse in anima*. (Jung, as cited in Kugler, 1997, p. 81)

It is the psyche, it is anima, soul, that rests between the extremes of idea and thing, and between the extremes of the constructed (linguistic) body and the body as mass, as object. Without this "between-ness," without psyche, without the animating force inhabiting bodies, what would the body as object be worth? What would be the living value of the body as mere sign, as semiotic side effect, as creature birthed from the womb of discourse? Contemporizing the terms of the opposition that Jung perceived, and his emphatic appeal to a living, ensouled reality, his mediating third position of *esse in anima* exists, "between what today would be called deconstruction and universalism. Psychic images point beyond themselves to both the 'historical particulars' of the world around us and the 'essences' and 'universals' of the mind and metaphysics" (Kugler, pp. 83–4).

For Jung, living reality is not the result, exclusively, of the objective behavior of things (their anatomy), nor is it a product of the formulated idea. It is the combination of both in a living psychological process. There is an affinity here between Jung's psychology as *esse in anima*, and the approaches of Fisher, Gendlin, Spretnak, Lakoff, Johnson, Romanyshyn, and others who champion a reclaiming of the experiential, animate body: "The psyche is living body, and living body is animated matter" (Jung, 1921/1971, p. 543 [*CW* 6 pt. 4 para. 961]). The body imbued of anima is not an anatomical object. A precondition of the anatomical object, it would seem, is that it exist without anima, without soul. A precondition of the corpus of a self-enclosed system of signs is also its de-animation. But where, exactly, is this animate body that exists betwixt and between?

To get a sense of where it might lie, let's return once more to the image of the grid. Imagine that you are a painter sitting before a canvas. In pencil you have drawn a diaphanous lattice of perfect squares upon the white cloth that you have carefully stretched over a rectangular wooden frame. You have drawn vanishing points and horizon lines and determined a fixed vantage point from which the work is to be viewed. You contemplate where exactly you might paint this body that is neither mere mass nor mere construct. Where might you place this subtle, felt body that exists in between the corpus of language and the anatomical body? Where might such a body be? Can you draw a point and call it mind, draw another point and call it matter, then place a third point between these two and call it the experiential body? In what feels like a momentary flash of brilliance you recall this idea of a vanishing point of reference. You recall a phrase from earlier on in the present text: Reference is the vanishing point for Saussure because this is where his project meets its own self-imposed horizon, the circumscription of its own possibilities, the frontier that, by virtue of its own spatial logic, cannot be traversed. It makes sense, then, to place this subtle body there, on the painted horizon of the canvas, there at the very limit where words touch the world of things . . . and yet, this feels slightly amiss, slightly off base. It seems conceptually accurate, but does not quite feel right. Placing the animate, felt body there is still placing it *within* a given frame, and doing so thereby implicitly accepts the assumptions that the frame is built upon. You lift your eyes from the canvas and look out upon a vast field populated by figures like Spretnak, Romanyshyn, Fisher, Foucault, Gendlin and others. Is such a body out there somewhere, not upon the grid of the canvas, but in the world the canvas would portray? This too feels amiss. You experience a moment of vertigo, as you sense yourself falling through a bottomless abyss of unresoluble conundrums, riddles that the intellect will simply never be able to resolve. You return your gaze once again to the vanishing point of the canvas, trying to imagine a place, there, just beyond and over the horizon of your linear perspective, just outside the purview of the canvas. You imagine yourself traveling far off into that simulated distance, till, after a very long journey, you arrive at the very body that is gazing at your canvas, which is also the body that is reading these words, and, perhaps, ultimately gives them meaning.

References

Abram, D. (1996). *The spell of the sensuous: Perception and language in a more-than-human world* (1st ed.). New York, NY: Pantheon Books.

Aho, J. A., & Aho, K. (2008). *Body matters: A phenomenology of sickness, disease, and illness.* Lanham, MD: Lexington Books.

Alexander, J. C. (1995). *Fin de siecle social theory: Relativism, reduction, and the problem of reason.* New York, NY: Verso.

Ball, J. M. (1910). *Andreas Vesalius, the reformer of anatomy.* Saint Louis, MO: Medical Science Press.

Berman, M. (1981). *The reenchantment of the world.* Ithaca, NY: Cornell University Press.

Bordo, S. (1987). *The flight to objectivity: Essays on Cartesianism and culture.* Albany, NY: State University of New York Press.

Brooke, R. (1991). *Jung and phenomenology.* New York, NY: Routledge.

Brooke, R. (2000). *Pathways into the Jungian world: Phenomenology and analytical psychology.* New York, NY: Routledge.

Butler, J. (1999). Foucault and the paradox of bodily inscriptions. In D. Welton (Ed.), *The body: Classic and contemporary readings* (pp. 307–13). Malden, MA: Blackwell.

Descartes, R., & Tweyman, S. (2002). *Meditations on first philosophy.* Ann Arbor, MI: Caravan Books.

Dillon, M. C. (1995). *Semiological reductionism: A critique of the deconstructionist movement in postmodern thought.* Albany, NY: State University of New York Press.

Fisher, A. (2002). *Radical ecopsychology: Psychology in the service of life.* Albany, NY: State University of New York Press.

Foucault, M. (1973). *The order of things: An archaeology of the human sciences.* New York, NY: Vintage Books.

Foucault, M. (1977). *Language, counter-memory, practice: Selected essays and interviews.* Ithaca, NY: Cornell University Press.

Foucault, M., & Gordon, C. (1980). *Power/knowledge: Selected interviews and other writings, 1972–1977.* Brighton, England: Harvester Press.

Foucault, M., & Rabinow, P. (1984). *The Foucault reader.* New York, NY: Pantheon Books.

Freud, S. (1901/1981). *The psychopathology of everyday life.* New York, NY: Norton.

Freud, S. (1905/1990). *Jokes and their relation to the unconscious.* New York, NY: Norton.

Freud, S. (1912/1958). The dynamics of transference. In J. Strachey (Ed. & Trans.), *The standard edition of the complete psychological works of Sigmund Freud* (Vol. 12, pp. 97–108). London, England: Hogarth Press.

Gendlin, E. T. (1992). The wider role of bodily sense in thought and language. In M. Sheets-Johnstone (Ed.), *Giving the body its due* (pp. 192–207). Albany, NY: State University of New York Press.

Gendlin, E. T. (1997). *Experiencing and the creation of meaning: A philosophical and psychological approach to the subjective.* Evanston, IL: Northwestern University Press.

Gendlin, E. T., & Kleinberg-Levin, D. M. (1997). *Language beyond postmodernism: Saying and thinking in Gendlin's philosophy.* Evanston, IL: Northwestern University Press.

Girard, R., & Doran, R. (2008). *Mimesis and theory: Essays on literature and criticism, 1953–2005*. Stanford, CA: Stanford University Press.

Jameson, F. (1972). *The prison-house of language: A critical account of structuralism and Russian formalism*. Princeton, NJ: Princeton University Press.

Johnson, M. (2007). *The meaning of the body: Aesthetics of human understanding*. Chicago, IL: University of Chicago Press.

Johnstone, A. A. (1992). The bodily nature of the self or what Descartes should have conceded princess Elizabeth of Bohemia. In M. Sheets-Johnstone (Ed.), *Giving the body its due* (pp. 16–47). Albany, NY: State University of New York Press.

Jung, C. G. (1921/1971). *Psychological types*. Princeton, NJ: Princeton University Press (original work published 1921).

Jung, C. G. (1959/1969). *Aion: Researches into the phenomenology of the self*. In R. F. C. Hull (Trans.), *The collected works of C. G. Jung* (Vol. 9). Princeton, NJ: Princeton-Bollingen (original work published 1959).

Jung, C. G. (1960/1969). *The structure and dynamics of the psyche* (2nd edn.). Princeton, NJ: Princeton University Press (original work published 1960).

Jung, C. G. (1961). *Memories, dreams, reflections*. New York, NY: Random House.

Jung, C. G. (1983). *The essential Jung* (A. Storr, Ed.). Princeton, NJ: Princeton University Press.

Jung, C. G., & De Laszlo, V. S. (1993). *The basic writings of C. G. Jung* (Modern Library edn.). New York, NY: Modern Library.

Kleinberg-Levin, D. M. (1988). *The opening of vision: Nihilism and the postmodern situation*. New York, NY: Routledge.

Kugler, P. (1982). *The alchemy of discourse: An archetypal approach to language*. Lewisburg, PA: Bucknell University Press.

Kugler, P. (1997). Psychic imaging: A bridge between subject and object. In P. Young-Eisendrath & T. Dawson (Eds.), *The Cambridge companion to Jung* (pp. 71–85). New York: Cambridge University Press.

Lakoff, G., & Johnson, M. (1999). *Philosophy in the flesh: The embodied mind and its challenge to Western thought*. New York, NY: Basic Books.

Lakoff, G., & Johnson, M. (2003). *Metaphors we live by*. Chicago, IL: University of Chicago Press.

MacNaughton, G. (2005). *Doing Foucault in early childhood studies: Applying post-structural ideas*. New York, NY: Routledge.

McNeley, J. K. (1981). *Holy wind in Navajo philosophy*. Tucson, AZ: University of Arizona Press.

Merleau-Ponty, M. (1973). *The prose of the world*. Evanston, IL: Northwestern University Press.

Norris, C. (1990). *What's wrong with postmodernism: Critical theory and the ends of philosophy*. New York, NY: Harvester Wheatsheaf.

Ricœur, P. (1977). *The rule of metaphor: Multi-disciplinary studies of the creation of meaning in language*. Toronto, Canada: University of Toronto Press.

Romanyshyn, R. (2000). Alchemy and the subtle body of metaphor: Soul and cosmos. In Brooke, R. (Ed.), *Pathways into the Jungian world: Phenomenology and analytical psychology* (pp. 27–47). New York, NY: Routledge.

Romanyshyn, R. (2001). *Mirror and metaphor: Images and stories of psychological life*. Pittsburgh, PA: Trivium.

Romanyshyn, R. (2004). *Technology as symptom and dream.* New York, NY: Brunner-Routledge.

Romanyshyn, R. (2007). *The wounded researcher: Research with soul in mind.* New Orleans, LA: Spring Journal Books.

Rowland, S. (2010). *C. G. Jung in the humanities: Taking the soul's path.* New Orleans, LA: Spring Journal Books.

Saussure, F. d., Bally, C., Sechehaye, A., & Riedlinger, A. (1986). *Course in general linguistics.* LaSalle, IL: Open Court.

Shelburne, W. A. (1988). *Mythos and logos in the thought of Carl Jung: The theory of the collective unconscious in scientific perspective.* Albany, NY: State University of New York Press.

Spretnak, C. (1991). *States of grace: The recovery of meaning in the postmodern age.* San Francisco, CA: Harper.

Spretnak, C. (1999). *The resurgence of the real: Body, nature, and place in a hypermodern world.* New York, NY: Addison Wesley.

Taylor, V. E., & Winquist, C. E. (2001). *Encyclopedia of postmodernism.* New York, NY: Routledge.

Whitmont, E. C. (1969). *The symbolic quest.* Princeton, NJ: Princeton University Press.

Zalewski, M. (2000). *Feminism after postmodernism: Theorising through practice.* New York, NY: Routledge.

Chapter 2

Abandoned earth, abandoned nature

Language theory as dream of departure

Lunar landings and gravitational pulls

In the summer of 1969, human beings set step on the moon's surface for the first time. Unchanged by the paltry atmosphere of that orbiting satellite, the boot prints left by Neil Armstrong and Edwin "Buzz" Aldrin lie there still, to this day, upon the barren lunar landscape. These same prints have also impressed themselves upon the landscape of the collective imagination, as have many other images of the Apollo 11 mission—the landing of the Eagle space module upon the wan, pockmarked face of that nearest celestial sphere; the stiff, doll-like suits with bulbous helmets bobbing along the rocky planes; a distant earth floating, half in shadow, just above the moon's horizon. In December of the previous year, the Apollo 8 spacecraft took the very first photographs of the earth from space. The hit single "Space Oddity," released a few months later by British pop icon David Bowie (1969), evinced a popular fascination with such images. Humans, standing firmly upon this planet, breathing in its air, drinking water from its rivers, lakes, and aquifers, and nourishing themselves upon its abundant biosphere could, for the first time, view the earth as an object seen from afar, as alien visitors might. Such a vision of the planet, according to Abram (2010), is now commonplace. In his book *Becoming Animal: An Earthly Cosmology*, he writes:

> Today many educated folks have ceased experiencing the earth as the rough ground that supports their steps and the wind pouring past their ears; for them the earth has become, first and foremost, that blue sphere flecked with clouds that they have seen in various NASA photos—images that were reproduced countless times and became the basis for a thousand corporate logos. For many persons the earth is now equated, in other words, with the earth *seen from outside*—with our planet as it might be seen by a transcendent god, or by a surveillance satellite. This "objective" view of the earth now conditions and supersedes our immediate experience of the rainswept land that enfolds us. (p. 92)

Shortly before NASA began taking such photos, and Armstrong left those boot prints upon the collective imagination, Rorty's *The Linguistic Turn*

(1967) went to print. In 1966, Foucault's *Les Mots et les Choses* was published to critical acclaim. One year later, Derrida's *De la Grammatologie* (1967a) was greeted by similar accolades.

No tangible relationship between these publications and the historic feat of the Apollo 11 lunar landing warrants their juxtaposition. No causal links unite these stellar works of postmodern discourse with NASA's technological triumphs. Yet an imaginative intelligence might find that the proximity in time of these disparate events does, serendipitously, mark a proximity of meaning: The Apollo 11's escape from the earth's gravitational pull closely paralleled another—the escape of language from the terrestrial gravity of an extralinguistic referent.

The metaphor of *escaping the terrestrial gravity of reference* is an imaginative way to speak of many things at once, and the image of the earth will serve this metaphor in multiple ways: It summons the very idea of our earthiness, that is to say, our *nature* as earthlings, as humans. Etymologically, the word *human* is related to the Latin *humus*, meaning earth or soil. Our species name is rooted in the earth. The image of our planet also lends itself to speaking of nature insofar as *nature*, the term, is derived from *natus*, the word for birth, from which we derive *natal*, *nascent*, and *native*. What is "natural" is considered to be inborn and inherent. It is not a post-natal acquisition, but innate. Instincts, therefore, as innate tendencies or impulses, are regarded as natural. Thus, there is an intimate connection between nature and birth, and by extension, place of birth or home. *Nature*, through *natus*, speaks to origins and beginnings. It is not a place we visit, it is home (Snyder, 1990). It is origin. A thing's nature has to do with where, and from what, it arose. The image of the earth, as our shared birthplace, our site of origin, our collective home intimates who we naturally are. Hence, the earth as image of human nature is doubly valid, insofar as it is both soil (*humus*) and place of birth (*natus*).

Nature, furthermore, is related to notions of the *essential*, the *intrinsic*, the *given*. What is natural for someone or something is essential or intrinsic to him, her, or it—given, not created, at least not by a human creator, though perhaps by a divine one. Yet the term has other connotations that must be kept in mind as we explore this metaphor of escaping the earthly gravity of linguistic reference. Ambiguous, polysemous, and protean, *nature* also denotes the living ecosystem not created by human beings, that is, the wilderness. It designates a world independent of human design and will, a world that is not machine, not artifact, not devised (Snyder, 1990). With these associations in mind, the image of departing the third planet from the sun, our birthplace, is pregnant with meaning.

Watch that planet slowly recede from view as we consider a pervasive sense in the works of Rorty, Derrida, and Foucault, that there simply is no human nature, or that such a notion no longer holds any real currency (Gendlin & Kleinberg-Levin, 1997; Pinker, 2002). It has no gravitational pull. In such thought, too, there is a corresponding critical attitude towards the inherent, the intrinsic, the essential, and the given. Thus, in employing the metaphor of the terrestrial pull of the referent, I intend to elliptically draw attention to a parallelism: The thought that disputes extralinguistic reference also disputes human nature—and several other closely related ideas. *In figuratively escaping the "pull" of the referent, so too does such thought escape the "pull" of nature.* Thus, Foucault avowed mistrust of the notion of human nature and understood it to be first and foremost "an epistemological indicator to designate certain types of discourse" (Chomsky & Foucault, 2006, p. 7). Derrida sought to dismantle this same notion, seeing it as merely one half of an opposition within polarizing language. The technique of deconstruction that he originated operates on the understanding that texts begin, not with natural givens but, rather, with cultural constructs that are blind to their own artifice (Johnson, 1981). Rorty (1989) openly professed a desire to get rid of any sense of intrinsic nature whatsoever, whether it might belong to self or world. For him, nature, human or otherwise, was a nefarious, dangerous idea that confused more than clarified.

Each of these men was also anti-essentialist. Rorty (1999) inveighed against finding anything intrinsic or essential to "tables, stars, electrons, human beings, academic disciplines, social institutions, or anything else" (p. 53). Anti-essentialism, in fact, was a key element of the philosophical therapy he considered his own writing to be. Foucault (1977) argued for an anti-essentialist conception of the human body, and Derrida's anti-essentialism informed a generation of French and Anglo-Saxon feminists (Brooks, 1997). From such viewpoints as these, human nature is not as close to us as human skin, or as essential to us as the air we breathe or the water we imbibe but, rather, something more analogous to the earth viewed from afar, and growing ever more distant.

Allusions to terrestrial gravity and imagery of astronautic endeavors—from men and women floating in their hermetically sealed tin cans far above the thinnest ether, to space shuttles lifting off from Cape Canaveral—are more than just imaginative ways of depicting a seeming escape from our earthly nature, our humanness. Much can be read into them, and their implications are multiple. For the metaphoric, imagistic language used here to describe space travel lends itself to speaking of yet other themes that arise with postmodern understandings of linguistic reference, themes such as *ground, foundations,* and *relativity.* This is testament to both the rich complexity of such imagery and the far-ranging implications of the debates on reference, and representation. For this reason, a thorough investigation, one that dares to reveal a complex symbolic image, also brings to light other more secondary or tertiary themes that may have initially seemed unrelated. Such themes include *self-invention, the critique of universals*, and *the correspondence theory of truth.*

In exploring these thematic correspondences, these associative clusters of thought and image surrounding both astronautic departures and theories of linguistic reference, I invite the reader to be a little unreasonable, a little irrational. My intent in the present writing is to present a commingling of image and idea, of mythos and logos, that aspires towards veracity, but not proof. So, feel images through as you think them through. Intuit their potential for meaningful disclosure, and sense them with skin, ears, tongue, eyes, and nose. If we follow the logic of an image, if we work it, and let our hands turn it over and again, like a curiously textured stone in our coat pocket, we may find, as Jung did, that "often the hands know how to solve a riddle with which the intellect has wrestled in vain" (Jung, 1960/1969, p. 86 [*CW* 8 pt. 1 para. 180]).

Astronautic bodies

> Having dominated the earth out of our increasing distance from it, we have come to believe that we are masters, and even creators. And in so doing, we have lost the sense that we are sponsored, which means supported, upheld, and already sent on the way. In this respect, we have lost something of the religious sense of human life, in the root meaning of that term, the sense that we are already bound, and connected to, and limited by something beyond ourselves. (Romanyshyn, 2004, p. 25)

The astronaut, like the corpse, forms part of a collective dream of departure from the animate (ensouled), experiential body. It is a figure in the process of cultural evolution that birthed a new, modern sense of self as detached spectator, and the body as spectacle and specimen. In this dream, the body as corpse is followed by the body conceived as machine, a corpse set in motion. Metaphors of mechanism came to predominate over those that drew parallels between the human body and the non-human world. Thus, the mechanical body possessed a mechanical heart, a pump to circulate the blood with clock-like precision, whereas previously "the prevailing opinion was that the blood ebbs back and forth within the body like the tides" (Romanyshyn, 2004, p. 136). Each organ came to possess a machine-like function, as the corporeal became mechanical. But a principle was needed to explain bodily movement and responsiveness to the environment. This need brought forth yet another understanding—one based on reflex, a principle that set the body in motion while simultaneously draining it of intention, desire, and passion. Thus, the body as corpse was resurrected as machine, and then vivified anew via reflex. Likewise, throughout history, one figure after another arose in the drama of estrangement from the body. The imagined perfection of the robot followed, then the transformed body of the present-day astronaut floating free of earth's gravity. Corpse, machine, robot, and astronaut, all are manifestations of a dream of ever-increasing distance from the living, animate body.

To understand how the dream of estrangement from the animate body is also the dream of departing earth, and the figure of the astronaut, close your eyes and take the time to simply imagine leaving your body, then floating a few feet above it. Allow yourself to move farther still, passing through the roof of a building, if you are in one, or perhaps beyond and above a canopy of treetops. As you move up into the thinning atmosphere, your body, and the objects surrounding it, appear progressively smaller. Soon, you will not see yourself at all. Move farther still and vast areas of terrain will come into view, until this vastness is so great that the planet itself is but a distant orb floating in the great cosmic void.

Another way of imagining this dream of departure and de-animation, or loss of soul, is by considering what it means for something to be *inside out*. The theme of the inside out runs like a thin thread throughout the recurrent images of this dream: The astronautic body is one that has been turned inside out, and is on the way to being discarded (Romanyshyn, 2004). In a similar vein, Abram, in the earlier description, tells of an earth *seen from the outside* that has come to supersede the immediate experience of our living enfolded within it. In these pages we've explored this sense of *inside out* in several ways, without ever quite naming it as such: The opening image of a corpse dissected is one of making the inside outside, quite literally taking out the innards. The final image of attempting to locate an experiential, or animate body, on a grid also played heavily upon a visceral sense of in and out. Likewise, exploring the dual meanings of the word *man* in the closing image of Foucault's *The Order of Things* (1973) required an understanding of *man* as existing, at times, *in* language, *qua* sign, and, at other times, *outside* language as its ostensible creator.

Inside out is a fundamental characteristic of the anatomical vision, a vision that not only turns the body into an object, but does so to the earth as well. When the body is turned inside out, when it is anatomized, so is the earth. This is not just a psychological truth, but an historical one as well: The anatomical corpse "was invented-discovered at that moment when, with Copernicus, we transformed the earth into an object in space; at that moment, then, when psychologically, humanity abandoned the earth to take up its place in the stars" (Romanyshyn, 2004, p. 147). The moment in which the earth as milieu, the earth as lived *in*, is transformed into an object *out* there, is also the moment in which the experiential body becomes anatomical. The astronaut, in his very being, manifests the psychological experience of distance as a physical fact. Through the astronaut, a dream of distance comes true, a dream of dissociation from the earthen ground beneath our feet.

The astronaut, understood in this way, is an exemplary image because it speaks to a dual departure from both the living body and the living planet, or what Abram (2010) referred to above as "our immediate experience of the rainswept land that enfolds us" (p. 92). The astronaut is, then, in a sense, doubly anatomical: It is the child of both a Vesalian anatomy of the body and a Copernican, heliocentric anatomy of the spheres. Just as the body as corpse is no longer the immediate, visceral experience of the body as the center of subjectivity, the earth as astronomical object is no longer the foundation upon which we human beings plant our feet. Both have become objects in space, to be seen, analyzed, measured, evaluated, and controlled. Both have been turned inside out. A new vision has displaced body and earth from the medieval, geocentric cosmos in which bodies were not machines, the heart was not a pump, and the dead were not subject to dissection.

The phenomenologist Edmund Husserl (Husserl, Merleau-Ponty, Lawlor, & Bergo, 2002) investigated this displacement, this modern sense of space, body, and earth brought about by Copernicus and others. In radical opposition to prevailing views of his era, and ours, Husserl took issue with the Copernican understanding of the earth's movement, an understanding that, to this day, is the very symbol of the victory of science over religious superstition and common-sense perception. He contended, rather, that our planet is not simply one heavenly body among many others floating in space (Abram, 1996). From a phenomenological standpoint, all bodies are first located relative to the ground of the earth. The earth is not 'in' space but, rather, provides it. The great philosopher went so far as to assert that the earth was not in fact in motion around the sun, or in motion at all, but contended that according to our sensory perception the sun traverses the sky of a stationary earth (Husserl et al., 2002). This is how we actually perceive it. This is what we experience. It is the actual phenomenon with which we are presented. Centuries after Copernicus, we still speak of the sun's rising and setting because, phenomenologically, experientially, this is what actually happens. We see the sun rise and set.

Yet the Copernican revolution rent mental concepts from bodily percepts (Abram, 1996); our educated minds tell us of the sun's centrality, and the earth's peripheral status, yet our body perceives something quite different. The Copernican legacy has taught us to mistrust this common-sense perception and trust the conception of the earth as both peripheral and moving. As a result, there is a cognitive dissonance between our geocentric experience and our heliocentric understanding. Richard Tarnas (1991) has described this schism with the felicitous, rich turn of phrase "post-Copernican double bind" (p. 418). Husserl attempted to overcome this double bind, contending that terms like *motion* and *rest* derive their meaning directly from our primary experience of being bodies in motion or at rest relative to the earth, which serves as an unshakeable foundation (Abram, 1996). The earth does not move, though it provides the space in which movement and rest can occur, or be seen, as in the case of celestial bodies like stars. The earth for Husserl is not one body among many floating in space, it is the experiential ground for all human beings (Husserl et al., 2002).

Phenomenology, first developed by Husserl, attempts to apprehend things in themselves, independent of any pre-existing theoretical framework, including our common assumption that we are subjects separated from objects. It is also an attempt to apprehend the mind as embodied (Rowland, 2010). Seeking to bridge the abyss between percept and concept, it is a philosophy of immediate experience in, of, and through both animate body and living planet. The earth's gravitational field pulls hard on phenomenology, so that it rests firmly upon a ground that is viscerally sensed, and intuitively known. Yet this philosophy of experience, in the latter half of the twentieth century and the beginning of the current one, has been eclipsed by the allure of language, semiotics, and the construction of knowledge (Abram, 2002). The linguistic turn has come to eclipse the philosophy of experience, and in a sense, even experience itself. This is perhaps most clearly perceived in the works of Jacques Derrida.

Derrida's unearthly theory of reference

> The problem of language has never been simply one problem among others. But never as much as at present has it invaded, as such, the global horizon of the most diverse researches and the most heterogeneous discourses, diverse and heterogeneous in their intention, method, and ideology . . . a historico-metaphysical epoch must finally determine as language the totality of its problematic horizon. (Derrida, 1976, p. 6)

The same year that Derrida published *De la Grammatologie* (1967a) he also published *La Voix et le Phénomène* (1967b), a work that sought to expose fundamental contradictions in Husserl's thought—aporia in the very phenomenology that championed the earth as primary point of reference. The chief intent of the work was to show that the theme of pure presentation, pure primordial perception espoused by phenomenology allied it with metaphysical presuppositions that this same phenomenology attempted to refute. On this reading, Husserl's thought suffered from a fundamental inconsistency, one that undermined the entire project. In contradistinction to pure primordial perception, Derrida (1973) affirmed that "perception does not exist or that what is called perception is not primordial, somehow everything 'begins' by 're-presentation'" (1973, p. 45n). Experience is indebted to representation. Perception itself is beholden to reproduction. For Derrida, what appears to be experientially given, upon closer scrutiny, reveals itself to be produced by the very act of representation (Habermas, 1987; Nash, 1994). The world does not present itself to us, and is not later *re*-presented by us. There is no self-presentation of meaning. There is nothing given in it, or intrinsic to it, that can be later depicted. Our perceptions and experiences of the world are always already re-presentations. What appears to be obvious or self-evident is not given by the nature of things, but constructed by way of culture, language, and history (Johnson, 1981). For Derrida, perception itself is meaningful only because it has been subsumed by a system of signifiers. Perception as presentation is not possible because perception is always already re-presentation (Dillon, 1995).

His critique is radical, in the sense of going to the very root of Husserl's thought: It challenges the essential notion within phenomenology that there is a domain of experience that can be called primordial, and that this domain might form the foundation upon which true understanding can rest (Dillon, 1995). Derrida undercuts the proposition that there is any sort of prelinguistic meaning that language can express. According to this critique, there simply is no immediate experience of the rainswept land, or of anything else for that matter, because the immediate is always already mediated. The primordial, the experiential, the perceptual, the sensual, the phenomenal, and the intuitive are reconceived, reconfigured, and appropriated in such a way that they are understood to be derivative rather than primary, compounded and produced rather than given. In this regard, Derrida's attack on phenomenology is an acute case of a general tendency within the linguistic turn, and exemplary of its enduring influence; for all fields within the wake of this turn, the presumed immediacy of perception, even the most seemingly immediate and indubitable perceptions of sense impressions can no longer serve as a court of last appeal (Habermas & Fultner, 2003). In this regard, Derrida's project is not merely a deconstruction of language; rather, more fundamentally, it is a deconstruction of the common-sense perception of the obvious (Johnson, 1981).

To understand Derrida's challenge to phenomenology (and how this might relate to questions of nature, earth, and ground), one needs to look no further than the concept of *difſérance*. Writing in the wake of the structuralist revolution initiated by Saussure, Derrida's critical appropriation of Saussure's theory of signification boldly accentuates two closely related elements of the Swiss linguist's thought: The value of linguistic signs as determined by intralinguistic relations, and the ambiguous or tenuous relationship between these signs and any actual referents. But whereas Saussure largely left aside the question of sign-to-referent relations in a conscientious attempt to delineate an area of study, Derrida radically, repeatedly, and explicitly undermines the very possibility that language might refer to anything outside of itself, to anything that might transcend the language system as such.[1]

For Derrida, it would seem, there simply is no way in which language might shed light on any reality other than a linguistic one, because everything is always already linguistic. Everything has always already been mediated by the production of signs. In a widely cited and controversial passage from *Of Grammatology* (1976) Derrida offers an explicit, vivid denial of any possible linkage between text and its other.

> If reading must not be content with doubling the text, it cannot legitimately transgress the text toward something other than it, toward a referent (a reality that is metaphysical, historical, psychobiographical, etc.) or toward a signified outside the text whose content could take place, could have taken place outside of language, that is to say, in the sense that we give here to that word, outside of writing in general. That is why the methodological considerations that we risk applying here to an example are closely dependent on general propositions that we have elaborated above; as regards the absence of the referent or the transcendental signified. (p. 158)

For Derrida, it would seem, text and its other, whether this other is metaphysical, historical, or psychobiographical, are fundamentally incommensurable and unbridgeable. There is no legitimate transgression, no justifiable moving beyond the parameters of the textual. The demands of his method, the spatial logic of his linear perspective, simply will not allow for any movement from language to its other, from text to an (absent) referent or reality. Meaning must be construed as *intra* and not *extra*-linguistic. It must be conceived as relational *within* an infinite matrix of signs and cannot leap, as it were, to something existing outside this relational web. There is no dictionary in which you will find "a word that detaches itself from these internal relationships and sends you sailing right out of the dictionary into a mythical, mystical thing in itself 'outside' of language, wistfully called the 'transcendental signified" (Derrida & Caputo, 1997, p. 100).

In the unbridgeable abyss between text and referent, lies *différance*, a neologism coined by Derrida, that is both deferral and differentiation (Johnson, 1981). A feature of the production of textual meaning, *différance* as deferral leads one down the unending chain of signification that cannot lead toward a referent, just as walking towards a forever-receding horizon cannot lead one to the sun; every step taken necessitates another step yet to be taken. Because the significance or value of each linguistic sign is dependent on its relation to other signs (as in Saussure), the ultimate meaning of a sign cannot be determined until the other signs to which it relates are reached. These signs, in turn, are subject to the same provisions. Since, then, for Derrida, to refer is to defer, the signified something that might be said to exist *outside* language, be prior to it, or at least not the result of it, is forever not yet here, forever elsewhere. The ostensibly mythical and mystical thing in itself, a.k.a., *the transcendental signified* always escapes. We are linguistic beings ensconced within a process of semiosis rendered infinite by way of deferral, a deferral which appears to prohibit the possibility of language pointing to any phenomena beyond itself.

The deferred reference of Derrida's semiotics undermines the basic project of phenomenology, and with it the sense that sign systems can speak to anything transcendent of themselves. The primordial, the experiential, the perceptual, the sensual, the phenomenal, and the intuited exist, in Derrida's thought, insofar as they are terms with meanings, but something of their *élan vital* has been taken away; perception that either does not exist, or is no longer primordial, that does not exist prior to its representation, as a primary something that can be spoken of or spoken from, is ersatz perception. Like a lifeless body, its form persists. The term "perception" remains, but its animating force does not. Its soul has departed. It has been, *ipso facto*, denatured, robbed of its quiddity.

Yet *différance* is not merely deferral, but also differentiation, a differentiation that precludes the possibility of identity; no word, no text, no reading of a text, can be identical with another, nor can a word or sign be identical with what it ostensibly represents. Here, too, we find echoes of Saussure, who believed that in language there are only differences "*and no positive terms.* Whether we take the signification [signified] or the signal [sign], the language includes neither ideas nor sounds existing prior to the linguistic system, but only conceptual and phonetic differences arising out of that system" (Saussure et al., 1986, p. 118, original emphasis). Only differences reside in language, and these differences are of a special variety, for they presume nothing positive. Sign systems work like a mathematics based entirely on subtraction and negative numbers, and this mathematics is itself radically segregated from any idea or sound that may be said to precede it. Nothing conceptual or phonetic within this mathematics can be said to originate outside of it. No infiltration is possible. Sounds and ideas present in language arise directly from it, as if by autogenesis.

Yet Derridean *différance* does not a Saussurian difference make. The former is a radical appropriation of the latter, an appropriation that goes to the very core of the signifier-signified dual character of the sign, so that even signs are non-identical with themselves: The signifier, the manifest word, is not identical with the signified, the concept. In fact, it cannot be. In order for Derrida's particular understanding of reference to work, there cannot exist an identity between these two so-called "component parts" of the sign. Words refer us to yet more words precisely because of their relationship of difference. Signs mark the place of difference (Spivak, 1976). For Saussure, this meant that language, all language, is based on the principle *this is not that.* Derrida suggests something far more radical: *This is not* (even) *this*, for *différance* is fundamental heterogeneity—thorough, deep, pervasive dissimilarity. Everything is alien to everything else. No two words, no two things, no two meanings are the same. Derrida's subsumption of the phenomenal, the experiential, the intuitive, and the sensual under the auspices of representation and signification is also a forceful subordination of identity to difference. It establishes the logical priority of the latter over the former (Dews, 1994).

This subsumption is another name for the semiological reduction, which Dillon (1995) sees as being the core thesis of postmodern thought. This reduction subverts the idea that language, conceived as a system of signifiers, arises from a level of experience that antecedes the mediations of language. It undermines any sense of a phenomenological grounding to statements that you or I might make. The only ground now is a linguistic one, and this ground, if it can be called such, is a forever shifting one, rife with relentless seismic activity. Language has subsumed experience, so that it is now merely "experience," that is to say, just one more signifier among many. If the phenomenal belongs under the rubric of the linguistic, or if the intuitively given is not given but, rather, produced via semiosis, then there is nothing for language to rest upon, except, perhaps, itself. There is no longer any ground beneath words. Language is in no way derived from an experiential life-world, what Husserl (Husserl et al., 2002) and other phenomenologists have called *die Lebenswelt.* It is not derivative, but constitutive. Whereas, for Husserl, terms like "motion" and "rest" must derive their meaning, first and foremost, from our embodied, sensory experience, for Derrida such an idea would appear to be a non sequitur.

Astronautic language and the meaning of ground

Language, à la Derrida, is astronautic. When the perceptual, the experiential, the intuitive, and the sensual, are no longer understood to be immediate, when perception does not exist in any primordial sense and everything begins by re-presentation, the earth ceases to be the immediate milieu that surrounds and sustains us. It appears only as a distant image, a mere depiction of itself, something seen through a window, or flashed upon an LCD screen. As immediacy is deferred, and the immediate is rendered mediate by an abyss of language that can, on principle, never be traversed, a dream of distance is enacted. As the perceptual, the experiential, the sensual, and the intuitive are transformed into objects (signs) within language, the earth (with all the myriad associations given to it in the present text), is transformed into an object in space. It is seen from the outside, and this view appears to supersede the immediate experience of living enfolded within it. The resulting body, an astronautic one, is isolated, insulated from its surround by a space capsule of signs, a spacesuit of semiosis. Within this dream of distance, though, the earth has not disappeared entirely. Within this dream of distance, the other of language exists, but it has grown so very remote.

Astronautic language does not touch the earth, but floats above it. Eluding the terrestrial gravity of an extralinguistic referent, it is language ungrounded. It is no surprise, then, that a recurrent image has arisen from within this dream of a turn towards language, an almost ubiquitously favored trope in various iterations crossing multiple disciplines: that of a lack of philosophical *grounds* or *foundations*. Accordingly, *postfoundationalism* is used as a blanket term to refer to post-positivist orientations informed by the linguistic turn. Books engaging such authors as Foucault, Derrida, Rorty, Gadamer, Habermas, and Fish, are given titles like *Critical Conditions: Postmodernity and the Question of Foundations* (Fairlamb, 1994). The image of a free-floating language, only tenuously, problematically, or dubiously related to a ground has become commonplace. It is a recurrent motif in a collective dream, and what you are reading is an attempt to amplify this motif, this image, flesh out its implicit sense, and follow the logic of its associative trails.

Deconstruction and post-structuralism relentlessly focus upon the problem of a philosophical ground, the problem of establishing a foundational principle for any act of interpretation. Such principles include so-called absolutes and metaphysical universals like *truth*, *reality*, *self*, and of course, *nature*. The semiological reduction eliminates an appeal to such transcendent entities and, as a result, we appear to be trapped in a sort of linguistic solipsism that prohibits any transgression of the text (Kugler, 2005). Since the text cannot be transgressed, and there is no direct appeal to the phenomenal world to adjudicate among texts, the result appears to be a radical relativism (Eagleton, 2003; Pinker, 2007; Reason & Bradbury, 2006). The radicality of this relativism resides, paradoxically, in its absolute character: When the signifier is cut off from the signified, when their severance renders the two utterly and thoroughly *different*, groundlessness itself is, paradoxically, grounded (Dillon, 1995).

The resulting relativism is also reductive, to the extent that it construes meaning as something produced by, and residing in, sign systems, within the strictly linguistic, *and nowhere else*. This relativism is reductive insofar as it contends that "from the moment that there is meaning, there are nothing but signs" (Derrida, 1976, p. 50). It is within this *nothing but* that its reductionism resides. Jung describes the *nothing but* temperament as an incubus "which is the insistent leitmotiv of all one-sidedness" (Jung, 1954/1969, p. 73 [*CW* 17 pt. 3 para. 156]), an issue to which we will return shortly. Language, understood in this way, appears to rest on an absence, an abyss, yet it is an abyss instituted by the very presumption that cleaves the sign into dual aspects, after having cleaved it from an entire referential context. The absolute relativism that lurks within this critique of absolutes is codified and instituted in the utter divide between words and what they mean.

Deconstruction's critique of grounds cannot be separated from the theme of origins; for Derrida, the two are virtually coterminous. The theme of origins permeates Derrida's work and throughout is associated with the idea of a firm ground, an abiding center, an absolute principle, the meaning of which is identical with its very presence:

> It could be shown that all the names related to fundamentals, to principles, or to the center have always designated an invariable presence – eidos, arche, telos, energeia, ousia (essence, existence, substance, subject) aletheia, transcendentality, consciousness, God, man, and so forth. (Derrida, 1978, pp. 279–80)

The fundamental principles that ostensibly ground all meaning have always been construed in terms of presence, a presence which the logic of *différance* discredits. Derrida deconstructs the very idea of an origin, of a moment when meaning was present to itself in all its plenitude, by showing that, in fact, it depends upon absence, upon a yet-to-come followed by a yet-to-come. Presence itself is an illusion, an epiphenomenon of the production of signs. The mistaken belief in the self-presentation of meaning—here and now, or in any here and now that ever was or will be— is what is termed *logocentrism*, a colossal blunder and delusion from which all of Western thought has suffered and continues to suffer (Johnson, 1981). Just as the conclusive moment never comes, the originary moment never was; the genesis of meaning resides in an absolute past that is never present and never could have been (Bennington, 2011). It is only through the very process of deferral—fundamental to the creation of all signification all the time—that the idea of an origin is even possible.

Another way that this critique of universals, absolutes, or philosophical grounds proceeds is by calling attention to an ostensibly problematic ambiguity involving the literal and metaphorical senses of these originary principles, or god-terms (Currie, 2013; Kugler 2005). Such terms suffer, inevitably, from a certain figurative duplicity: Their metaphoric sense cannot be thoroughly teased away from their literal sense, regardless of the author's intention. Even the most abstract of notions always conceal a sensible figure, and metaphors are always sedimented within these abstractions (Derrida, 1982). Metaphors masquerade as literal expressions imbued with veritative pretense, the presumption of speaking truth. Yet they cannot make good on the presumption because of their very status as metaphor. Because of this problematic ambiguity, this duplicity, the reader of any text is always confronted with a certain semantic indeterminacy within it (Kugler, 2005) and is forced to choose between metaphorical and literal senses of key words (De Man, 1979). Given that these originary principles or transcendental terms serve as cornerstones supporting entire theories or worldviews, their fundamental indeterminacy and ambiguity undercuts the integrity of the texts they appear in. The simultaneously literal and metaphorical significance of key terms provides an opportunity for the deconstruction of meaning, a dismantling of authorial intent through exposing the ways in which a text compromises its professed intentions.

Deconstruction has relentlessly focused on the metaphoric nature of all language (Currie, 2013). The problematic ambiguity between metaphoric and literal senses is, from the viewpoint that it espouses, another instance of the difference between signifier and signified: Words do not mean what their manifest form suggests, and the full meaning that they pretend to convey is always yet to come. There is always something more to it, always cause to believe that there is no easy, direct route leading from one aspect of the sign to another. Deconstruction is the repeated refutation of the belief that the link between signifier and signified is "one of natural necessity, of analogical participation, and of resemblance" (Derrida, 1982, p. 13). *Différance*, in its guise as radical differentiation, in its emphasis on fundamental dissimilarity and heterogeneity, undercuts this logic of resemblances at the heart of metaphor, which, as Derrida rightly claims, "has always been defined as the trope of resemblance" (p. 13). Metaphors are always an attempt to show how two or more disparate objects resemble one another. For Derrida, metaphor—which in its root sense is a carrying-over, a transference of meaning from one figure to another—is implicated in logocentrism, or what is also called a metaphysics of presence. Metaphor is merely metaphysics by another name (Derrida, 1982). The very logic of *différance* vitiates the pretense that metaphor might lead to a meaning that would serve as a firm foundation for knowledge or understanding.

A person can believe that the metaphoric nature of a statement undermines its pretension to speak truth. One can see the ambiguity involving the literal and metaphorical senses of originary principles or god-terms as being problematic. You or I can perceive the plurivocity or polysemy (multiplicity of meanings) of such terms as rendering impossible the philosophical justification of absolutes or universals. But perhaps in doing so, we suffer from the psychological one-sidedness that Jung refers to above.

A less one-sided approach might also see this same ambiguity, this same polysemy as a gift, or a nugget of wisdom, embedded in an associative matrix that has been built up over time. This is a fundamentally different understanding of metaphor. Case in point: *ground* is a key term in the book you are reading and one of its root metaphors. It serves as a linchpin without which the text does not cohere. It is also used in both a literal and a metaphoric sense: *Ground* is, at times, to be understood metaphorically as a basis for belief, action, or argument. Yet, at other times, it is understood literally, as in the sentence "Today many educated folks have ceased experiencing the earth as the rough ground that supports their steps" (Abram, 2010, p. 92). At times, too, I have intentionally obscured and conflated the metaphoric and literal senses of the word (as in the third sentence of this paragraph) in order to suggest the idea that there is a direct relation between a view of texts or language as ungrounded—that is to say, not having a basis for belief—on the one hand, and an alienation from the literal ground, on the other. The term *ground* is ripe for deconstruction. It possesses the figurative duplicity and ambiguity involving literal and metaphorical senses that deconstruction tirelessly directs its critical gaze upon.

A contrary view sees a gift, or a nugget of wisdom, within this term, within this metaphorical expression laden with ostensibly problematic ambiguity. Such a view is akin to Jung's belief that in neurotic fantasy there lie a hidden treasure. If we imagine the story of a lack of philosophical grounds as being just such a neurotic fantasy (and the present book as an attempt to understand this fantasy), we might also imagine a hidden treasure within it, something potentially curative or redemptive. For Jung, illness itself is an attempt at healing and for this very reason he exhorts us to not be like the neurotic who "flings away as absolutely worthless [that which] contains the true gold we should never have found elsewhere" (Jung, 1964/1970, p. 170 [*CW* 10 pt. 2 para. 361]). This belief in a hidden treasure, of buried gold at the heart of our pathologies, is consonant with Jung's general understanding of the *telos* of both neurosis and symptom. Our neurotic symptoms have meaning and purpose. At their very core, they preserve an impulse towards psychic wholeness. As we will address further on, they are emissaries of the Self, whose function is to restore the integrity of the psyche by changing "the false attitude of the ego" (Jung, 1964/1970, p. 170 [*CW* 10 pt. 2 para. 361]).

Following Jung's thinking, one might imagine the fantasy of a lack of grounds as a symptomatic expression of a neurosis whose core thematic content also contains gold. Perhaps, then, the entire issue of grounds as posited by the deconstructive critique is also imbued of meaning and purpose. Shrouded within it is psyche's attempt to move us towards wholeness. This fantasy of groundlessness, like all neurotic symptoms, has arisen because we have lost touch with the other side of our nature and lost any sense of the urgency of its problems (Jung, 1953). On this line of thinking, the fantasy of groundlessness is an envoy from that other, neglected, side of ourselves.

We can find the gold in this fantasy, its gift, when we let the metaphor speak in such a way that it leads us back to its literal sense. Then, *the metaphor of a "lack of philosophical grounds" becomes an opportunity to renew our relationship with the literal, physical ground upon which we plant our feet.* It becomes a summons to the very earth that sponsors, supports, and upholds us. We begin to see that the literal and the metaphorical coincide, and that this coincidence marks the site of an opportunity, not merely to deconstruct a text, but to find something of value and healing within it. When we allow ourselves to perceive by way of a symbolic attitude, the absence of philosophical grounds becomes a calling. The multiple senses of *ground* reveal themselves to be less a logical incongruity than a felicitous opportunity for insight, less an occasion to deconstruct meaning than a chance to renew it. The approach that I am suggesting acknowledges that grounds are lacking, but in a sense that the deconstructive critique is ill-equipped to perceive, precisely because of its unilateral attitude, its one-sidedness. It is blind to the hidden treasure: the call to the "immediate experience of the rainswept land that enfolds us" (Abram, 2010, p. 92), the plea to return to the earth as the rough ground that supports our steps.

If we are merely content to deconstruct the metaphor, and nothing else, we throw away the gold, we miss the metaphor's (the symptom's) healing potential. We are trapped within the false attitude of the ego. This false attitude is precisely the desire to deconstruct, and thereby disempower, the metaphor of *ground*, in this case, or the metaphor at work within any other god-term or philosophic universal. The deconstructive approach to the *ground* metaphor misses the fact that such a metaphor might serve to correct this false, one-sided attitude.

But in what way does the deconstructive approach embody such an attitude? It subordinates identity to difference, establishing the logical priority of the latter over the former and then proceeds to construct an entire method of textual analysis around this subordination. It construes the primordial, the experiential, the perceptual, the sensual, the phenomenal, and the intuited as terms with meanings, yet undermines any sense that they have an existence beyond the terminological. It construes meaning as being a purely *intra*-linguistic affair in which the *extra*-linguistic can play no part, can make no claims upon our understanding. It boldly affirms that "perception does not exist or that what is called perception is not primordial, somehow everything 'begins' by 're-presentation'" (Derrida, 1973, p. 45n). This one-sidedness privileges mediacy over immediacy. In doing so, it undercuts any sense of the innate and inherent, the intrinsic and the essential, and implicitly exalts the acquired and cultivated, the extrinsic and incidental.

If we return to the opening image of this chapter once more, that of astronauts escaping the pull of terrestrial gravity, and consider all that this image was intended to hold, there is, I think, a growing coherence. It is a metaphorical expression of the disappearance of philosophical grounds. This absence of ground coincides with a particular understanding of linguistic reference. There being no ground upon which our linguistic interpretations might rest, such concepts as self, truth, reality, and most importantly, nature, are disenfranchised. Nature is left behind, and with it, any sense of the intrinsic, the inherent, the implicit, the essential, or the given. Also left behind, as Abram (2010) notes, is a conscious relationship to the ground, the very earth beneath our feet, which is also, quite literally, our cosmic place of origin. Simply stated: No extralinguistic reference—no ground, no foundation, no earth, no nature, no origins. This coherency has been arrived at by way of a certain rationality of argument, one that explicates a particular understanding of linguistic meaning as operating through differentiation and deferral. Yet it has also come about by an association of images, and a playfulness with metaphor. As in the previous chapter, a symbolic attitude that attempts to integrate both rationality and imagination, or logos and mythos, has been at play. This symbolic attitude does not limit itself to arguing ideas at face value. Thus, I have not so much argued for, or against, Derrida's theories, as much as I have attempted to place them within a dream narrative, or a cluster of symbolic associations that feels, to me, both intuitively justified, and rationally tenable. The dream deciphered here, within the linguistic theories that purport a lack of grounds for interpretation, suggests that such tropes are symptomatic expressions of a pervasive estrangement from the land.

Rorty's version of space travel

Kindred in spirit, though differing in his specific rhetorical tools and strategies, Rorty, like Derrida, and Saussure before him, undermines the notion of extralinguistic reference. In the writings of the three authors, language appears insular, self-enclosed, segregated from, or only dubiously related to, its other. This insularity is twofold: While the importance of intralinguistic relations (relations immanent to the system of signs) is emphasized, the ostensible relationship that said system may have with any extralinguistic referent is called into question and undermined. Whereas Derrida puts forth a theory that renders deeply problematic the possibility of such a referent (if not outright denying it), Rorty prefers to show ways in which theories of reference are muddled, misguided, and of little use. It is not surprising, then, that he takes a highly critical attitude to the very idea of nature, and affiliated notions like the *inherent*, the *essential*, the *intrinsic*, and the *given*. In doing so, he forms part of a deconstructive postmodernism that takes aim at these very same *bête noirs*. Though not, in any technical sense, a post-structuralist or deconstructionist, he nevertheless shares their general ethos of dismantling past orthodoxies and undermining long-held assumptions by way of critiquing such concepts as reference, representation, and correspondence.

Language as mirror is a metaphor best abandoned. Such is the argument put forth by Rorty in his classic work *Philosophy and the Mirror of Nature* (1979). For Rorty, the language-as-mirror metaphor speaks to the (supposed) capacity of language for representation. The mirror re-presents what it reflects. An accurate mirror produces accurate representations of the objects before it. Accurate language accurately represents. Philosophy from Descartes to the present day has been the self-proclaimed caretaker of mirrors; its *raison d'être* has been to act as arbiter of accurate representations:

> To know is to represent accurately what is outside the mind; so to understand the possibility and nature of knowledge is to understand the way in which the mind is able to construct such representations. Philosophy's central concern is to be a general theory of representation, a theory which will divide culture up into the areas which represent reality well, those which represent it less well, and those which do not represent it at all (despite their pretense of doing so). (Rorty, 1979, p. 3)

If knowing is representing accurately, then an understanding of how representations are constructed is necessary. Philosophy, equipped with its knowledge of this construction, can distinguish between more, or less, valid representations. It can act as the judge of a mirror's fidelity to what it ostensibly reflects.

Yet Rorty advocates abandoning this central concern over accuracy of reflection, arguing that theories of representation, theories that rely on a scheme-content distinction in which the scheme of language purports to represent a content outside itself, are more trouble than they are worth. In his disavowal of this distinction, a distinction that is synonymous with the philosophy as mirror metaphor, he argues against the usefulness of any theory of linguistic reference, any theory that would purport to explain how language adheres to the world. He has reiterated his advocacy against such theories over a large body of work (Rorty, 1979, 1989, 1998, 1999). In so doing, he has critiqued terms such as *reference*, *representation*, and *correspondence* in the name of calling into question the mirror metaphor. Underlining some of the conceptual difficulties in speaking of *reference*—the very equivocity and ambiguity of the term, and its facile confusion with other notions such as *talking about*—he concludes that theories of reference are hopeless. Forever the self-proclaimed pragmatist, he does not so much refute the possibility that language "hooks onto" the world, or couples with something other than itself, as much as he claims that theories as to how this occurs are more problematic than they are valuable. Language, for him, simply should not be thought of as an interface, or as something that represents. (Rorty, 1967).

Central to this skepticism as regards any theory that would link language and world is the observation that such theories arise from the very theoretical milieu that they attempt to stand outside of and explain; any such theory can only justify itself in terms of pre-existing theories as to what the world is made of. This creates the dubious situation of using a part of one's present theory to justify and endorse the remainder of it (Rorty, 1979). For Rorty, the search for an adequate theory of reference requires the impossible—an Archimedean point outside of our representations, a vantage point from which we can objectively assess both our representations and their relations with the objects they purport to represent. The upshot of this is that our accounts "of how the things in the content reach up and determine the reference of the representations making up the scheme, our theory about what the world is made of will produce, trivially, a self-justifying theory about that relation" (p. 295).

In response to this, one might rightly ask whether it is possible to accept reference, representation, correspondence, or interfacing in the absence of a theory that explains how these things come about. One can, for example, believe in one's own existence without accepting Descarte's doctrine of the *cogito*: I think, therefore I am. Many people believe that they *are*, that they exist, without having to accept theories to prove the fact. (I include myself among such folk.) Although it may very well be true that an illusory transcendental standpoint outside our present set of representations would be necessary to provide an irreproachable theory of reference, accepting that reference takes place, or that words can in some way portray, hook up with, or correspond to a world they ostensibly speak of, does not require a theory. One can, for example, explain reference, representation, correspondence, and other related notions as simply forming part of the mystery of language (Girard, 1978). Ignorance of mystery leads to extreme, irreconcilable beliefs: Language is the hermetic confine within which all things unfold, or, conversely, it is the perfect tool that flawlessly mirrors. Acceptance of mystery allows that it is both: a sterile captivity, and a fecund opening, a labyrinthine enclosure, and a simple, direct call to experience.

Rorty, apparently, is not inclined to accept such mysteries. For him, it is truly problematic that theories of reference and representation arise from the very same theoretical corpus they seek to explain; this has serious consequences well beyond the philosophy of language and effects epistemology in general, because nothing can serve as a justification without reference to what has already been accepted. Yet it is impossible to find a way outside of our own pre-existing beliefs and language in which we already find ourselves embedded in order to test our beliefs. Once we set aside problematic theories of word-world relations and see them as extraneous to questions of justification, we can abandon the search for privileged representations, and in this very act, abandon the goal of a theory of knowledge (Rorty, 1979).

Admonishing the reader to renounce such self-justifying, muddled theories of reference and representation that perpetuate the philosophy-as-mirror metaphor and scheme-content distinction, Rorty (1979) promotes a pure philosophy of language that understands how language works, which he sees as fundamentally different from the question of how it might directly refer to the world. In promoting such a philosophy, he has campaigned against presuppositions "that bits of the world 'make sentences true' and that these sentences in turn represent those bits" (Rorty, 1967, p. 372). He has passionately argued against the very idea that true sentences might be true because they in some way correspond to a given state of affairs, or the facts of a given matter. To this end, he repeatedly cites philosopher Donald Davidson approvingly, at times in passages evocative of Saussure and Derrida in their emphasis on intralinguistic relations. For Davidson, it is better not to think that "individual words must have meanings at all, in any sense that transcends the fact that they have a systematic effect on the meanings of the sentences in which they occur" (Davidson cited in Rorty , 1979, p. 303).

At the risk of caricature, portraying Saussure, Derrida, and Rorty in terms of the map-terrain or scheme-content metaphor so often employed by the latter figure, one might say that Saussure does not address the relation between map and terrain because maps are his interest; Derrida's semiological reductionism suggests that we cannot know if maps have any relationship with terrain because map-making erases the terrain—that is, all we can ever know are the maps, and Rorty advocates a view that holds there is no useful way of comparing any relationship between map and terrain—trying to form a theory of such relations is too problematic, not useful, and based on metaphors best discarded. In terms of the central metaphor of the present work, one might say that all three men have, to varying degrees, simply departed the terrain. To abandon reference is to abandon terra.

As I have endeavored to show through the metaphor of space travel, when the ground is left behind, and language is no longer rooted in it, having seemingly lost its referential and representational capacity, the very idea of nature is undermined. To leave the ground is also to leave home, to leave both *natus* and *humus* behind, and with it, any sense of the intrinsic, the inherent, the implicit, the essential, or the given. Not surprisingly, then, Rorty (1989) explicitly links representation and nature: Once one "does not view language as a medium for either expression or representation . . . he is able to set aside the idea that both the self and reality have intrinsic natures, natures which are out there waiting to be known" (p. 11). In a similar vein, he implores the reader to relinquish the question of the adequacy of any language for a given task, whether it be the task of expressing human nature, or expressing the nature of any nonhuman reality. Likewise, with the issue of correspondence:

> for this talk of correspondence brings back just the idea my sort of philosopher wants to get rid of, the idea that the world or the self has an intrinsic nature. From our point of view, explaining the success of science, or the desirability of political liberalism, by talk of "fitting the world"

> or "expressing human nature" is like explaining why opium makes you sleepy by talking about its dormitive power. To say that Freud's vocabulary gets at the truth about human nature, or Newton's at the truth about the heavens, is not an explanation of anything. (Rorty, 1989, p. 8)

Words cannot fit the world or, at least, it is of no value to believe that they can. It is best to rid oneself of any sense that language might correspond to any given state of affairs, that statements may be considered true by virtue of their agreement with particular situations, circumstances, or conditions. Once the logic of correspondence has been undermined, for this philosopher, all thought of nature, all thought of the intrinsic, is vitiated. On his view, to affirm that a statement is true because it corresponds to the facts of the matter is hopelessly redundant and risibly tautological. Yet the question may still arise, for the reader who has not succumbed to Rorty's argument, what, if anything, his own words can be said to express. Can Rorty's explanation explain anything if we set aside all sense that his words may correspond to a given state of affairs? If Freud's (or Jung's, or anyone else's) language cannot get at the truth of human nature, can Rorty's language get at the truth of this inability?

Note

1 In an interview with Richard Kearney (Kearney & Ricoeur, 1984), Derrida vehemently denies that deconstruction amounts to a suspension of linguistic reference. He expresses utter astonishment as to the sheer number of critics who understand deconstruction as a denial of reference, one that would suggest that there is nothing beyond language. Rather, he acknowledges that deconstruction merely "tries to show that the question of reference is much more complex and problematic than traditional theories supposed" (p. 123). His critique is, in his own words, not the denial of, but "the search for the 'other' and the 'other of language'" (p. 123). The present work does not suppose that Derrida's extensive and relentless problematization of reference amounts to a denial of the other of language. It attempts to interpret the form of thought that would render the other of language so distant or hidden as to require a search. The referent exists for Derrida but, like the transcendental signified, it somehow is always absent, and "the thing itself" always escapes. Indeed, such a need to search for the other of language suggests the very image that is the primary metaphor of the present chapter: the earth seen from afar and growing ever more distant.

References

Abram, D. (1996). *The spell of the sensuous: Perception and language in a more-than-human world* (1st edn.). New York, NY: Pantheon Books.

Abram, D. (2002). Foreword. In A. Fisher, *Radical ecopsychology: Psychology in the service of life* (pp. ix–xix). Albany, NY: State University of New York Press.

Abram, D. (2010). *Becoming animal: An earthly cosmology*. New York, NY: Pantheon Books.

Bennington, G. (2011) *Not half no end: Militantly melancholic essays in memory of Jacques Derrida*. Edinburgh, Scotland: Edinburgh University Press.

Bowie, D. (1969). Space oddity. On *David Bowie* [CD]. London, England: Phillips/Mercury.

Brooks, A. (1997). *Postfeminisms: Feminism, cultural theory, and cultural forms*. London, England: Routledge.

Chomsky, N., & Foucault, M. (2006). *The Chomsky-Foucault debate: On human nature*. New York, NY: New Press.

Currie, M. (2013) *The invention of deconstruction*. New York, NY: Palgrave Macmillan.

De Man, P. (1979). *Allegories of reading: Figural language in Rousseau, Nietzsche, Rilke, and Proust*. New Haven, CT: Yale University Press.

Derrida, J. (1967a). *De la grammatologie*. Paris, France: Les Editions de Minuit.

Derrida, J. (1967b). *La voix et le phénomène*. Paris, France: Presses Universitaires de France.

Derrida, J. (1973). *Speech and phenomena, and other essays on Husserl's theory of signs*. Evanston, IL: Northwestern University Press.

Derrida, J. (1976). *Of grammatology*. Baltimore, MD: Johns Hopkins University Press.

Derrida, J. (1978). *Writing and difference*. Chicago, IL: University of Chicago Press.

Derrida, J. (1982). *Margins of philosophy*. Chicago: University of Chicago Press.

Derrida, J., & Caputo, J. D. (1997). *Deconstruction in a nutshell: A conversation with Jacques Derrida*. New York, NY: Fordham University Press.

Dews, P. (1994). Adorno, poststructuralism, and the critique of identity. In S. Žižek (Ed.), *Mapping ideology*. (pp. 46–4). New York, NY: Verso.

Dillon, M. C. (1995). *Semiological reductionism: A critique of the deconstructionist movement in postmodern thought*. Albany, NY: State University of New York Press.

Eagleton, T. (2003). *After theory*. New York, NY: Basic Books.

Fairlamb, H. L. (1994). *Critical conditions: Postmodernity and the question of foundations*. Cambridge, England: Cambridge University Press.

Foucault, M. (1966). *Les mots et les choses*. Paris, France: Editions Gallimard.

Foucault, M. (1973). *The order of things: An archaeology of the human sciences*. New York, NY: Vintage Books.

Foucault, M. (1977). *Discipline and punish: The birth of the prison*. New York, NY: Pantheon Books.

Gendlin, E. T., & Kleinberg-Levin, D. M. (1997). *Language beyond postmodernism: Saying and thinking in Gendlin's philosophy*. Evanston, IL: Northwestern University Press.

Girard, R. (1978). *"To double business bound": Essays on literature, mimesis, and anthropology*. Baltimore, MD: Johns Hopkins University Press.

Habermas, J. (1987). *The philosophical discourse of modernity: Twelve lectures*. Cambridge, MA: MIT Press.

Habermas, J., & Fultner, B. (2003). *Truth and justification*. Cambridge, MA: MIT Press.

Husserl, E., Merleau-Ponty, M., Lawlor, L., & Bergo, B. (2002). *Husserl at the limits of phenomenology: Including texts by Edmund Husserl, Maurice Merleau-Ponty*. Evanston, IL: Northwestern University Press.

Johnson, B. (1981). Introduction. In J. Derrida, *Dissemination* (pp. vii–xxxiii). Chicago, IL: University Press.

Jung, C. G. (1953). Two essays on analytical psychology. In R. F. C. Hull (Trans.), *The collected works of C. G. Jung* (Vol. 7). Princeton, NJ: Princeton-Bollingen.

Jung, C. G. (1954/1969). *Psychology and education*. In R. F. C. Hull (Trans.), *The collected works of C. G. Jung* (Vol. 17). Princeton, NJ: Princeton-Bollingen.

Jung, C. G. (1960/1969). *The structure and dynamics of the psyche* (2nd edn.). Princeton, NJ: Princeton University Press (original work published 1960).

Jung, C. G. (1964/1970). Civilization in transition. In R. F. C. Hull (Trans.), *The collected works of C. G. Jung* (Vol. 10). Princeton, NJ: Princeton-Bollingen.

Kearney, R., & Ricœur, P. (1984). *Dialogues with contemporary continental thinkers: The phenomenological heritage: Paul Ricœur, Emmanuel Levinas, Herbert Marcuse, Stanislas Breton, Jacques Derrida*. Manchester, England: Manchester University Press.

Kugler, P. (2005). *Raids on the unthinkable: Freudian and Jungian psychoanalyses*. New Orleans, LA: Spring Journal Books.

Nash, K (1994). The feminist production of knowledge: Is deconstruction a practice for women? *Feminist Review*, *47*, 65–77.

Pinker, S. (2002). *The blank slate: The modern denial of human nature*. New York, NY: Viking.

Pinker, S. (2007). *The stuff of thought: Language as a window into human nature*. New York, NY: Viking.

Reason, P., & Bradbury, H. (Eds.). (2006). *Handbook of action research: Concise paperback edition*. Thousand Oaks, CA: Sage.

Romanyshyn, R. (2004). *Technology as symptom and dream*. New York, NY: Brunner-Routledge.

Rorty, R. (1967). *The linguistic turn: Essays in philosophical method*. Chicago, IL: University of Chicago Press.

Rorty, R. (1979). *Philosophy and the mirror of nature*. Princeton, NJ: Princeton University Press.

Rorty, R. (1989). *Contingency, irony, and solidarity*. New York, NY: Cambridge University Press.

Rorty, R. (1998). *Truth and progress*. New York, NY: Cambridge University Press.

Rorty, R. (1999). *Philosophy and social hope*. New York, NY: Penguin Books.

Rowland, S. (2010). *C. G. Jung in the humanities: Taking the soul's path*. New Orleans, LA: Spring Journal Books.

Saussure, F. D., Bally, C., Sechehaye, A., & Riedlinger, A. (1986). *Course in general linguistics*. LaSalle, IL: Open Court.

Snyder, G. (1990). *The practice of the wild: Essays*. San Francisco, CA: North Point Press.

Spivak, G. C. (1976). Preface. In J. Derrida, *Of grammatology* (pp. vii–xc). Baltimore, MD: Johns Hopkins University Press.

Tarnas, R. (1991). *The passion of the Western mind: Understanding the ideas that have shaped our world view*. New York, NY: Harmony Books.

Chapter 3

Earthrise

The ecocentric critique of dissociated reference

Being claimed by the land: advocates of the earth and the human-nature identity

Let us return again to the opening image of our last chapter. It is the summer of 1969. Neil Armstrong and Edwin "Buzz" Aldrin are impressing their boot prints upon the pallid terrain of our nearest natural satellite and, almost simultaneously, upon the collective imagination. From the moon, the crew of Apollo 11 see the half-shadowed sphere that is our home, our place of origin, the birthplace (*natus*) that is soil (*humus*). Over the black horizon of this pock-marked lunar landscape the distant earth rises. Yes, from a lunar perspective, *the earth rises*, just as, from an earthly perspective, so does the sun.

To speak of an earthrise, perhaps, pays equal homage to both Copernicus and Husserl, to the founder of an anatomy of celestial spheres, and the dogged originator of a geocentric logic. The statement of the earth's rising contains both an acknowledgment of the radical de-centering brought about by the transformation of the earth into an object in space, and a testament to the compelling immediacy of perception: Certainly, that we may witness the earth *rise*, attests to the undeniable validity of heliocentric astronomy, just as the technological feat that made such a witnessing possible attests to the immense power of the scientific zeitgeist of which Copernicus is a primary representative. Yet, to say that the earth *rises* is also an acknowledgment that, from an earthly perspective, the sun rises as well. The statement speaks to the same compelling immediacy of perception that Husserl called attention to: Phenomenologically, the sun does, in fact, rise and set upon the earth's horizon. Just as there is a certain phenomenological truth to the sun's traversal of the sky of a stationary earth, likewise it is true that the earth traverses the sky of a stationary moon.

In meditating upon this image of an earthrise, using an associative logic to discern something of the meaning that inheres within it, it is important to acknowledge that such a complex symbolic image need not carry only a sense of estrangement. The symbol of our alienation from nature, and psychological distance from our place of origins can also serve as an image of our longing and love. Symbolic images contain incalculable possible meanings. They are symbolic precisely because their meaning is inexhaustible. They allude to that which is withheld from present knowledge (Jung & de Laszlo, 1993), and just as we might imagine that within neurotic fantasy there lies a hidden treasure, within the image of our estrangement there may lie something potentially curative and redemptive. Just as the absence of philosophical grounds has the potential to become a calling, so does the image of earth seen from afar. There is meaning and purpose here that goes beyond mere allusion to alienation, dissociation, and disembodiment. At its core, this image, as both symptom and symbol, holds within it an impulse towards psychic wholeness. Such is the *telos* of our pathologies, being, as they are, attempts at healing (Jung, 1964/1970).

Photos of the earth's rising, taken by the earlier Apollo 8 mission, appeared for the first time in print in January 1969. Although it is true to say, with Abram, that such images of the earth, *seen from outside*, now condition and supersede much of our immediate experience of the terrain we walk upon, it is also true that such images are widely credited with inspiring an eco-renascence. Fifteen months after the publication of these photos, on April 22, 1970, the first Earth Day was celebrated (Poole, 2008). This date is now widely credited to be the beginning of the modern environmental movement. Later that year, the United States government founded the Environmental Protection Agency. The photos had a lasting effect on environmentalists the world over. Conflating and playing upon both literal and metaphorical senses of the word *earthrise*, one might imagine the earth's rising as an allusion to more than a physical relation of celestial bodies or a lunar perspective on the earth's trajectory. The earth's rising might also allude to the birthing of earth-based disciplines: the "rising" of modern-day environmentalism, which itself helped to inspire fields like ecocpsychology, psychecology, ecocriticism, ethology, and ecology—all modes of thought with a certain geo-logic or eco-logic, that is to say, all ways of understanding the earth as a living ecosystem within which we human animals have evolved.

If we try to imagine an understanding of language inspired by this rising of the earth, we might envision an understanding that would have no qualms with speaking of the essential, the innate, the intrinsic, or the given. It might champion the very idea of nature, and even, specifically, human nature. It would not postulate a system of signs that was fundamentally ungrounded, or dissociated from lived experience. It would have some way of speaking of word-to-world relations, whether in terms of reference, representation, linking, or even, perhaps, that great binding agent, Eros. In contradistinction to astronautic language, this language might be called ecological—language understood as a relation between the human species and the ecosystem of which it forms an integral part, between human organisms and the folding terrain they wander. Such an understanding might find its way into various disciplines, not the least of them phenomenology, but also, of course, disciplines with a geo-logic or an eco-logic. Within the context of this dream of departure from the terrestrial gravity of linguistic reference, it could not be otherwise.

So it is, perhaps, no surprise that many of the voices critiquing the seeming severance of language from referent and signifier from signified are voices of those who champion the earth and the vital importance of our relationship to all of the living creatures upon it. They are voices that come from fields like ecopsychology, which conceives psychological well-being within an environmental context, understanding that to do otherwise, to conceive health in terms that are not firmly planted in an appreciation for the ecological system that birthed us, is ultimately self-destructive (Brown, 1995). Among the most strident advocates of a renewed relationship with the earth, nature, and the wild are individuals calling for an understanding of language that takes issue with semiological reductionism (Abram, 1996; Fisher, 2002; Shepard, 1995; Soulé & Lease, 1995).

It is essential to the project of ecopsychology that it possess an understanding of language that fundamentally differs from the dictates of deconstruction and post-structuralism (Fisher, 2002). This, in part, is due to a need to conceive of extralinguistic space, something that seems precluded by Derrida's (1976) claim that "there is nothing outside the text" (p. 158), nor any experience that does not begin by way of representation. Without this space, without a sense that our experience is not completely and utterly beholden to representation, there is no way for us to find *meanings* in nature that are anything other than the repetition of pre-existing linguistic forms (Fisher, 2002). In contrast to such a view, one that cannot envision an opening, or an outside, to linguistic construction, one might focus upon the extra-referential character of language. Extra-referentiality speaks to how terms not only refer to other terms within a system (infrareferentiality), but also how they reflect differentiations present within the world they ostensibly describe. It is this extra-referential aspect of language that brings to light "some of the meaning that inheres in the way the *things themselves* internally relate" (Fisher, 2002, p. 129). The *thing itself*, on this view, does not always escape, as in Derrida, and differentiation is not merely the result of *différance*. Discreet objects do not acquire their delineation, their demarcation simply as a byproduct of semiosis; they are not merely derivative of the production of signs. Rather, differentiation exists in the perceived world. Terms like "aardvarks" and "possums" have meaning not merely by virtue of relations between signs but also, and perhaps more importantly, by virtue of the actual living creatures that these words refer to. Language understood in this way does not create a world of differentiated objects, rather, it is an elaboration of an already existing differentiation (Fisher, 2002).

This focus upon extra-referentiality takes issue with a linguistically reductive disposition insistent that "if there is anything 'out there,' we cannot know it because we are shut up in the concentric prisons of cultural bias and sensory apparatus. Therefore, it is impossible to know nature at all" (Soule & Lease, 1995, p. 149). Contact with nature is forever deferred; only contact with its sign is possible, and this sign may be little more than a placeholder in certain types of discourse. This understanding is but one exemplar of a very longstanding bias of exalting words while devaluing nature that can be traced back to ancient Greece and the citified teachings of both Socrates and Plato (Abram, 1996). The difference between the ancient Greeks and the deconstructionists of the present day is that the latter go much farther, "claiming that living nature and wilderness are illusory—just some biologists' narrative, banal, ersatz, or, at minimum, coterminous with history" (Soule & Lease, 1995, p. 149).

There is reason for a far-reaching critique of much of contemporary hermeneutics influenced by the linguistic turn—such a hermeneutics listens to the voices of texts, cultures, and historical artifacts, but renders nature mute, for, as Rorty claims, "nature has no preferred representation" (Rorty, cited in Fisher, 2002, p. 38). Put differently, such hermeneutics puts nature in brackets: The épochè of the semiological reduction consists precisely in setting aside everything that exists outside of the human text, an entire phenomenal world that includes the very body and nature that is championed by ecopsychology. An important task of the ecopsychologist is to reopen the pathway between language and its other, particularly the "other" of the natural world itself, so that it may, in a sense, speak to us (Fisher, 2002). If we are unable to do this, then a crucial asymmetry is lost: "[T]he living world outside of human language, the world of creeks and porcupines and leaves, even if revealed through language, is the given, primary reality, the ultimate social context to which our speaking must in good health remain faithful" (p. 132). The deconstructive critique understands such an asymmetry as a form of logocentric bias, and sees in all so-called "given, primary realities" an opportunity to dismantle cultural prejudices. Yet in doing so, it appears to commit a similar offense to the one it condemns, privileging culture over nature, which is a violation of the latter.

No longer placing culture over nature in a conceptual hierarchy entails not assuming that the extraordinary diversity of human cultures undermines any possibility of a universal human nature. Just because we are cultural beings does not mean we are not also born of the earth. The denial of human nature by way of an appeal to cultural differences rests on a misconception of culture that fails to acknowledge a depth of our experience that transcends any particular culture (Fisher, 2002). No longer privileging culture over nature also involves seeing the natural world not merely as a set of resources to be placed in service of human needs and desires—"a narcissistic culture, however, takes the *reverse* view, insisting that the world of nature serve *it*" (p. 119).

The philosophical invalidation and conceptual neutering of *nature* that undermines any sense of the inherent, the essential, or the given cannot be teased apart from the conviction that "reality is . . . invented by words" (Shepard, 1995, p. 17). Reality is an invention because a person's experience of it, on this view, is so thoroughly beholden to representation, so comprehensively entwined with it, that what appears to be intuitively given is, in fact, fabrication, construction, production. Words are thus "a barrier behind which is a vast, unknowable enigma—or perhaps nothing at all" (p. 17). One cannot say. Who knows? The barrier is absolute. It precludes a retrievable domain of experience. Both *différance* and Rorty's neo-pragmatic attack on reference, hit this barrier with equally sonorous thuds; for each, nothing can escape the semiotic in which it is found. Texts, in one form or another, ultimately circumscribe everything. The life cycle of honeybees, the complex ecosystems of tropical rainforests, the decomposition of dead bodies, the visceral sensation of panic, and the pre-Columbian trading customs of Native Americans are all neatly confined under the rubrics of language games, truth regimes, or metanarratives. All "are subordinate to the arguments for or against their existence" (p. 21) in the same way that the phenomenal is subordinate to the linguistic.

We can understand the destruction of nature as part of a two-pronged assault that is both overt and covert, devastating the earth overtly in the form of an ecological crisis, and attacking it covertly in the form of ideologies that lead to social and psychological crises (Soulé & Lease, 1995). Thus, this violation of nature has a Janus face: It is directed both inward and outward, towards the human and the non-human. The attack takes place on two fronts—the physical, on the one hand, and the social or ideological, on the other. One attacks the biosphere and all of the plants and animals that help form it, bulldozing it over to create space for shopping malls and apartment complexes, stadiums and power plants. The other front justifies this physical assault ideologically. Ideas pave the way for pavement. When the very concept of nature has been neutered by way of a semiologically reductive approach, nature as a living, breathing reality that is both external and internal can be easily violated. When "nature" is subsumed into a textual body, it is more easily bulldozed into submission. A principal tool of this violation is deconstruction (Soulé & Lease, 1995; Spretnak,1999).

The siege upon nature is not monolithic, but multivalent. There are physical, ideological, social, environmental, and psychological elements to this attack, and these elements are all inextricably related to one another. The undermining of the idea of human nature as a set of intrinsic, inherent, innate qualities, dispositions, tendencies, and dynamics is not ultimately separable from a disturbed and disturbing relationship to nature *qua* wilderness, the living ecosystem not created by human beings, the world apart from the productions of human design and civilization. This attack, this siege, this undermining is also the creation of a distance: The earth, with all the myriad associations given to it in the present text, is now, seemingly, little more than a remote, untouchable orb floating in vacuity, a sign among signs, with no real referent to speak of.

Then again, such an image might equally serve as a calling to relinquish this ostensible primacy of culture over nature, a primacy made possible by a privileging of sign over referent, signifier over signified, and the linguistic over the phenomenal and intuited. Heeding this call allows for a much-needed acknowledgment of nature as an establisher of the limits that come with being incarnate, finite beings subject to death and decay—limits of endurance, lifespan, suffering, hunger, and comprehension that violently clash with "our society's consistent denial and narcissistic hatred of limits" (Fisher, 2002, p. 119) and also, perhaps, clash with the limitless interpretative possibilities proffered by an ungrounded system of signs. Heeding the call, in stark contrast to semiological reductionism, bows reverently to the perennial truth that "we belong to the natural order . . . so that we are claimed by it, are limited by it, and feel its demands within our bodily experience" (p. xv).

Without a sense of our own intrinsic, innate needs and limitations, a word like *trauma* has little meaning (Fisher, 2002). Without a sense of our fundamental human nature, it is difficult, if not impossible, to conceive of developmental needs, such as boundary setting and a healthy emotional life, and without a conception of these needs and limitations, they are all the more easily violated. If what we understand to be our nature is, nevertheless, expressed in terms that are specific to a given culture and a given language, this mediation need not be the absolute mediation of *différance*. The word *culture*, traced back to its Latin roots, refers to a tending of natural growth. Culture is cultivation. It is not possible without the land. Culture is predicated upon the very earth that is our place of birth, on the *natus* of nature. It is possible to seek ever-more primordial terms, terms that attempt to express what is most elemental in our makeup while nevertheless acknowledging that our experiences are historically and culturally mediated. Likewise, there is no need to malign culture in the name of nature; rather, the two can be understood as "internally related moments within a unified and processual reality" (Fisher, 2002 p. 119).

Linguistic mediation does not have to be understood as the absolute mediation of *différance*, which disallows a transgression of the text, and prevents any direct appeal to the world to adjudicate among texts. As Jung comments in a footnote to *Two Essays on Analytical Psychology*, *absolute* means cut off or detached. If something is absolute it is unconnected. Thus, an absolute god "would be of no consequence at all" (Jung, 1953, p. 235n [*CW* 7 pt. 2 para. 394]) since, being completely disengaged, it would not be able to touch its creation. Mediation via history, culture, and language does not have to exclude the possibility of speaking of transhistorical and transcultural human characteristics, or preclude a retrievable domain of experience. Language and culture can, in a sense, touch creation. To believe otherwise, I think, may only serve to prevent a rapprochement with nature. From an ecological point of view, this would be tragic, given that "sanity is grounded in the reality of the natural world; that the ecological crisis signifies a pathological break from this reality; and that the route out of our crisis must therefore involve . . . a psychological reconciliation with the living earth" (Fisher, 2002, p. xiii).

This sense of absolute mediation, one that defers any contact between language and its other, makes it appear as though followers of deconstructive postmodernism possess "no glimmer of earth, of leaves or soil. They seem to live entirely in a made rather than a grown world" (Shepard, 1995, p. 20).

They appear to believe "that 'making' language is analogous to making plastic trees, to be always on the edge of supposing that the words for things are more real than the things they stand for" (p. 20). Thus, even the very notion of simulacra is at risk of falling apart. Words are not like photos that, to some degree, simulate and testify to a primary reality. How could they be? Words can only simulate and testify to other words, like avant-garde painting in which "the simulacra become images without resemblances except to other images" (p. 20).

Rootless consciousness: Jung on pathology as alienation from nature

Throughout Jung's entire opus there is a deep concern for the loss of connection with nature (Jung & Sabini, 2002). One of his favorite metaphors for this loss of connection involves a severed relation to foundations or ground. For example, he writes, "It is as if our consciousness had somehow slipped from its natural foundations and no longer knew how to get along on nature's timing" (Jung & Sabini, 2002, p. 68). Jung employs imagery of a gap, a distance, or a divide between humans and the ground, human beings and the earth, when speaking of a divorce from the natural world. Though he never uses the term, one might call *astronautic* the consciousness that he more often than not describes as *rootless*. Such a consciousness is one that has abandoned the earth *qua* nature. It has no roots, lacks a foundation, or does not touch the ground. Such a consciousness is not *down to earth*, and is too enthralled by its own abstractions, its own verbiage. It is "an intellect that has grown estranged from human nature" (p. 125), one that has succumbed to the tyranny of words and is completely dependent upon them, so much so that "the danger that faces us today is that the whole of reality will be replaced by words" (p. 138). It is to this spellbound intellect that Jung attributes the appalling atrophy of instinct in modern human beings, particularly the city dweller, who lacks all contact with living, breathing nature. For Jung (1958), this loss of connection, this rootless condition, was not merely a passing concern; it is at the very core of his understanding of pathology, and forms a key element in his ongoing psychological critique of the West, as well as his critique of modernity. Pathology is synonymous with a severed relation to the ground, with all of the associations given to it in the present text.

The grave danger that Jung saw in his contemporaries, and in himself, lies in their alienation from their own instinctual ground, that is, simultaneously, the very ground that the city dweller no longer touches. It is this loss of instinct on the part of citified folk that is the fundamental cause of psychological pathology. Jung is unambiguous and direct on this point: "In the last analysis, most of our difficulties come from losing contact with our instincts, the age-old forgotten wisdom stored up in us" (Jung, cited in Lacourt, 2010, p. 79).

Nature, in Jung's way of framing things, is the primordial foundation upon which the conscious, language-bearing intellect rests. Pathology involves the dissociation of the latter from the former. Illness is a form of extirpated consciousness. For such a consciousness, the great danger is that it may lose its relation to its earthly origins (Jung, 1928) and succumb to the fascination with *isms*. Yet this rootless condition is, in some sense, the result of the natural tendency of consciousness to attempt to emancipate itself from the unconscious psyche. This emancipation is both necessary and dangerous, for the former (consciousness) risks completely forgetting its ultimate dependence on the latter (unconscious psyche), much like an astronaut who has forgotten that his or her view of the earth as a distant planet, as an object *out there* depends, first, on that planet having provided a foundation for take-off. It is the emancipation of a consciousness that risks losing the sense of having been sponsored, supported, upheld, sent on its way, yet also one that is forever tied, related to, and limited by something beyond itself. Consciousness, as Jung tells us, is proud of this emancipation, but ignores the fact that "although it has apparently got rid of the unconscious, it has become the victim of its own verbal concepts" (Jung & Sabini, 2002, p. 72). All of our great advancements must be paid for with a loss of instinct, and a loss of a sense of reality, to the very degree that we remain in a primitive dependence on words. Such an emancipation is, thus, also an incarceration. Perhaps it is even what one could call, to borrow from Jameson (1972) again, an incarceration in a prisonhouse of language.

Jung associates this dependence upon words with a discriminating activity that ruptures any possible sense of unity, one that divides and subdivides things into their smallest components, an activity that, in terms of the present text, anatomizes as it atomizes:

> This rupture of the link with the unconscious and our submission to the tyranny of words have one great disadvantage: the conscious mind becomes more and more the victim of its own discriminating activity, the picture we have of the world gets broken down into countless particulars, and the original feeling of unity, which we integrally connected with the unity of the unconscious psyche, is lost. This feeling of unity, in the form of the correspondence theory and the sympathy of all things, dominated philosophy until well into the seventeenth century. (Jung & Sabini, 2002, p. 72)

The discriminating activity breaks the world down into myriad separate, divisible things. Like *différance*, which precludes the possibility of identity, it ceaselessly differentiates. It interminably sees particulars and particles. Yet the feeling of unity, interrelatedness, and integrality of these particles is lost. From the perspective of the discriminating intelligence, things are not sympathetic to one another, that is to say, there is no affinity, no mutuality, relationship, likeness, or correlation between them. Any sense of correspondence, and the affiliated concepts of agreement, similarity, association, congruity, and resemblance disappear into the shadows created by the glaring light of discrimination. Any sense of conversation also disappears, for *correspondence*—from the Latin *cor*, meaning *with* or *together*, and *respondere*, meaning to respond, to answer—is, at root, conversation.

Consciousness, which Jung is fond of referring to as a Promethean conquest, is a turning away from, and opposition to, instinct. It is, almost by definition, in opposition to nature. The rootless condition of consciousness is accompanied by a dangerous *hubris*, an inflated, exaggerated belief in ones own self-importance and powers of discernment. This rootless condition is also accompanied by a sense of *meaninglessness*, a psycho-spiritual malaise. For Jung (1983), the great pathology in need of healing is the condition of a soul that has lost its meaning. This loss is part and parcel of the loss of connection with the instinctual. The great danger in both individual and collective development of conscious discrimination is that it can lead to a one-sidedness and deviation from what is innate, intrinsic, and inherent to human beings. Such a deviation is a theoretical impossibility for a thinker like Rorty. It is conceptual humbug, given his insistence that speaking of any intrinsic nature, whether of self, world, others, or anything else, is an endeavor best abandoned. Yet, for Jung, there is always a tension between the freedom of conscious choice and one's instincts, the former making possible the transgression of the latter. Consciousness that does not heed instinct acquires an enormous Promethean debt, one that must be paid eventually, with interest. This payment often takes the form of neurosis, hysteria, psychosis, splitting, fragmentation, and a plethora of both physiological and psychological illnesses.

Nature, on Jung's view, is what one must align oneself with. To deviate too greatly from it is sickness, madness, premature death, and decay. Its voice is heard in our dreams, those weird and wondrous emanations of sleep that arise when consciousness is weakest. Dreams speak in the language of nature, a language incomprehensible to us, not, as Freud (1901/1981) would have it, because its meaning is censored or veiled, but because we have simply forgotten its lexicon. It is in need of translation to the seemingly rational words and concepts of present-day speech unencumbered by a more primitive and mystical participation with things.

> Dreams are impartial, spontaneous products of the unconscious psyche, outside the control of the will. They are pure nature; they show us the unvarnished, natural truth, and are therefore fitted, as nothing else, to give us back an attitude that accords with our basic human nature when our consciousness has strayed too far from its foundations and run into an impasse. (Jung & Hoffman, 2003, p. 79)

Consciousness can travel far, too far, and is at times in need of guidance. Implicit to Jung's view is the sense that consciousness cannot simply construct any story it pleases. If its constructions are not built firmly upon the ground, they fall apart, and a neurotic dissociation takes hold. If consciousness tells a story that does not correspond to an actual state of affairs, there are consequences. Consciousness must live in alignment with forces that are greater than itself, forces that are not invented or constructed by any individual or culture. The realization of this can be disappointing. It frustrates our yearning for mastery, intelligibility, and control.

Psychological pathology, as understood by Jung, bears a striking resemblance to semiological reductionism: A consciousness enthralled by words, bereft of contact with its instinctual ground, and suffering from a lack of meaning could also describe an intellectual ethos that has reduced everything to semiotics, dismissed the very idea of nature as an ersatz human fabrication, and risks, at least by some accounts, collapsing into nihilism. Jung sought to actively reveal what this reductionism merely passively reflects: the alienation of a language-bearing consciousness from its experiential, instinctual foundation. On this reading, the *isms* that profess a language unable to refer to, hook up with, or represent any reality, essence, nature, or phenomena are the philosophical codifications of pathology, symptoms in the form of intellectual theories, truly delusions of reference. Semiological reductionism, on this reading, reflects dissociation and fragmentation in its attempt to reveal the true workings of language. As such, it is the justification and systematization of an estrangement, an apologetics of aberration. It dissociates itself from nature by rejecting it on principle, the principle of an ungrounded system of signs bereft of any referential capacity. It replicates in the realm of theory the very condition that Jung sought to heal with his psychology.

From this viewpoint, *différance* is more the symptomatic expression of an alienation than a plausible account of the working of signs and signifiers. It is more symptomatically telling than theoretically credible. The reigning anti-essentialism of a deconstructive postmodernism appears like yet another vain attempt to escape nature's call by way of philosophically invalidating it, conceptually neutering it. It is but one example of a very old tradition within Western culture—that of dissociating from, and attempting to conquer, both nature and instinct (Lacourt, 2010).

Attempts to disparage the very idea of anything innate, inherent, intrinsic, or given are but thinly veiled efforts to conquer nature by rendering it mute. What better way to silence nature than to nullify it entirely, perpetually defer its presence, postpone its call, fence it off behind chain-linked signifiers? What better way to suspend its imperative than to place it within the safe confines of human-made construction? Jung, who was highly critical of collective desires to dominate, would have been deeply suspicious of an attempt to de-potentiate nature by way of its deconstruction, by way of its semiological reduction. Such a de-potentiation, as he knew, was ultimately illusory. Conquest was not his approach, but rather, reconciliation, and he viewed askance any ideology that might serve such a conquest. Thus, he wrote of the typical European of his day that "his task is to find the natural man again. Instead of this, there is nothing he likes better than systems and methods by which he can repress the natural man who is everywhere at cross purposes with him" (Jung & Sabini, 2002, p. 126). Semiological reductionism constitutes such a system or method.

You may have noticed that in some of Jung's writings cited here, the term "nature" (*natur* in German) is being used to speak of all those essential qualities, tendencies, and characteristics that make the human animal what it is. Yet it is also being used, at times, to speak of the living ecosystem not created by human beings, the wild, something that Jung mentions the city dweller, specifically, has little contact with. It takes on the meaning of a world separate from the products of civilization, a world not created by human beings. At times, Jung and I use the term one way, then another, and quite often both simultaneously, playing upon the ambiguity and polysemy present in both the English and German variants. Jung often uses the term to refer to multiple senses, employing an indistinctness of meaning similar to that of the word "ground" as previously discussed. He speaks of nature as a literal place, a world apart, with inhabitants that are other than human. He also speaks of nature in another, perhaps more metaphorical, sense. Rather than see this polysemy as merely a knotty, difficult challenge to understanding, or an opportunity to deconstruct, and ultimately render impotent, the notion of *nature*, one might also see in this multiplicity of meanings both insight and acumen.

What the dual and dueling senses of *nature* suggest is less a logical incoherency or cultural bias in the English and German languages, or Jung's writings, than a fortuitous prospect to discover meaningful connections. Jung's ambiguous use of these multiple senses of the word *nature* simply suggests that what is essential, inherent, and given in human beings is, in fact, the rainforest, the desert, the prairie, the entire living biosphere. As Peter Levine (2010) remarks, we possess an "internal savannah, one populated by ancient instincts that manifest as coherent behaviors, sensations, feelings, and thoughts" (p. 234). Or as Ian McCallum (2008) explains, "The animals . . . are in our blood. The landscape is in our skin. We too, gnash and gnaw; we sound our alarm calls and our cries of territory, sexuality, and discovery" (p. 60).

Nature exists both within and without. Both senses of *nature* speak to what is not created by humans, what exists beyond our conscious intent, what appears to be given, pre-existing human intervention. The polysemy of *nature* reminds us that we are not solely of our own creation. We humans are of the wild. To alienate ourselves from one aspect of nature is to alienate ourselves from the other, for "the depths of mind, the unconscious, are our inner wilderness areas" (Snyder, 1990, p. 17) and the outer wilderness areas are our depths of mind. This is why "the nature around us can provide insight regarding the kindred 'nature' within" (West, 2007, p. 17). As without, so within.

As within, so without. And because this is so, any attempt to heal the psyche in isolation from the ecosystem that birthed it is madness.

What Jung's conflation of meanings points to is a sense that what is essential, innate, and inborn in human beings is the wild—we are the kith of stiff lizards in frozen desserts, the kin of moles burrowing about their subterranean dens. Jung (1956/1962) affirms our collective affinity with the reptilian, the mammalian, the vegetative, all of which form part of our phylogenetic heritage. Consciousness cannot disregard the dictates of this heritage for too great a time; the facts of nature cannot in the long run be violated, and no higher principle exists than that of being in agreement with nature's laws (1921/1971). This is the fundamental principle behind leading an optimal, fulfilling human life.

Acknowledging affinities: speaking to, with, and about non-human others

In his book *The Spell of the Sensuous*, Abram (1996) puts forth a vision of language in which word and world once participated in the most intimate of relationships, but have since been severed from one another: Pictographs, from which the modern alphabet evolved, echoed in their form the sensible entities for which they stood; to write of an ox was to draw a simple picture of an ox. The animal, and the sign that represented it, were intimately related; pictographs referred the reader to a living being that could be immediately perceived by the senses. However, with the advent of the alphabet, this direct relationship between word and world was diminished. An intimacy was lost. An estrangement began. Unlike a pictograph, an individual letter does not so directly portray any sensible phenomena in the world, except perhaps the sound that it represents. Though a limited number of consonants reflected elements of nature, like the flight pattern of cranes, increasingly this reflection has faded; an *X* does not draw our attention to any object or living being existing in the world that we co-inhabit. Rather, it draws attention to itself, and the relationship it has to other letters in a given word.

Although this shift is perhaps subtle, the consequences are profound. On Abram's telling, with the dawn of the alphabet, a schism between word and world begins, and a concomitant growing muteness of the natural world. As the human voice begins to articulate itself by way of words formed in letters, "the other animals, the plants, and the natural elements—sun, moon, stars, waves—are beginning to lose their own voices" (Abram, 1996, p. 101). No longer can we hear the whispering brook warn of coming danger. No longer can we read omens in the clouds, or hear the query in a crow's caw. The sensitive observer who sees animals in the cumuliform and stratiform sky sees only a curiosity. The ancient hermeneutic endeavor of reading nature's vicissitudes has gradually been replaced by a world in which nature seems to have nothing to say, a world that signifies nothing, and is therefore insignificant. Thus the divorce that Abram describes is twofold; as human language extricates itself from the world of the senses, nature's language grows mute to human ears. Language slowly becomes more and more an exclusively human affair. I say slowly, for the tale of the divorce of word and world is a long one. The abstraction of language from its sensuous surround takes us from the original formation of a pictographic language by Phoenician traders, to the innovation of the aleph-beth by Hebrew scribes, to the adaptation of this aleph-beth by the Greeks and the formation of the Western alphabet, to the recognition of language as a formal system of signs in the semiotics of Saussure.

Saussure's semiotics is important for Abram's account because it inaugurates an understanding of linguistic meaning as a product of differences *within* a system of language; words possess meaning less because of what they might refer to in the world and more because of differences they possess in relation to other words. From pictographic representation to modern-day semiotics, language, once born directly from the sensuous world, has now ostensibly subsumed that world, converting it into a mere *something* within an abstract system of distinctions. With Saussure's understanding of language, we are brought close to our current era in which an entire world of representation, of mental landscapes, and linguistic formulations seems to float above a material world to which it has no clear relation. Abram portrays the situation thus:

> The apparently autonomous, mental dimension originally opened by the alphabet—the ability to interact with our own signs in utter abstraction from our earthly surroundings—has today blossomed into a vast, cognitive realm, a horizonless expanse of virtual interactions and encounters. Our reflective intellects inhabit a global field of information, pondering the latest scenario for the origin of the universe as we absently fork food into our mouths, composing presentations for the next board meeting while we sip our coffee or in order to network with other bodiless minds. (1996, p. 265)

Such an abstraction from earthly surroundings is passively reflected, codified, and raised to the level of method by a semiological reductionism that posits a system of signs floating independently of any referential ground. Abram, like Jung, perceives the way in which language can seemingly divorce itself from the realm of experience and the phenomenal. Both men acknowledge alienated, astronautic language, language that does not touch the earth. For both, this alienation is not absolute, nor is it a matter of course. Neither understands this divorce as benign or inevitable. Rather, it is indicative of a greater ill, symptomatic of a deeper malaise. Alienated language is for both Jung and Abram a symptom of alienated being, not an inevitable outcome of semiotic deferral, nor the felicitous result of transcending metaphysical, essentialist thinking.

For Abram, this alienation of language, this extirpation of human signs from their generative matrix, is of the same lineage as the belief that language is a solely human affair, and that a greater, non-human world does not, and has never, spoken to us. Could it not be that the words we now speak arose at some point as "a stuttering reply not just to others of our species but to an enigmatic cosmos that already *spoke to us* in a myriad of tongues?" (Abram, 2010, p. 4) Our civilized assumption is to believe that words are merely human artifacts but, "what if meaningful speech is *not* an exclusively human possession?" (p. 4, original emphasis) Then, it is difficult to construe it as a grid superimposed upon a primary order with which it has only a tenuous relation, à la Foucault. A world that speaks to us contrasts starkly to one that has been cut up into the discernible components of a general anatomy. Abram describes a community of subjects, a web of relationships that includes the more than human world, within which language arises—not a mute void, but an entire population of sentient others. Such a description speaks directly to the aforementioned root sense of correspondence as a *responding with*, as a dialogue made possible by similarity, mutuality, relationship, likeness, and correlation. It implicitly alludes to what Jung referred to above as *the sympathy of all things*, the sense that between everything, and everything else, there is affinity, association, congruity, and resemblance even amidst variance, dissociation, incongruousness, and difference.

To perceive a speaking world is to share a sensibility with all indigenous cultures that conceive of human beings as embedded within a living matrix. Australian aborigines live in a world *animated* by spirits, sentient subjects living within the rocks and rivers, canyons and gullies of their native soil. Such features of the terrain are not merely geological objects for them. They are physical manifestations of the movements of ancestral beings (Tacey, 2010). They have meaning. They speak. Practitioners of earth-based spiritual traditions live in an ensouled world in which all the parts belong to an interconnected whole of subjects speaking to one another (Starhawk, 2004). Those who live in an animate world do not merely speak *about* it. They speak *to* it and *with* it. This may be difficult to understand for many of us who have been brought up within a literate culture, but indigenous peoples often see plants, animals, and natural bodies such as lakes, rivers, and mountains as subjects capable of expression with whom one might have a conversation (Abram, 2010).

As odd as this speaking *to* and *with* may seem to the contemporary sensibility of many, present-day ethology suggests that the seemingly meaningless cacophony that many might hear in the forests and glades, savannahs and prairies, is no less significant than the most lively of human conversations (McCallum, 2008). There is evidence for interspecies communication in fields ranging from trans-species psychology to ethology and neuroscience (Bradshaw & Cater, 2010): Lions roar their territorial claim, and hyenas vocally beg to differ. Predators learn the calls of their prey. Mimicry abounds, as does communicative subterfuge, for example, when monkeys belt out a warning of imminent danger in order to fool their playmates. Monkeys, in effect, cry wolf. Domesticated dogs bark and paw their owners to inform them of impending epileptic attacks. Symbiotic relationships abound in which one species evolves a complex understanding of the sounds, behaviors, and habits of others. This interspecies communication involves humans as well, at least those humans who have not forgotten such an ability. The Andaman islanders, for example, who still possess a Neolithic culture, were able to preemptively flee the 2004 tsunami that devastated the Bay of Bengal, apparently by reading the behavior of the non-human cohabitants in their surround (McCallum, 2008).

An interspecies community composed of bonobo apes and humans has refuted the conceit that language is an exclusively human affair (Bradshaw, 2010). In this community, the bonobos have proven themselves capable of not merely mimicking human language, but rather using it as a medium through which to learn complex concepts, including such concepts as rights. In doing so, they have demonstrated "that humans can no longer claim linguistic or even epistemic authority" (p. 177). Nor can we, in light of such discoveries, view ourselves as alien to our animal kin. There is evidence for interspecies communication of emotion by way of the same neurons that make this possible between human beings (Murrow, 2010). Such findings have helped undermine the pervasive rationale of an absolute difference between humans and other animal species. Findings of trans-species similarities in responses to imminent threat undermine this rationale all the more. This modern discovery of interspecies communication is, of course, a re-discovery of what is commonplace in many pre-modern, traditional cultures for which communication between humans and their non-human brethren is a given (West, 2006).

The rationale of absolute differences involves speaking *about* rather than *to* and *with*. It involves a distancing. Talking *about* implies a certain remoteness. Our civilized tendency to speak *about* a world, rather than *to* or *with* it, resides in our having "taken our primary truths from technologies that hold the world at a distance" (Abram, 2010, p. 7). The blessing of technological truths becomes a bane only when such truths are not "carried carefully back to the lived world, and placed in service to the more-than-human matrix of corporeal encounter and experience" (p. 7). In terms of one of the primary metaphors threading its way through this book, astronauts must return home and not imagine that this home is merely the third planet from the sun. To do so would be to forget the very act of departure—the fiery push against a solid earth that makes the vision of earth as object even possible. Anatomists of both body and language must remember that their vision is predicated upon distance. To forget this is the danger, since "this animal body, for all its susceptibility and vertigo, remains the primary instrument of all our knowing, as the capricious earth remains our primary cosmos" (p. 8).

For indigenous, oral peoples, it is clear that their words spring forth from the earth and they share an affinity with the chirps, gobbles, croaks, roars, cackles, songs, and screams of other species. It is those cultures that have become adept at speaking *of* and *about* the world without speaking *to* it and *with* it for whom language becomes ungrounded:

> When oral culture degrades, the mediated mind loses its bearings, forgetting its ongoing debt to the body and the breathing earth. Left to itself the literate intellect, adrift in the play of signs, comes to view nature as a sign, or a complex of signs. It forgets that the land is not first and foremost an arcane text to be read, but a community of living, speaking beings to whom we are beholden. (Abram, 2010, p. 287)

The mind that forgets its debt to body and earth becomes disoriented. When the debt is forgotten, body and earth become, seemingly, mere signs to be deciphered, conceptual abstractions within a constructed code. A sentient world can be spoken for, but cannot speak for itself. A community of beings can be spoken *of*, but not *with*, not *to*.

Yet we share affinities with these beings to which we are beholden. We are kindred in nature. Our affinities do not reside merely in being creatures that speak, but also in our response to overwhelming fear, helplessness, and loss. How humans respond to threats to their survival is surprisingly similar to that of other species. Touch a potato bug where it is soft and sensitive and it will coil up into a ball. Touch a human in this way and he or she may do the same. Vastly different species share common action patterns and instinctive responses. Like other animals, we are susceptible to trauma, and able to heal ourselves from it in remarkably comparable ways. Such is the testament of renowned trauma theorist Peter Levine (2010), whose approach to healing is based on the understanding that human beings are first and foremost instinctual beings—human animals. And it is this animal nature of ours that makes us both vulnerable to trauma and capable of robust recovery in response to it.

We are not unlike the proverbial deer in the headlights, frozen at the sight of an oncoming car. Humans do this too, as do other animals. We are scared stiff, paralyzed with fear, immobilized by imminent danger. We play possum. We still ourselves as an instinctual response, one that is also available to lizards and leopards, serpents and sea otters (Levine, 2010). Collapsing in a state of utter helplessness is another such response. Both paralysis and collapse form part of the experiential matrix of trauma response in humans. Both are common to the experience of other animals as well. Drawing heavily from the insights of ethology, Levine tirelessly draws parallels between animal and human behavior, reminding us that emotions like grief and anger, feelings like disgust and lust, and behaviors like mating and caring for the young are not merely universals among human beings. They also resemble the behaviors of other mammals. It should be noted here, that *universals* are one of the favorite targets of deconstructive postmodernism. For the true believers of such an approach, to propose that universal characteristics might exist, not only among humans, but also among humans and other species, is not merely a venial sin, but a mortal one.

The colorful, plumed display of peacocks; the courting dance of scorpions; or the pre-coital strutting of the males of many species are not so very different from human rituals of seduction: "Anyone who has seen a well-executed rendering of a dance such as the tango or samba has witnessed an exquisitely instinct-rooted mating ritual" (Levine, 2010, p. 233). The mourning customs of elephants are not that different from those of humans (Bradshaw & Buckley, 2010). Although there may be a danger in naively extrapolating from animal to human behavior, the evidence supporting strong, deep, persistent human-animal affinities is simply too overwhelming. Human beings share fixed action patterns that we have inherited from a long evolution that is not separable from the evolutionary paths of our reptilian, mammalian, and avian brethren. This past is not separable from the evolutionary paths of any creature living upon the planet. This is what Jung (1958) means when he speaks of our phylogenetic heritage. Such a heritage is evidenced in the development and structure of the human body, and can be seen in a phylogenetic tree that connects human beings with invertebrates, protozoa and other life forms.

A dissociation from nature, the belief in the absolute otherness of non-human animals, is also a dissociation from the living, sentient body, without which "nature becomes something out there to be controlled and dominated. Disembodied, we are not a part of nature, graciously finding our humble place within its embrace" (Levine, 2010, p. 286). Distinguishing between two senses of *body* in German, Levine echoes a crucial differentiation made in Chapter 1, the differentiation between *körper*, the physical body as object, and *leib*, the living body. This *leib* has been largely abandoned as we have become, collectively, enamored of our own abstractions, hypnotized by our own verbiage, and psychologically distant from the natural world not created by human beings.

The word "nature" in the sense used by the eco-logically minded cannot be understood as merely "an epistemological indicator to designate certain types of discourse" (Chomsky & Foucault, 2006, p. 7). Nor can it be understood, as does Rorty (1989), as something that an ideal philosopher should want to disregard. The intrinsic, inherent, and instinctual traits of human beings, for those imbued of an ecological sensibility, runs far deeper than this. To the deconstructive pretense that everything human is *always already linguistic*, they respond with an equally adamant *always already animal*. Yet the social sciences often demonstrate an aversion to the human-as-animal supposition, namely by way of eliminating concepts of instinctual behavior from their vocabulary (Levine, 2010). Words like *instinct*, or those that allude to anything organic, innate, or intrinsic to the human condition are puritanically purged from social science disciplines that prefer more technologically attuned words such as *drives*, and *mechanisms* (Stevens, 1997). Instincts are used to explain animal behavior, but not human behavior. The metallic, mechanistic ring of a word like *drive* is preferable to the all-too-chthonic *instinct* with its connotations of animality. This purification of vocabulary leads to a forgetfulness of the ways in which human behavior, although modifiable through conscious intent, is also primal and universal (Levine, 2010). This universality cannot be reduced to the merely human. There are basic patterns of behavior, for example, that can be seen in both human and non-human infants. Mammal babies of all species, including humans, do not need to be taught "that the taste of sugar is 'good' and a hard pinch or a tummy ache is 'bad.' The ingestion of sugar is necessary for energy production, hence the pleasure attraction; while the pinch can cause tissue damage, feels painful" (p. 242) and is, for this reason, to be shunned. Good and bad cannot be understood as mere impositions of a binary language system that creates such dichotomies, dichotomies that can be deconstructed and neutralized by way of a literary-philosophic technique. This sense of good and bad is an inherent part of what makes the human animal what it is.

The implicit and explicit appeal to our kindred relationship with non-human species is antithetical to any line of thought that would deny nature its due. In contrast to an ethos of affinity, Derrida envisions an unbridgeable gap between human beings and non-human others, an abyssal rupture that cannot overcome the dualistic construction of non-human animals as absolute other (Woodward, 2008). By way of *différance*, he places an insurmountable chasm between text and referent and places this same chasm between human selves and non-human others. As immediacy is deferred, and the immediate is rendered mediate by a system of signs that can, on principle, never be traversed, others become absolute, untouchable others. As the perceptual, the experiential, the sensual, and the intuitive are transformed into objects (signs) within language, not only the earth, but the earth's inhabitants become distant objects. Then there is no sense of interspecies connection as exists in shamanism (Woodward, 2008). There is no way of acknowledging intergenerational and interspecies relationships through practices of drumming, chanting, and singing that invoke the living spirits of both ancestors and animals (Cumes, 2010). In shamanic understanding, through the throwing of bones, animal sacrifice, and prayer, illnesses are healed by way of healing those interspecies soul connections between humans and other beings, including the deceased. But this is exactly the connection that is lost to the abyssal rupture of semiotic deferral; what is absent from the vision that severs language from referent is not only the animate (ensouled) human body, but the animate world. What is lacking is *anima mundi*, an understanding of the entire natural universe as alive, which is perhaps the most ancient form of the human experience of being in the world (Starhawk, 2004).

As a challenge to the Derridean vision of the utter alterity of non-human animals, many writers sense kinship between humans and non-human others, so that "their knowledge productions become 'relational epistemologies'" (Woodward, 2008, p. 3). Such knowledge productions undermine the logic of differences that has permeated our relationships with other animals, a logic that grants to humans all epistemic authority, all power to know, while granting no agency to non-human others, as the traditional beliefs of indigenous cultures do. Such cultures have a greater sense of *we* that includes other species, while the more modern logic of absolute difference conceives in terms of more polarizing notions of "self" and "other." Derrida, despite himself perhaps, shares more in common with this latter approach. Though making a laudable attempt to acknowledge the subjectivity and agency of non-human others, an attempt to acknowledge the animal gaze as a sentient one, he conceives this sentience as, regrettably, forever inscrutable (Derrida & Mallet, 2008). As with the aforementioned claim that for Derrida, "the thing may *be* in itself, but it cannot manifest itself except by way of representation" (Dillon, 1991, p. xxii), it seems that animal subjectivities may *be* in themselves, but they can only manifest by way of our human representations of them. The perceptual veil that has alienated us from animal kin has been identified, and perhaps some vague forms have been discerned through its gossamer lace, but it has not been rent asunder.

Loosening oppositions

Yet it would be a mistake to depict too radical an opposition between defenders of the earth, professed champions of an eco-logic, on the one hand, and a deconstructive postmodernism informed by the linguistic turn, on the other. There can be no doubt that deconstruction has represented an important challenge to a conservative power structure that uses the very idea of "nature," to defend the presumed universality of Western values. Post-structuralism and deconstruction have relentlessly analyzed the ways in which the West has divvied up almost everything into opposing qualities and then prioritized one side of the opposition (West, 2007). In doing so, they have brought into stark relief the ways in which generations past and present have imagined such opposing qualities as being natural, given, and inherent at the expense of seeing the extent to which they are projections of the cultural mind that conceives them. From this perspective, post-structuralism's virtue is that it calls out the privileging of likeness over otherness, and the reverberations of this privileging throughout entire conceptual systems. It disrupts and undermines the ruthless logic of binaries imposed upon a world that may not, of its own accord, possess these binaries. In focusing on the peculiar ways in which some languages and cultures cleave reality into distinct, mutually exclusive, and conflicting pairs organized hierarchically, it has been able to draw out, and call into question, these pairs as mere projections. They are not, or may not be, the ostensibly innate or essential characteristics that they pretend to be.

As projections, these oppositional pairings precede, influence, and determine a good deal of what an individual, or a people, seemingly find in their encounters with a world, a reality. Thus, undoubtedly, as Rinda West (2007, p. 24) points out, "our ideas about what to expect when we venture into wilderness shape the ways we experience the wild. Some theorists go so far as to suggest that we cannot know anything meaningful about what is 'out there.'" The predominant, strongly accentuated divergence between nature and culture that exists in Western languages prefigures and prejudices what is found on the prairie and in the shopping mall, in the bog and in the classroom, on the ocean floor and on the football field. It not only prefigures and prejudices what you or I find there, it is the very prefiguring that establishes such binaries as prairie/mall, bog/classroom, ocean floor/football field, all of which are variations on the nature/culture binary. Once the projective quality of these oppositions is acknowledged, then it is much easier to understand how "Western culture has constructed one way of looking at nature, while African and American Indian cultures understood nature quite differently" (p. 53). Such an understanding of the social construction of knowledge suggests that nature is a product of human design, "from the drained fens of England to the deserts of what was once the Fertile Crescent" (p. 24).

In both structuralism's and post-structuralism's understanding of the relationship between the two elements of the sign, some see an opportunity to unmask the crimes of empire. The distance between signifier and signified that is believed to be more prominent in European languages, makes these languages "well suited to the tasks of conquest and control, lying to the domestic audience about the rapacity of empire and proclaiming to the conquered that their condition is natural" (West, 2007, p. 43). Because, by contrast, in traditional cultures words are more closely related to their experiential surround, because they exist in relation to the natural world and are not exclusively human tools, they "have the power to conjure the things, events, or conditions they name, [and] it is much more difficult to lie" (p. 43). As in Abram's tale of the growing schism between word and world that comes with alphabetic languages, West sees a similar disjunction: European tongues are forked. In their slithery slippage from signifier to signified, they evince an uncanny capacity for subterfuge. The tenuous, problematic, perhaps even non-existent relationship between words and what they purport to refer to—the relationship which has formed the very subject of the present inquiry—on this reading is more the province of a particular group of languages whose history is inseparable from conquest. The extended meditation upon this slippery relationship in the guise of postmodern language theory plays an important role in undermining the pretensions of empire.

Yet, notwithstanding the ostensibly beneficial effects of this meditation, the positive role that such theory has had in dismantling empire's ethic, there is also a blind spot—a privileging of culture over nature that would seem to repeat and reinforce the very sort of hierarchical dichotomy that this theoretical disposition intends to dismantle. There is a contemporary debate in literary studies regarding the validity of speaking of human nature. Within that debate, "most theory that clusters around the term *post-modernism* starts from the premise that culture has the decisive influence on human experience: one cannot locate essential characteristics, because everything is traceable to the particulars of history, class, gender, and race" (West, 2007, pp. 8–9). To those who would deny any and all attempts to speak of the essentially human, one can beg to differ. Many ecocritics believe that blank-slate, nature-skeptical theorists should pay more attention to the work of ecology and evolutionary biology (West, 2007). If they were to do so, they might be led to recognize the influence of a shared biological history and the formidable tendencies people have to react according to patterns common to all. Literary studies themselves speak to these common patterns as well. Granted, "three thousand years' worth of written texts suggests that the social forces of history, class, gender, and culture have a resounding influence on the development of character" (p. 8). Yet that same written record also suggests "a number of themes that recur across cultures, representing common human experiences, suggesting that something in our biological makeup inclines humans to respond in similar ways" (p. 8). Responding to postmodernist critiques of Jung as anachronistically essentialist and Eurocentric, particularly in his belief in a shared psychic substrate or collective unconscious, West contends that such a belief is simply a way of recognizing the immense power of our phylogenetic history, a way of conceptualizing our innate dispositions to respond in particular ways to common or universal human situations.

Like West, literary theorist and ecocritic Rowland (2005, 2006a, 2006b, 2010) offers a subtle, complex, and thoroughly nuanced reading of post-structuralism and its relation to both ecocriticism and the eco-logic of Jung's writings. Central to this reading is a contrast between two mythic sensibilities—that of the sky father and the earth mother. Bequeathed by Christianity, the sky-father mythos is monotheistic, conceives of divinity as divorced from the natural world and earthly processes, and is dissociated from femininity and matter. Within this Christian, patriarchal ethos, "nature does not speak; culture speaks of and for nature" (Rowland, 2005, p. 107). Humans are alien to nature, and this alienation has been evinced in textual practices of the Church that have created a notion of god made manifest through the much-venerated word. Nature is thus reduced to a symbolic presence only, an "object" mediated by language and symbolic systems designated as purely human. In the West, this father-god mythology triumphed over that of an ancient, animistic, mother-earth mythology that imbued the world with a multiplicity of voices, and valued interdependence and relation over independence and separation (Rowland, 2006b). In contrast, the transcendent sky-father privileged "rationality, discrimination, and separation over connection and relating" (p. 286).

On Rowland's reading, the animistic mother-earth mythology with its multiplicity of voices has not disappeared. When theology divorced God from his creation, animism did not so much die as shift location, moving from the natural world to the textual world: "Once nature spoke to us, now texts do" (2006b, p. 287). Once whispering brooks warned us of coming danger, and omens could be read in the clouds. Now such reading takes place before books and computer screens. As a result of this shift, "the marginalized cultural forms connecting humans to nature have re-surfaced in surprising new 'ground:' poststructuralism" (p. 285). Because post-structuralism reads texts for their multiplicity, for their myriad voices, "it emphasizes plurality and diversity. In arguing that meaning is always unstable, that signifiers slip away from signifieds, poststructuralism is an animistic vision of cultural production" (p. 288). As such, it represents a fundamental change from the mythos of the sky father towards "the ontological perspective of the earth-mother" (p. 289). Therefore, it could be argued that within post-structuralism there is a return to animism "with the many voices of nature shifted to texts" (2005, p. 108). Such a return, understandably, would ally post-structuralism with ecocriticism.

This alliance, however, is not without its limitations. Rowland contrasts literary theory that emphasizes language as an enclosed system, on the one hand, with the critical orientation of ecocriticism, on the other, noting that the former suffers from a "semiotic fallacy with ethical implications" (p. 105). One central implication of this fallacy is that it tends to think of human culture and language as existing apart from the natural world, rather than being intimately woven into the very fabric of that world. The semiotic fallacy risks rendering nature mute and moot—both silent and beside the point. Theory that has not moved beyond the linguistic turn has succumbed to "the 'semiotic fallacy'. In other words, it is assumed that because mountains and waters are human at the point of delivery, they exist only as signified within human culture. Thus they have no intrinsic merit, no value and no rights" (Coupe, cited in Rowland, 2005, p. 105). The semiotic fallacy conceives of language as an enclosed system. Anything that may touch upon this system cannot truly infiltrate it or permeate it. Nothing that is conceived in language can have a reality greater than its linguistic conception. Even mountains and waters become human constructs without any inherent quality, character, or being beyond their construction.

On the one hand, the return of animism is a boon for the ecocritic, yet on the other, this semiotic fallacy remains problematic: "The question stubbornly lingers: how to get from texts to nature, to hear the authentic voices of the 'other' from beyond human technological culture" (2005, p. 109). Post-structuralism may be a form of animism, but it is one of a peculiar variety in which nature itself has become cultural "by the fact that our only relation to it is one of our cultural framings of it" (2006b, p. 290). Curiously, one can hear in this reading of a semiotic fallacy, and in the idea of nature becoming cultural, echoes of the very sky-father mythos that reduces nature to a symbolic presence, an object mediated by purely human language. One can sense, too, inklings of astronautic distancing. The semiotic fallacy seems to operate within post-structuralism as a great caveat that prevents the authentic voices of nature from a full-throated articulation.

Rowland's framing of nature having become cultural, and post-structuralism as a surprising case of nature's voice speaking through texts, raises many questions that have been implicit and explicit in the present and preceding chapter. Where is nature? Is it a signified something nested wholly within culture? Or does it include culture within itself? Are nature and culture adjacent to one another? Are culture and nature two "internally related moments within a unified and processual reality" (Fisher, 2002, p. 119)? In asking these questions, are we approaching the same paradox of the inner and the outer explored earlier through Foucault's work? There, both *body* and *man* are understood as recent inventions, constructs, existing *within* a semiotic, yet a contrary sense also implies itself, a sense in which both body and man exist, as it were, *outside*, or prior to, this semiotic. In what sense can nature be both inside a system of signs, and as such a product of a particular culture and moment in history, and, at the same time, be intrinsic order, innate dynamic, inherent characteristic, as well as a biosphere, a vast web of living beings not created by human intent? How can nature be *nature* (the term), and can it ever be only that?

These questions will not be answered here. Rather, this chapter will end by way of paradox. And it will end, as it began, by way of image—an image that, perhaps, intimates a deeper sense or purpose to this figurative departure from earth as nature, as ground. Please imagine the globe once more, floating in the vast void of space. Allow this image to be imbued with the meanings given to it here: the earth as place of origin and birth, the earth as home. Let it allude to what is essential, intrinsic, inherent, but also all that is sensual, primordial, phenomenal, perceptual, and intuitively given. Let it summon a vague sense of earthiness, but let it also be an image of wholeness, as circular, spherical objects often are (Jung & Von Franz, 1964). Let it be a big blue eye looking back at you as you look at it, a sentient being that perceives you in your act of perceiving. Allow this image to speak and say what it will, not only what has been said in the present text, but what the image says to you beyond the parameters and associations established here. See the earth, as if from afar, as one of an infinite number of planetary bodies in a seemingly limitless cosmos, merely one among many, and, at the same time, the very special and truly unique planet that it is, to any and all of its inhabitants. As you let this image of our planet reverberate through your felt, living body, and evoke what it will within your imagination, hear these closing words that open onto new meanings to this dream of departure, and the return made possible by such a dream:

> In realizing our cultural-psychological dreams of distance, even to the point where distance can become departure forever or perhaps destruction, a curious event, perhaps unexpected, has occurred. In leaving the earth, we have, it seems, become more aware of it. Seen from outside the envelope of its protective atmosphere, seen from space, the earth can be *seen*, for the first time in the history of humanity, as home. And perhaps that is the most radical meaning of return: technology as homecoming. For it is only in leaving one's home, in departing from it, that the possibility of return arises. It is only in our distance that the possibility of remembering home takes place, the possibility of taking up in a new way what was, the possibility of recovering as a destiny what was heretofore a heritage. (Romanyshyn, 2004, p. 203)

References

Abram, D. (1996). *The spell of the sensuous: Perception and language in a more-than-human world* (1st edn.). New York, NY: Pantheon Books.

Abram, D. (2010). *Becoming animal: An earthly cosmology*. New York, NY: Pantheon Books.

Bradshaw, G. A. (2010). Bicultural living among apes. *Spring: A journal of archetype and culture: Minding the animal psyche, 83,* 161–182.

Bradshaw, G. A., & Buckley C. (2010). The art of cultural brokerage: Recreating elephant-human relationship and community. *Spring: A journal of archetype and culture: Minding the animal psyche, 83,* 35–59.

Bradshaw, G. A., & Cater, N. (Eds.). (2010). *Spring: A journal of archetype and culture: Minding the animal psyche, 83,* v.

Brown, L. (1995). Foreword. In T. Roszak, M. E. Gomes, & A. D. Kanner, *Ecopsychology: Restoring the earth, healing the mind* (pp. xiii–xvi). San Francisco, CA: Sierra Club Books.

Chomsky, N., & Foucault, M. (2006). *The Chomsky-Foucault debate: On human nature*. New York, NY: New Press.

Cumes, D. (2010). Sangoma medicine—how it works. *Conversations in the field, 1*(6), 1–8.

Derrida, J. (1976). *Of grammatology*. Baltimore, MD: Johns Hopkins University Press.

Derrida, J., & Mallet, M.-L. (2008). *The animal that therefore I am*. New York, NY: Fordham University Press.

Dillon, M. C. (1991). *Merleau-Ponty vivant*. Albany, NY: State University of New York Press.

Fisher, A. (2002). *Radical ecopsychology: Psychology in the service of life*. Albany, NY: State University of New York Press.

Freud, S. (1901/1981). *The psychopathology of everyday life*. New York, NY: Norton.

Jameson, F. (1972). *The prison-house of language: A critical account of structuralism and Russian formalism*. Princeton, NJ: Princeton University Press.

Jung, C. G. (1921/1971). *Psychological types*. Princeton, NJ: Princeton University Press.

Jung, C. G. (1928). *Contributions to analytical psychology*. New York, NY: Harcourt, Brace.

Jung, C. G. (1953). Two essays on analytical psychology. In R. F. C. Hull (Trans.), *The collected works of C. G. Jung* (Vol. 7). Princeton, NJ: Princeton-Bollingen.

Jung, C. G. (1956/1962). *Symbols of transformation: An analysis of the prelude to a case of schizophrenia*. New York, NY: Harper.

Jung, C. G. (1958). *The undiscovered self*. Boston, MA: Little Brown.

Jung, C. G. (1964/1970). Civilization in transition. In R. F. C. Hull (Trans.), *The collected works of C. G. Jung* (Vol. 10). Princeton, NJ: Princeton-Bollingen.

Jung, C. G. (1983). *The essential Jung* (A. Storr, Ed.). Princeton, NJ: Princeton University Press.

Jung, C. G., & De Laszlo, V. S. (1993). *The basic writings of C. G. Jung* (Modern Library edn.). New York, NY: Modern Library.

Jung, C. G., & Hoffman, E. (2003). *The wisdom of Carl Jung*. New York, NY: Citadel Press.

Jung, C. G., & Sabini, M. (2002). *The earth has a soul: The nature writings of C.G. Jung*. Berkeley, CA: North Atlantic Books.

Jung, C. G., & Von Franz, M.-L. (1964). *Man and his symbols*. Garden City, NY: Doubleday.

Lacourt, J. A. (2010). My father was a bear: Human-animal transformation in native American teachings. *Spring: A journal of archetype and culture: Minding the animal psyche, 83*, 79–98.

Levine, P. A. (2010) *In an unspoken voice: How the body releases trauma and restores goodness*. Berkeley, CA: North Atlantic Books.

McCallum, I. (2008). *Ecological intelligence: Rediscovering ourselves in nature*. Golden, CO: Fulcrum.

Murrow, B. (2010). Developing beyond a narcissistic relationship with animals. *Spring: A journal of archetype and culture: Minding the animal psyche, 83*, 279–96.

Poole, R. (2008). *Earthrise: How man first saw the earth*. New Haven, CT: Yale University Press.

Romanyshyn, R. (2004). *Technology as symptom and dream*. New York, NY: Brunner-Routledge.

Rorty, R. (1989). *Contingency, irony, and solidarity*. New York, NY: Cambridge University Press.

Rowland, S. (2005). *Jung as a writer*. New York, NY: Routledge.

Rowland, S. (2006a). Jung and Derrida: The numinous, deconstruction and myth. In A. Casement & D. J. Tacey (Eds.), *The idea of the numinous: Contemporary Jungian and psychoanalytic perspectives* (pp. 98–116). New York, NY: Routledge.

Rowland, S. (2006b). Nature writing: Jung's eco-logic in the coniunctio of comedy and tragedy. *Spring: A journal of archetype and culture: Psyche and nature, 75*, 275–97.

Rowland, S. (2010). *C. G. Jung in the humanities: Taking the soul's path*. New Orleans, LA: Spring Journal Books.

Shepard, P. (1995). Virtually hunting reality in the forests of simulacra. In M. E. Soulé & G. Lease (Eds.), *Reinventing nature? Responses to postmodern deconstruction* (pp. 17–29). Washington, DC: Island Press.

Snyder, G. (1990). *The practice of the wild: Essays*. San Francisco, CA: North Point Press.

Soulé, M. E., & Lease, G. (Eds.). (1995). *Reinventing nature? Responses to postmodern deconstruction*. Washington, DC: Island Press.

Spretnak, C. (1999). *The resurgence of the real: Body, nature, and place in a hypermodern world*. New York, NY: Addison Wesley.

Starhawk. (2004). *The earth path: Grounding your spirit in the rhythms of nature*. San Francisco, CA: HarperCollins.

Stevens, A. (1997). *The two-million-year-old self*. New York, NY: Fromm International Publishing.

Tacey, D. (2010). Ecopsychology and the sacred: The psychological basis of the environmental crisis. *Spring: Journal of archetype and culture: Minding the animal psyche, 83*, 329–51.

West, R. (2006). Land minds: Images of psyche and shadow in two American Indian novels. *Spring: A journal of archetype and culture: Psyche and nature, 76*, 19–40.

West, R. (2007). *Out of the shadow: Ecopsychology, story, and encounters with the land*. Charlottesville, VA: University of Virginia Press.

Woodward, W. (2008). *The animal gaze: Animal subjectivities in southern African narratives*. Johannesburg, South Africa: Wits University Press.

Chapter 4

Promethean postmodernism

Stealing fire from the god-terms

The titanic impulse to deconstruct

There is something Promethean about semiological reductionism: To deconstruct the god-terms is to steal their fire. Insofar as this deconstruction relocates meaning within the play of human signs and thereby eliminates an appeal to such transcendent entities, originary principles, and metaphysical universals as truth, reality, self, center, unity, origin, nature, and archetype, it has taken something of their *élan vital*, their life-giving flame. Insofar as it acknowledges the primordial, the experiential, the perceptual, the sensual, the phenomenal, and the intuited only as terms with meanings, but endows them with no reality beyond the terminological, it steals their fire.

The divine absolutes, once personified and embodied in the mythic deities of the Greek pantheon, gradually evolved into more abstract, philosophical forms (Tarnas, 1995)—the very metaphysical universals and originary principles that have become the prime targets for deconstruction. Greek philosophers gave these gods and goddesses their metaphysical, ideational outline, sublimating and transfiguring them into principles, abstractions, and intellectual articulations. The god-terms thus descended directly from the gods and goddesses; the words now used to refer to absolutes and essences are the conceptual elaborations of mythic figures (Tarnas, 1995). Derrida (1982) expresses this fact in his own way when he claims that metaphysics is the mythos of an idiom. There are gods in our ideas and deities live on in the root metaphors of our language (Hillman, 1975). The linguistic formulations of the timeless universals informing any concrete particular are the contemporary representatives of figures embodied in myth (Tarnas, 1995). There is an intimate relation of consanguinity between these universals and the divinities of old; thus, for Homer, the Greek tragedians, Plato, and others, "knowledge of events means knowledge of the universals in the events, i.e., knowledge of the Gods" (Hillman, 1975, p. 247n).

Yet these linguistic formulations cannot allude to any fundamental reality informing any concrete particular if one is "trapped in the solipsism of language—unable to transgress the text" (Kugler, 2005, p. 19). The undermining of extralinguistic reference disempowers the god-terms, deprives them of their ability to shed light upon any existing state of affairs. If, as Rorty (1989) would have it, such terms are no longer understood as being adequate to the task of properly expressing or representing the nature of the human species, or any nonhuman reality, then they are no longer emissaries of the gods, no longer envoys of powers, dynamics, forces that do not reside exclusively within the confines of a purely human language. This quality of being an emissary, a messenger, an envoy of the gods is described by Hillman (1975) as an angelic quality. There are angels in words, and a new angelology is required if we are to renew our faith in the communicative power of language. Without these angels in our words, "—and angel means originally 'emissary,' 'message-bearer'—how can we utter anything but personal opinions, things made up in our subjective minds?" (Hillman, 1975, p. 9). How can we transgress the text, and "how can anything of worth and soul be conveyed from one psyche to another, as in a conversation, a letter, or a book, if archetypal significances are not carried in the depths of words?" (p. 9).

The semiologically reductive approach attempts to overcome a seemingly naïve faith that sees in words envoys of meaning, representatives of truths, powers, facts, that cannot be reduced to the words themselves. The postmodern Promethean endeavor places meaning's flame solely in the hands of *homo linguisticus*. Its titanic impulse is to liberate humankind from the tyranny of metaphysics as it deconstructs the philosophical tradition that preceded it (Girard & Doran, 2008). Much like the titan of antiquity, who sought to free humanity from the tyranny of the gods, this latter-day Prometheanism attempts a liberation from the oppression of the metaphysical. Deconstructive postmodernism, on this reading, is a new variation of a very old story. As such, it belongs to the realm of archaic myth, and the fire it steals is an ancient one.

In the protean, yet strangely consistent, Promethean story, this Greek titan is, at heart, a rebel, one who often represents the powerless in the perpetual battle against authoritarian regimes (Dougherty, 2006). This is true, to varying degrees, in versions of the story created by Hesiod, Plato, Aeschylus, Mary Shelley, Percy Bysshe Shelley, Lord Byron, and many others throughout the years. Prometheus is the fierce advocate for humankind against the oppressive tyranny of the gods. More than any other Greek deity, he intervenes on behalf of humankind, allying himself with its cause (Kerényi, 1997). Benefactor of the human race (Radin, Kerényi, & Jung, 1969), it was he, more than any other figure in Greek mythology, who stood up for human beings against Zeus' abuse of power (Dougherty, 2006).

Edward Edinger summarizes this myth as follows:

> Prometheus presided over the procedure of dividing the meat of sacrificial victims between gods and men. Previously there had been no need for division because gods and men ate together . . . Prometheus tricked Zeus by offering him only the bones of the animal covered by a layer of enticing fat. For man he reserved all the edible meat. Zeus, angered by this

> trickery, withheld fire from man. But Prometheus slipped into heaven, stole the fire of the gods, and gave it to mankind. In punishment for this crime, Prometheus was chained to a rock where every day a vulture tore at his liver and every night it was healed again. Punishment was also sent to his brother Epimetheus. Zeus fashioned a woman, Pandora, whom he sent to Epimetheus with a box. From Pandora's box emerged all the ills and sufferings that plague mankind—old age, labor, sickness, vice and passion. (1992, p. 24)

Contemporary Prometheanism, of course, has no gripe with Zeus. He is, as with every other deity possibly named, merely a cultural artifact, a signifier whose meaning grows more irrelevant as time passes. Oppression does not emit from the heights of Olympus. Now it takes the guise of the ominously named "regimes of truth" (Chomsky & Foucault, 2006, p. 169) that cannot be understood without referring to political power, for these regimes consist of "the ensemble of rules according to which the true and the false are separated and specific effects of power attached to the true" (Chomsky & Foucault, 2006, pp. 169–70). The oppression to be combated takes the form of power/knowledge, the effects of which are as diffuse and entrenched as they are dangerous (Foucault & Gordon, 1980). Knowledge and power have come to form a single, though hydra-headed, beast: "It is not possible for power to be exercised without knowledge, it is impossible for knowledge not to engender power" (p. 52). Such statements are Promethean insofar as the myth focuses, precisely, on the use and abuse of power.

The current Promethean rebellion is not against the bearded patriarch and son of Chronos, but, rather, against a logocentrism that, it is said, the entirety of Western philosophy to date has been founded upon (Manithottil, 2008). This logocentrism is a form of violence (Lawlor, 2002), or at least harbors it, for there is a deep, epistemic violence that is forever, or always already, at work within the very production of both meaning and truth (Cleary, 1992). The oppression from which deliverance is sought no longer possesses the name of a god or goddess. It goes by the names of god-terms such as "meaning," "logos," "power/knowledge," "metaphysics," "essentialism," and "nature." The authoritarian regime to be rebelled against now is a regime called "truth" and deconstruction is a weapon that takes aim at the very idea of truth (Girard & Doran, 2008). This regime, the metaphysics associated with it, and the veiled deities that find their clandestine home within it (in the form of god-terms), are to be annulled and invalidated. Their force is rendered void by way of a movement that replaces them all, and puts language itself in their stead, thereby establishing sign systems as primary and originary, while simultaneously making gods, goddesses, truths, and essences secondary and derivative. Thus, for a thinker like Derrida, language, by way of *différance,* displaces the gods, and Being itself, as the origin of truth (Dillon, 1995). Derrida simultaneously appropriates and subverts Saussure's understanding of the difference between signifiers so as to vitiate *all* possible truth claims. The only truth left is, perhaps, the absence of truth, although even this is not entirely certain (Girard & Doran, 2008). The titanic rebellion against the authoritative regime of truth appears to affirm its own truth, yet because this rebellion is absolute and all-encompassing, it subverts even its own authority. Indeed, deconstruction has instigated a crisis of authority (Currie, 2013) just as Prometheus did.

The Promethean myth is one of disruption—disruption of tradition, structures, and limits. It is a story of the defiance of authority, the rebellion against all established forms, the breaking of the chains of human bondage, the transcendence of all limitation. The titan-protagonist of this myth challenges all orthodoxy and custom, as well as royalty, aristocracy, institutionalized religion, and political oppression (Tarnas, 1995). The consummate rebel, Prometheus epitomizes the spirit of political revolution (Camus, 1991). Yet such descriptions, with only minor alterations, if any, might also speak to the iconoclastic, anti-authoritarian, and ostensibly progressive spirit of deconstructive postmodernism. It is distrustful of norms, inherent values, established hierarchies, authoritative standards and practices, as well as consensual codes and conventions (Eagleton, 2003).

Its disruption of tradition and overthrow of past limits and structures takes place via the question of reference; when language is severed from its referent, when meaning is understood as a production of signs, a process of semiosis, and nothing more, then both moral values and epistemic assumptions appear to be a question of random, free-floating cultural traditions (Eagleton, 2003). Once traditional beliefs and customs are understood as free-floating and ungrounded, the moral values and limits espoused by them are overthrown *in toto*, relativized to such a degree that they are rendered inconsequential. Thus, in deconstructive theory, Western humanistic and ethical values (being logocentric) have become meaningless (Girard & Doran, 2008). The postmodern variation of the Promethean disruption of tradition takes place at the level of disrupted reference. This disruption, in turn, allows for the rejection of the transcendent authority of *all* authors at *all* times (Girard & Doran, 2008).

Titanism, that is to say, the titanic mentality, violates all limits; it is characterized by boundlessness, and excess. The titanic does not do nuance. Like a tidal wave, it washes away everything in its path and expresses itself through excess (Lopez-Pedraza, 2012). So, contemporary Prometheanism does not merely undermine *an* authority, but, rather, subverts the vary possibility of *any* authority and *any* authoritative statement, except, perhaps, its own. Like the titan of old, an intellectually and politically revolutionary figure, it strives to overturn all certainties, all that has been formerly thought of as given or true. Embodying the fall from absolute foundations and frameworks, its rebellion is, ironically, absolute. Promethean postmodernism offers a scorched-earth approach to truth-claims, incinerating all epistemological certainty, except, perhaps, its own.

The *post* in post-structuralism and postmodernism alludes to the notion of progress, a movement forward and beyond both structure and modernism, a movement beyond tradition. There is no *post* without an *after*, a *subsequent*, a *later*—all terms that carry with them both a sense of temporality and a moving forward, an advancement. Deconstruction, too, partakes of this sense of progress, this moving beyond structure that is also, ostensibly, a movement beyond metaphysics. This is indicative of its Prometheanism insofar as Prometheus, whose name means foresight or forethought, is a figure that speaks to progressive impulses. He is an embodiment of the urge to move away from a rigid, inhibiting orthodoxy (personified in the despotic rule of Zeus) and towards a better future. He is the mythic incarnation of the urgent demand for freedom and the endless search for new horizons (Tarnas, 1995). Prophetic Prometheus, gifted with foreknowledge, is the deity who understands that the present order must be surpassed (Kerényi, 1997). Although deconstructionism is largely ambivalent on the question of progress—since it would seem to deny such a thing could be anything but the imposition of an arbitrary norm—deconstructionists nevertheless espouse a belief in the progressive dismantling of Western metaphysics (Girard & Doran, 2008). The Promethean purpose of deconstructive postmodernism is perhaps even more clearly apparent in Rorty's (1999) own description of neo-pragmatism, which he construes as an apotheosis of the future, a deification of the yet-to-come, that also involves an abandonment of the very idea of nature. Both classical and neo-pragmatism possess

> a willingness to refer all questions of ultimate justification to the future, to the substance of things hoped for. If there is anything distinctive about pragmatism it is that it substitutes the notion of a better human future for the notions of "reality", "reason" and "nature". One may say of pragmatism what Novalis said of Romanticism, that it is "the apotheosis of the future." (p. 27)

The forward-looking attitude that aspires to leave nature behind is a Promethean one. It attempts to overcome the powers of reality and reason so as to institute its own power.

The progressive intent thus far described coincides with a fundamentally negative conception of structure, tradition, metaphysics, and universals. Deconstructive postmodernism has an essentially distrustful conception of god-terms; the gods and goddesses it conceives are punitive, inhibiting, unjust, despotic, and prejudicial. They are not the granters of boons. Why even attempt to deconstruct a benevolent god? Why steal the fire of a god-term if it is the giver of gifts, or the imparter of wisdom? The desire to deconstruct a god-(term) only arises when it is perceived to be a threat, a hindrance, a malevolent power. The tenor of the more semiologically reductive variety of postmodernism brought forth by the linguistic turn construes all governing systems as oppressive and, inverting the polarity, sees positive value in what has been cast out. Yet, in doing so, it replicates the very binary thinking that it attempts to transcend (Eagleton, 1996). For Promethean postmodernism, *power* is always *power over*. It always oppresses, as does all system and law, thus "words like 'norm', 'Law', 'authority', [and] 'power' echo somewhat ominously in its collective consciousness" (Eagleton, 1996, p. 56). Its negative attitude towards structure, tradition, metaphysics, and universals forms part of a general ethos, a primary disposition.

Prometheus liberates humans not only from tradition. He is not merely a rebel against a culturally conservative power structure. He is the immortal prototype of human rebellion, the mythic embodiment of an affirmation of fate (Kerényi, 1997). But his revolt is broader and deeper than this, for he is also the personification of a rebellion against nature itself (Orfanos, 2006). Before Prometheus, men were mere beasts. They had no tools, no technology, no skills, no crafts. It is he who provided humanity with the raw materials for culture that, so the story goes, allows for a transcendence of nature. The titan not only shifts power relations between humans and gods, but humans and the natural world as well. The emphasis in one direction or the other changes from one variation of the myth to another. Hesiod's account of the tale emphasizes a revolt against the gods, while Aeschylus focuses upon the human desire to surpass the ostensibly inferior state of the merely animal. Before the intervention of this cosmic dissenter, men lived like animals. Thus, his story is one of hope and an impulse that moves from "primitive" nature towards sophisticated culture (Dougherty, 2006). Yet those of his kind, the titans, are synonymous with human arrogance at its height, an arrogance that employs technology in a battle against nature itself (Shearer, 2009). This is why Jung spoke of a Promethean conquest that is a turning away from, and opposition to, everything instinctual and natural (Jung & Sabini, 2002). This is why he referred to the specifically *Promethean* debt of the consciousness that does not heed instinct, a debt that must be paid for eventually.

The thought that disengages language from world, sign from referent, and signifier from signified, shares something of this impulse to liberate humans from nature, namely by neutralizing and invalidating the very concept. It does this through an understanding of linguistic reference that allows for no ground, no foundation, no instinct, no inherency. The Promethean impulse in postmodernism dismisses the very idea of nature as an ersatz human fabrication, disparaging everything innate, intrinsic, or given. It silences nature by perpetually deferring its presence, postponing its call, and fencing it off behind chain-linked signifiers. Those who have embraced this impulse cleave language and culture from a "nature" rendered obsolete by a semiotic technique, a Promethean trickery. The Promethean tale, as a story of self-definition, an overcoming of nature's authority, is truly an *opus contra naturam*, a work against nature. Jung notes that in both the East and the West people are desperate to conquer the "mere naturalness of life. It is the assertion of mind over matter, the *opus contra naturam*, a symptom of the youthfulness of man, still delighting in the use of the most powerful weapon ever devised by nature: the conscious mind" (Jung & Sabini, 2002, p. 128).

Prometheus is thus the personification of the human struggle vis-à-vis nature and the gods, a mythic image of the very real human need for self-definition, mastery, control, and autonomy. This is the spiritual impulse that "emerged so decisively in the later, modern development of the Western psyche, that impelled the evolving human self to break free from all cosmic determinism to forge its own autonomy" (Tarnas, 1995, p. 93). Deconstructive postmodernism participates thoroughly in this spirit by envisioning an autonomy of the text that breaks free of all cosmic determinism, depicting both "cosmic" and "determinism" as merely the result of *différance*, merely *flatus vocis*, words without correspondence. As such, not only does it fall perfectly in line with the autonomy-seeking trajectory of the modern mind, it may even represent the apex of such a trajectory. The postmodern, then, is *most* modern.

This self-definition and mastery is implicit in theories of reference that emphasize the productive capacity of language over its reflective capacity, theories that grant a disproportionate constitutive power to the language user and the linguistic community that he or she forms a part of. Such theories understand the differentiation and demarcation of discreet objects (whether physical or metaphysical) as a byproduct of semiosis, a result of *différance*, something derived from the production of signs. They do not comprehend language as a medium that elaborates differentiations already present in the perceived world. Rather, they sever the signifier from the signified and construe the latter to be formed, rather than revealed, by the text. Foucault's conception of the body which appears, at times, to deny it any ontic status independent of a language that ostensibly constructs it is one instance of this productive capacity of language being privileged over its reflective capacity. The body, on this view, is but a term in a semiotic, or the complex effect, of many terms, a cultural artifact, the net result of the interpretation and production of signs. Such an understanding appeals, I believe, to a desire for self-definition, mastery, and control insofar as it places language users in the position of seemingly divine creators, for even "man" is understood as the invention of those who employ language (what shall we call them?).

The semiological reduction places the purloined flame and pilfered power of the gods and goddesses squarely within the realm of purely human signs. When signifiers produce, rather than reflect, signifieds, when the reality of the world itself seems to rely upon our discourse about it "then this seems to lend the human animal, however 'decentered', an imposing centrality. It makes our existence appear less contingent, more ontologically solid, and so less of a prey to mortality" (Eagleton, 2003, p. 162). When signifiers produce, rather than reflect, referent-signifieds, and when it is we who speak for a world that cannot speak for itself, there is no sense in which, collectively or individually, we might be defined by circumstance, defined by fate, defined by nature or gods or anything other than the particular sign system that we ourselves produce and employ.

In a particularly revealing passage, Rorty (1998) touches upon these themes of self-definition, mastery, and control in terms of human answerability to the non-human, and a wresting of power from God:

> I take the linguistic turn in philosophy . . . to be a turn away from the very idea of human answerability to the world. I agree with Heidegger that there is a straight line between the Cartesian quest for certainty and the Nietzschean will to power. So I think that modern European philosophy amounts to an attempt by human beings to wrest power from God – or, more placidly put, to dispense with the idea of human answerability to something nonhuman. It involves what Heidegger lamented as "forgetfulness of Being." Like Nietzsche and Derrida, I think of such forgetfulness as a thoroughly good thing, and of what Heidegger called the "humanism" of modern philosophy as an equally good thing. I regard the need for world-directedness as a relic of the need for authoritative guidance, the need against which Nietzsche and his fellow pragmatists revolted. (p. 143)

These few sentences warrant extended reflection because they touch upon several points that have been explored in the current and past chapters. For Rorty, the linguistic turn is a turn away from human answerability to something non-human. We have already explored this same theme in terms of speaking *to*, *with*, and *about* non-human others. Unlike when I speak *to* or *with* someone or something, when I speak *about* someone or something, I have no need to respond to him, her, or it. Speaking *about* does not imply the same sort of two-way communication that is implied by speaking *to* or *with*. I do not expect a response from what I speak about. I expect a response from whatever, or whomever, I speak to or with.

When humans live in a world that they do not have to answer to, it is a dumb world, a speechless world, one that requires no answerability, no response-ability. When we humans no longer feel ourselves as having to answer to non-human others, it is because they can pose no questions to us. This lack of a need to answer, for Rorty, is, in fact, the benign intent not only of the linguistic turn, but much of modern Western philosophy from Descartes to Derrida—to move beyond the need for answerability. This intent is framed in terms of a quest for certainty and a will-to-power, a power that must be wrested from God, which in Rorty's phrasing appears to be synonymous with everything non-human. God is the quintessential other. This wresting of power from God is also a transcendence, a moving beyond the need for any authoritative guidance. Rorty's framing, like my own, draws a parallel between a world that grows increasingly mute, and the corresponding sense of a deity or deities that have seemingly lost their hold upon us. His framing, like my own, sees this as a process at work at the birth of modernity, with Descartes, and follows through into the postmodern present. Where we differ is in the sanguine faith that this is, in fact, a *thoroughly* good thing.

Prometheus is a titan of stratagem and artifice. He is a trickster (Hyde, 1998), who is intellectually clever, deviously astute, and capable of crafty deception. In an act of sacrificial subterfuge, he stealthily outwits Zeus by offering him only the bones of an animal, concealed by a layer of alluring fat. This fatty heap of skeletal remains is intended to represent something other than what it actually is; it is intended to appear to be nourishing meat. Without this simple act of presenting something as what it is not, there is no Promethean story to be told. The titan's offering to Zeus thus plays a double role of sorts—that of what it is (bones and fat), and that of what is represents (all the flesh of an animal). There is something analogous at work in Derrida's oeuvre, and it goes by the name of *sous rature*. Something that is *sous rature* is under erasure. This notion of being under erasure permits Derrida's philosophical "offerings" to play a similar double role. It allows him to employ a term, without having to answer for its implications (Dillon, 1995). Sous rature is expressed typographically by a simple crossing out of terms; *under erasure* thus becomes *~~under erasure~~*. This textual innovation has become the "typographical expression of deconstruction" (Taylor & Winquist, 2001, p. 113). It allows one to plant an idea in the reader's mind while simultaneously disavowing its consequences, thus Derrida can write: "that the sign ~~is~~ that ill-named ~~thing~~, the only one, that escapes the instituting question of philosophy: 'what is . . . ?'" (Derrida, 1976, p. 19). Writing in this way allows the author to affirm that the sign is an ill-named thing that escapes what, for him, is the instituting question of philosophy, the question of Being, and, simultaneously, to deny that the sign "is" at all, and that it is a "thing" at all. His denial erases his affirmation when needed. When there is no such necessity, then the affirmation remains intact. Signs are, thus, not so ill-named that they cannot stand in for what the philosopher-savant intends to communicate. Yet they are also just ill-named enough that he can claim them to be incapable of communicating his intent. An intelligent reader who has not succumbed to the charms of Derrida's mischievous, extravagant, and brilliant prose, might ask her- or himself if it is not so much the sign that escapes such instituting questions as much as it is the author himself.

Such a doubling-up of affirmation-negations makes deciphering Derridean texts a notoriously onerous task. It is difficult to know what it actually means to agree or disagree with him (Garver, 1977). His technique of writing under erasure is similar in spirit to his aforementioned appropriation-subversion of Saussure's structural linguistics. Both Derrida's writing under erasure and his appropriation-subversion leave him open to the criticism that the coherency of his critique of metaphysics is undermined by his appropriation of the very tools of that same tradition (Garver, 1977).

It appears that his argument succeeds at the price of failure and cannot be put forth without, in this very act, being rescinded.

Apotheosis, inflation, hubris: Jung's critique of the Promethean ego

> Men have always needed demons and cannot live without gods, except for a few particularly clever specimens of homo occidentalis who lived yesterday or the day before, supermen for whom "God is dead" because they themselves have become gods—but tin-gods with thick skulls and cold hearts. (Jung, 1953, p. 71 [*CW* 7 pt. 1, para. 110])

The *spiritus rector* of Jung's work could not be further from that of Rorty's afore-cited, thoroughly Promethean text, with its jubilant affirmation of human usurpation of divine will. At the very heart of Jung's entire critique of modernity is a profound skepticism that such usurpation is possible or even desirable. In this regard, his thinking shares an affinity with Rene Girard's (1965): "For two or three centuries this has been the underlying principle of every 'new' Western doctrine: God is dead, man must take his place" (p. 56). The mythic figure that this trenchant critic of deconstruction speaks of in describing such doctrines is no other than Prometheus himself. What Jung fears in modernity is precisely its titanic drive to utterly disempower all deities, its blind desire to render all gods and goddesses impotent and set human beings in their stead. Jungian analyst Jerome Bernstein (2005) expresses his own concern, one entirely consonant with Jung's, when he describes a Western ego that is "unchecked by any power outside itself and prone to profound and dangerous inflation" (p. xvi). What both men find most dubious is the belief that what has been called "god" is something that can, or should, be done away with, deconstructed. Virtually Jung's entire opus can be understood as an attempt to translate into a more contemporary language the truths embedded in religious, mythic, alchemical, spiritual, and mystical texts in such a way that contemporary readers can feel the full force of what, in other times, were referred to as gods, spirits, daemons, incubae, succubae, sprites, ghosts, goblins, and every other variety of seemingly supernatural or divine being. To the secular intellect that imagines itself beyond such superstitious, anachronistic beliefs, Jung (Jung, Hull, & De Laszlo, 1991) warns that "what we have left behind are only verbal specters, not the psychic facts that were responsible for the birth of the gods. We are still as much possessed by autonomous psychic contents as if they were Olympians" (p. 366). The verbal specters can be deconstructed, subdued by way of a literary-philosophic technique, but what these specters allude to remains ever potent, even more so in fact, because now they have become "phobias, obsessions, and so forth; in a word, neurotic symptoms. The gods have become diseases; Zeus no longer rules Olympus but rather the solar plexus, and produces curious specimens for the doctor's consulting room" (p. 366).

One can leave behind the verbal specter, leave behind the signifier, but the signified-referent remains. One can deconstruct the god-terms, but the phenomena to which they allude persist. The power wrested from the gods and goddesses of yore somehow endures and, in fact, may even grow stronger in direct proportion to the perceived abrogation of divine authority. The ego may believe itself to have vanquished the powers beyond its ken, but this is an impossibility. These powers, which for Jung emanate from the unconscious psyche, not only persist, but are even strengthened by the belief that they have been overcome. Because the unconscious not only contains libido, or psychic energy, but is in fact the spring from which this energy arises, there can be no ultimate conquest, no final overcoming of the gods, or more precisely, the psychic facts that gave birth to them (Jung, 1953). It is precisely the moment when the ego believes itself to have dominated, to have *deconstructed*, the unconscious that it finds itself most possessed, most at the mercy of powers that exceed its comprehension. Jung's word for this type of phenomena is *enantiodromia*—the process by which something turns into its opposite—the moment, in this case, when the imperious ego's ultimate conquest becomes its abject, inevitable defeat. And the defeat *is* inevitable, for it is "a delusion to think that by some kind of magical theory or method the unconscious can be finally emptied of libido and thus, as it were eliminated" (Jung, 1953, p. 285 [*CW* 7 pt. 2 para. 473]). It is precisely when I believe myself to be subject to no force, no truth, no dynamic, no divinity, to nothing greater than myself that I am most vulnerable to possession by the very forces I believe myself to have vanquished and transcended. The enantiodromia suffered by the ego that would attempt domination by way of such magical method, or by any other means, Jung (Jung, Hull, & De Laszlo, 1991) likens to a Promethean punishment upon the rocks:

> The stronger and more independent our consciousness becomes, and with it the conscious will, the more the unconscious is thrust into the background, and the easier it is for the evolving consciousness to emancipate itself from the unconscious. Gaining in freedom, it bursts the bonds of mere instinctuality and finally reaches a condition of instinctual atrophy. This uprooted consciousness can no longer appeal to the authority of the primordial images; it has Promethean freedom, but it also suffers from godless hybris. It soars above the earth and above mankind, but the danger of its sudden collapse is there, not of course in the case of every individual, but for the weaker members of the community, who then, again like Prometheus, are chained to the Caucasus of the unconscious.(p. 341).

In this passage, Jung encapsulates much of the admonitory intent of his psychology, and much of its clarion call to an awareness of, an engagement with, the primordial, the instinctual, and the divine. Promethean freedom is real, and relative. It is not without negative consequence. Consciousness tends to want independence, but this independence is a paradoxical and, in many ways, illusory one. The commanding freedom that a Promethean attitude offers is shadowed by the specter of collapse and bondage.

The disengagement of sign from referent, the institution of an abyss between language and its other, offers precisely a Promethean freedom, a freedom that allows one to soar, astronautic, above the earth, and all that it represents—home, origin, nature, essence. Yet this soaring also means that ideas, interpretations, and truth claims can no longer be grounded. The titanic liberation of the semiological reduction allows, seemingly, for an elevation over and above the human body, an elevation which bursts the bonds of instinctuality. Yet when the bond between language and referent is rent asunder, the very idea of instinct is rendered moot. When Derrida (1978) writes of "the joyous affirmation of the play of the world and of the innocence of becoming, the affirmation of a world of signs without fault, without truth, and without origin" (p. 292), he is telling a Promethean tale, one in which there exists no truth, no origin, no greater *something* that humans might be subject to or bound by. Yet, this god(term)less hubris is at risk of suffering a collapse; signs, having no ground upon which to rest, buckle like a house with rotting foundation. The semiological reduction implodes into nihilism (Cheetham, 2005; Fisher, 2002; Gendlin, 1992; Smith, 2003). The Promethean pretension of deconstructive postmodernism would liberate *homo semioticus* from subservience to the gods and goddesses of old, but like all Promethean endeavors, it is bound to an ambiguous outcome of liberation paid for through suffering and eventual submission to the flouted divinities.

A pathological egomania is, for Jung (Jung, Hull, & De Laszlo, 1991), the danger in not acknowledging the gods as present and powerful. Sickness he understands, primarily, as a psycho-spiritual malaise imbued with a sense of meaninglessness. For him, the great illness in need of healing is that of a soul that has lost its meaning (Jung, 1983). The ego's mania, which involves an inflated (that is to say, hubristic) belief in itself, and an infringement on divine authority, inexorably leads to its humbling, or humiliation, its metaphoric bondage to rock. The neurotic power psychology of the ego, in its attempt at an apotheosis, a self-divination, eventually ends in ruin.

For Jung (Jung, Hull, & De Laszlo, 1991), to serve a mania is abhorrent and undignified, while serving a god is an act of religious devotion full of meaning and purpose. As an act of submission, it is also an acknowledgement of a higher, spiritual being or value. Yet this is precisely what Prometheus refuses to do. He is the exemplar of a refusal to pay homage to the gods, a repudiation of sacrifice in their name. He is, in a sense, the personification of irreverence. His attitude is irreligious. Jungian analyst Rafael López-Pedraza (2003) articulates this attitude by way of a comparison between the two most infamous tricksters of Greek mythology, Hermes and Prometheus. Both are thieves, yet whereas Hermes sacrifices his plunder to the gods, the Promethean theft is a theft *from* the gods through a faux sacrifice. One personifies a truly religious attitude. The other embodies an equally anti-religious attitude. Hermes is the messenger of the gods, a true psychopomp, who mediates between divine and human realms. He also evinces, at times, a vulnerability that the titan does not. Prometheus, in contrast, hides his weakness, seeks to dominate and control, and in the unbridled chaos of his titanic nature, is possessed of ambition for power. He is a rebellious braggart, suspicious of "the archetypal forms of life, forms he is keen in finding ways to blackmail or destroy" (p. 65).

Hermes and Prometheus, thieving tricksters that they both are, nevertheless represent fundamentally different attitudes. Hermes the mediator is not Prometheus the power-driven. What might this mean for hermeneutics, the interpretive art that bears Hermes' name? Could deconstructive hermeneutics be, in a sense, a misnomer, an application of the moniker of one mythic being when another quite different one is clearly at work? Derrida replaces the *hermeneutic* circle that moves between the divine and the human with an interpretive circle that moves solely within a human realm. This is another way of saying that its movement is restricted to an infrareferential sphere; signifiers refer only to other signifiers. Language is not responsive to something that transcends it, something that would, in its transcendence, also serve as a ground. In contrast, Derrida sees Heidegger's hermeneutic circle, which is responsive to something transcendent to itself, as being, regrettably, still trapped within onto-theology—an ontology of God, a theology of Being—with which no Promethean thinker can rest well (Dillon, 1995).

As with Rorty, once the extralinguistic is denied, or once the ability of language to represent or refer to the extralinguistic is refuted, so is the divine. When there is no thing to which, or of which, language can speak, then there is no responsiveness, no answerability, and no divinity either. Grounds and origins disappear, or are denied. To explain why this might be, what relation exists between the question of reference and the question of God, it is instructive to look at the etymology of the word *religion*. Related to the Latin *religāre*, *religion* is rooted in the idea of *being bound*. *Religāre* is a yoking, a binding, a linking. When there is no binding of word and world, sign and referent, then the religious sense is lost. The divinity in the word, its angelic quality, disappears. Onto-theology then becomes a philosophical fault to be remedied.

Prometheus must refute the gods and goddesses, must rebel against the archetypal forms of life. The Promethean-technological mindset, having dominated the earth, believes itself master and creator, and loses all sense of being sponsored, supported, upheld. It has lost the religious sense, of being bound, tied to, and limited by something greater than itself (Romanyshyn, 2004). With these reflections in mind, it would seem that deconstruction embodies a different mythic sensibility than one corresponding to Hermes, a sensibility that has less to do with the psychopomp that travels between human and divine realms, and is bound through sacrifice, and more to do with the titanic, the unhinged, the unbound. Mythologically speaking, deconstruction is less hermeneutic than Promethean.

Stanton Marlan in his provocative, richly descriptive work, *The Black Sun: The Alchemy and Art of Darkness* (2005) has noted that the supposed absence of a transcendental signified, for Derrida, appears to imply a sort of negative theology, though he acknowledges that Derrida himself does not agree with this characterization. On Marlan's reading, which follows along post-structuralist lines, "a transcendental signified (for our purposes read as Self)" (p. 183) must be put under erasure. The Self, in Jung's writings, was a concept that continually evolved, though he often gave it the sense of "an all-embracing totality" (Marlan, 2005, p. 187) from which the ego arises and to which it belongs. This totality, in turn, Jung directly associates with the concept of God (Jung, 2002; Jung, 1959/1969). This Self, God, and the concept of totality are all comparable if not completely synonymous in his thinking. Thus, in his last great work, *Mysterium Coniunctionis*, he remarks that "the self can be distinguished only conceptually from what has always been referred to as 'God,' but not practically" (Jung, 1977, p. 546 [*CW* 14 pt. 6 para. 778]). In that same work, speaking of Adam as a symbol for the totality of the psyche, Jung adds that Adam was a symbol of the Self and an image of the irrepresentable Godhead. Explicating Derrida's thought and its relevance to Jung's conception of Self, Marlan writes:

> When we speak of God or Self, we are naming something whose Being is never fully present and cannot be captured in any signification. Even to speak of it as having a core or as being something is problematic. In Jungian language, we speak of images of the Self, but what does it mean to speak of this Self as if it existed as a kind of independent presence or transcendentally signified object or being? We have seen that, in negative theology, trying to name such transcendental "objects" always falls short and that they can be referred to only in terms such as Divine Darkness, which does not seem to refer to any "thing" at all. If no word or sign can capture the transcendental notion of God or Being or the Self and so on, then the words or signs that refer to it must be put under erasure—or crossed out—since the word is inaccurate. However, since all signs or words are necessary but also share the same lack, the convention has been to print both the word or sign and its deletion. Derrida gives this example: "[T]he sign ~~is~~ that ill-named ~~thing~~ . . . that escapes the instituting question of philosophy." (Marlan, 2005, p. 184)

Marlan's affirmation that God or Self can never be fully captured in any signification parallels Jung's reference to an irrepresentable Godhead. Jung is well aware that such terms as *God* or *Self* fall short. They share the same lack. No term or series of terms, no matter how complex and vast, can confine or fully represent what he attempts to intimate with the word *Self*. Both

Self and *God* point to an ineffable, "something" or, better yet, some process that both transcends and encompasses the ego.

The Self cannot be fully captured in words, but this does not lead Jung to believe that there is nothing to be said, or that the concept must be erased, or that one cannot offer a thousand analogies that in some way approximate or insinuate it. The concept stands, albeit with the understanding that it alludes to a mystery that will never be fully described, captured, or confined in words. For Jung, the Self is "the indescribable totality, which though it is inconceivable and 'irrepresentable' is none the less necessary as an intuitive concept" (Jung, 1977, p. 155 [*CW* 14 pt. 3 para. 181]). For Jung, the Self is indescribable in the sense that it is inexhaustibly describable. No description can exhaust its meaning. No word or sign can capture this transcendental notion, yet the words or signs that refer to it need not be put under erasure, or crossed out, even though they are inadequate.

Marlan, having accepted the basic presumptions of post-structuralist understandings of reference, follows Derrida's convention of *sous rature*, putting the Self under erasure. He accepts the supposition that because God or Self cannot be captured in language, because our speaking always falls short, our attempts to allude to such "things" must be put under erasure. Words like *Self*, or *God*, or *Being* must be effaced by virtue of their inability to capture that to which they ostensibly refer. However, words like *Divine Darkness* do not appear to suffer from this inability, or the inability is for some reason not problematic. Darkness can be divinized, and its divinity need not be erased.

The typological conventions used by Derrida vis-à-vis the verb *to be* are instructive; it is either crossed out, erased, as in the above cited text, or placed in quotes: "This which is called X . . . 'is' neither this nor that, neither sensible nor intelligible" (Derrida, cited in Marlan, 2005, p. 183) or again, "It 'is' not and does not say what 'is'" (Marlan citing Derrida, 2005, p. 183). Derrida's replacement of a *hermeneutic* circle that moves between the divine and the human with an interpretive circle that moves solely within the realm of the human does so by erasing Being (which appears to imply a theology, a greater transcendent something to which humans must respond). Or, alternatively, it does so by reducing ontology to grammatology, by reducing Being to 'being.' This is, precisely, the semiological reduction. This is the metaphoric theft of divine flame, a theft that can also be stated in the simplest of terms as: Derrida places (linguistic) mediation before being.

Marlan's reading of post-structuralism parallels both Dillon's and my own in identifying the question of reference as being determinative of Derrida's problematization of an onto-theology—an ontology of God, a theology of Being. The absence of the transcendental signified implies the absence of God, Self, or Being. From the perspective I am putting forth here, this is precisely the Promethean aspect of semiological reductionism;

no supreme being can exist beyond the linguistic categories of any given system of thought. Yet, having accepted Saussure's and Derrida's understanding of meaning arising *exclusively* from the binary, diacritical play of signs, Marlan's thinking proceeds within the confines of a post-structuralist framing that will not allow for the privileging of any terms. Terms like *Self*, *God*, and *Being* "cannot be privileged or given status outside the language system from which they have been drawn" (Marlan, 2005, p. 186). To do so would involve giving them a privileged ontological position, around which the other elements in the linguistic system must revolve. A privileged term would allow for the idea that meaning might be implicated in something other than the infrareferential play of signs of a synchronic linguistic system.

Once this diacritical understanding of language is accepted, a term like Jung's *Self* can only be meaningful, plausible, viable, in relation to the *No-Self*, the very *black sun* to which the title of his work alludes. For Marlan, the erasure of Self is a logical consequence of the Derridean and Saussurean insight that a word like *Self* can only derive meaning from or against *No-Self*. His thinking in this regard advances with an admirable, reasoned coherency, the rationale of which I do not wish to question here, so much as to point out that it proceeds from the premise that terms like *Self*, *God*, *Being*, but also *reality*, *truth*, *center*, and *essence* can *only* derive their meaning through the binary oppositions of a human language system, that at no point can meaning arise from a province other than linguistic polarities. But what if that premise is not true? What if that premise itself forms part of a mythic disposition bent on overcoming, conquering, vanquishing nature, timeless verities, and philosophical universals? What if the terminological effacement of god-terms is the latest incarnation of the titanic desire to efface the gods? What if it bespeaks, to use Rorty's phrasing, the negation of the very idea of human answerability to something nonhuman?

Despite these reservations regarding Marlan's understanding of such terms, his fundamental intuition of associating Derrida's deconstruction with the alchemical phase of *nigredo* is sound. An encounter with the blackness of the alchemical *nigredo* is an experience of the suffering psyche in the process of decomposition. Deconstruction, alchemically and symbolically speaking belongs to the realm of the black sun, and the blackness of "*putrefactio*, *mortifactio*, the *nigredo*, poisoning, torture, killing, decomposition, rotting, and death [that] all form a web of interrelationships that describe a terrifying, if most often provisional, eclipse of consciousness or of our conscious standpoint" (p. 11). Or perhaps it is more accurate to say that this realm of the black sun coincides with an element in deconstruction, or a particular moment in its alchemical-mythological unfolding. This moment, construed by way of the mythic tale of Prometheus is the moment of the titan's bondage to stone, which will be addressed further on.

In the shadow of collapsed binaries: titanic technology and cyborgian hybrids

Within the titanic dream of a departure from animate body and animate earth, which is also the dream of conquering nature, gods, and goddesses, an image has arisen in recent years, one of hope for some, and abject horror for others: a human/machine hybrid known as the *cyborg*. We have seen this image before in a different guise. His bulbous helmet has bobbed along the rocky lunar planes of our collective imagination; it is the astronaut, who is not merely the image of departure and distance from earthly ground but also the image of human-machine hybridity. He is, in a sense, the material, physical manifestation of the human-as-machine metaphor born of the inert Vesalian body. As mechanical metaphors have come to dominate everyday speech, as well as the social sciences, including psychology, we have come to equate our experience with mechanical, robotic, and computational processes. Viewing the human body as mechanism has become commonplace, so much so, that we are inclined to forget that we see by way of this human-as-machine metaphor. We speak of defense mechanisms, without so much as a silent inner recognition that to speak this way is to use metaphor, and one of a particular type that draws parallels between human beings and their mechanical creations.

Glen Slater (2006), in his sapient *cri de coeur* "Cyborgian Drift: Resistance is not Futile," illustrates how the human-machine hybrid that is the cyborg has become not only a technological possibility, but, for many, an ideal. The ubiquity of the metaphor of body as machine has led not only to its thoughtless promulgation as literal truth, but also to its adoption as an image of human perfectibility. It is a short step from believing that each human organ possesses a machine-like function, to believing that these organs can, and should, be replaced by machines, thereby creating a new cyborgian creature. These steps are, in fact, being taken, as genetics, nanotechnology, and robotics converge into the new field of GNR technology, making science fiction science fact. As nanotechnology penetrates the human brain and the speed and patterns of neural connections are altered, the frontier between human and machine grows ever-more indistinct. As nano-sized robots are injected into the bloodstream to repair tissue, combat disease, and play the role of replacement parts for ailing human bodies, it is difficult, perhaps, not to share the hope of cyborg enthusiasts that see in such innovations the prospect of greater health, intelligence, and immunity to disease. The cyborgian dream allures with promises of diminished suffering, and perhaps even a transcendence of mortality. Yet, the result of these innovations, given the direction they are headed in, is a largely synthetic body qualitatively different from what is known as the human body at present.

Many devotees of human-machine hybridization actually envision, and hope for, an absolute end to bodily based existence; there is a belief that what is essential in any human life amounts to information that can be downloaded into cyberspace where one can live forever. Organic existence can be dispensed with entirely. Human-machine hybridization is but one step in a process of disincarnation that may, it is believed, end with a complete abandonment of the human organism, its total abstraction into the realm of binary code. Rather than understand this process of disincarnation as an end to the human race, many visionaries of a thoroughly technologized future, appropriately denominated *post-humanists*, see it as a form of salvation from the limitations of the mortal, organic body. They envision a victory over death by redefining what counts as life. There is a certain irony, or poetic duplicity in this post-humanist dream that evokes Foucault's simile, explored earlier, of *man as a face drawn in the sand*. By way of this image, Foucault equates and conflates human beings with their self-representations. True to his nominalist creed, he intimates that when the representation of something disappears, so does that which it ostensibly represents. The reader of Foucault's text who lets the word "man" resonate with the established, though antiquated meaning of "human beings" is left with an apocalyptic and genocidal image: humans reduced to rubble, detritus as diminutive as grains of sand. In this same vein, Foucault goes on to construe man as an event within a knowledge that transcends his temporal dimensions: Man is merely a new wrinkle within that knowledge. Post-humanists, in their fantasies of cybernetic immortality, proceed by a similar inverted reasoning. Only the terms and technologies have been updated: Man understood as a wrinkle within a particular form of knowledge has become the human being as binary code within a cybernetic informational matrix.

Slater, who makes no mention of the linguistic turn or post-structuralism in the text in question, sees the path leading towards this post-humanist future, as resting primarily upon two reductive assumptions. One is the aforementioned mechanistic, computational, machine-derived imagery used to describe human beings. The other involves a "privileging of the intellect over other aspects of being—animal sensation, instinct, aesthetic response, intuition" (p. 180). Given that the intellect would seem to be more closely analogous to silicone-based forms of "intelligence," this is perhaps not surprising: Aspects of the human being that are less easily "replaced" by synthetic means are considered secondary or irrelevant by those who dream of an eventual transfiguration of our current, human, organic form. Slater notes, repeatedly, that this abandonment of bodily, incarnate existence bespeaks another abandonment: "The departure from the body and being in the world is also a departure from soul. Without a bodily existence in the world there is no soul" (p. 177). What is being discarded by way of the cyborgian dream, this latest variation upon the dream of the body's abandonment, is soul. It is anima and animus. What is being left behind is an ensouled, animate body. To prevent this, Slater affirms the need for a declaration of ultimate values and the preservation of certain qualitative states, among them, "sensual awareness, erotic bonds, embodied thought, beauty, wisdom, limitation, imagination, empathy, reflection, artistic expression, and playfulness" (p. 187). Without these, the cyborgian drift, the unquestioned creep towards a human-machine hybridization, or worse, the complete replacement of humans by their technological creations, may be a *fait accompli*.

The values that Slater cites are also, roughly speaking, the very characteristics that specialists in artificial intelligence still find vexingly difficult to program into their silicone-based creations. Moods, emotions, embodied thought, a sense of importance or value are all attributes that resist the transformation into binary code required by such so-called "intelligence" (Dreyfus, 1992). Perhaps this is why enthusiasts of AI simply choose to ignore these non-cognitive aspects of the human mind, aspects that may be better described as psychic or psychological, and that resist categorization as mere "information." What is to be counted as human, or as human consciousness, must be conceived in such a way that it can be transferable to an artificial domain if the dream of human/machine hybridity is to be fulfilled. If cybernetic technology cannot emulate human minds, let alone the fullness of what we understand as human *being*, then our understanding of mind must be forcefully altered to fit a particularly restrictive cognitive paradigm. The realization of the human-as-machine dream requires both a carving away of all human characteristics that do not fit the pretense of the human-as-machine metaphor, and a simultaneous elevation in importance of those characteristics that both humans and computers appear to share in common. The fundamental assumption that human beings are essentially information processors, and that the information processed can be systematically formalized in a way that parallels human capacities is required if the metaphor is to be made materially manifest.

Others envision the cyborg somewhat differently. There is little sense of horror, repugnance, or revulsion. Donna Haraway (1991), for example, argues for *pleasure* in the confusion of boundaries between humans and machines and for *responsibility* in their construction. This pleasure of confused boundaries is evident in the very form by which she elucidates the theme of cybernetic organisms; Haraway weaves back and forth between the literal and the figurative, the factual and the fictional, the acerbically astute and the boldly utopic. Her image of the cyborg, at times, stands in for a habit of mind, a way of being, that is contemporary and endemic: "By the late twentieth century, our time, a mythic time, we are all chimeras, theorized and fabricated hybrids of machine and organism; in short, we are cyborgs. The cyborg is our ontology" (p. 150). At other times, Haraway's cyborg represents not so much a current habit of mind, or a way of being, as much as a literal human-machine interfacing. Yet this distinction, on her reading, appears less than important. Indeed, the blurring of such distinctions is precisely what the image of the cyborg is meant to hold. The cyborg is the exemplar and harbinger of a growing ambiguity brought about by technological innovation that renders obsolete the boundaries between natural and artificial, mind and body, and in fact all distinctions that previously applied to organisms and machines. Cybernetic-human hybrids represent the collapse of many long-held oppositions once believed sacrosanct.

Astutely, Haraway construes this collapse as taking place within the ideological space created by a postmodern, post-structural "textualization" that reconceives both machine and organism as coded text. She employs the image of the cyborg as yet another postmodern strategy to disrupt the oppositional pairings that make the human/machine distinction possible. Her intent is to subvert the very certainty of what is considered to be natural, a process already well under way, as this certainty has already been "undermined, probably fatally" (p. 153) by post-structuralism. In her view, the transcendent authorization of interpretation that has grounded Western epistemology has been lost, and with it the seemingly common-sense distinction between the mechanical and the organic. Textualization has subverted the machine-organism dichotomy. The mechanical and the organic can now be understood as merely two poles in a fundamentally arbitrary system of signs. Though some may see this as a blatant disregard for the lived relations that ground linguistic play, as Haraway herself acknowledges, on her reading the validity of such an assertion need not be cause for a negative outcome. Rather, it is the felicitous result of an overcoming of Western metaphysics.

Whereas Slater sees in the cyborg a potential death knell for the human species, foretelling the sad demise of creators at the hands of their machine creations, Haraway sees the portent of a worthy subversion, the welcome herald of a fatal undermining of what counts as nature. This is a point, however, in which the author clearly revels in her professed pleasure of confused boundaries, for she also states that the cyborg is "the awful apocalyptic *telos* of the 'West's' escalating dominations of abstract individuation, an ultimate self untied at last from all dependency, a man in space" (pp. 150–51). Yes, a "man" in space, an astronaut, untied from all dependency, and floating just outside the firm grasp of earth's gravitational pull. Without doing any injustice to Haraway's reading, this gravitational pull might also be understood as the gravitational pull of reference. Once this is overcome, so is the distinction between the natural and the artificial. Once the signified is raised in importance over the level of the referent, and the signifier is elevated over and above the signified, the linguistic body is bled of all content. It loses its *élan vital*, its animating force. Then, there is little distinction to be made between organic and artificial bodies.

A certain parallel exists—imprecise perhaps, yet redolent—between Slater's account of a privileging of the intellect over other aspects of being, such as animal sensation, instinct, esthetic response, and intuition, on the one hand, and the deconstructive privileging of signifiers over signifieds, and signs over referents, on the other. It is this latter privileging that subsumes the phenomenal, the sensual, and the intuited under the rubric of the linguistic and conceives nature itself as constructed—a mere epiphenomena of the play of signs. It renders dubious any sense of the immediacy of our experience as embodied beings and vitiates any sense of this experience as primary or given. Both the post-humanist and deconstructive privileging are evocative of a primary dissociation that cleaves the language-marshaling intellect from a feeling, sensing, intuiting, self. Slater's invocation of ultimate values in an attempt to stave off the cyborgian drift is another parallel worthy of mention; such values could just as easily be invoked in response to a semiologically reductive approach that seeks to steal the fire from the god-terms. If this invocation is an *explicit* challenge to the post-humanist Promethean endeavor that conceives human beings as little more than binary code, it is also an *implicit* challenge to the deconstructive ethos that relocates all meaning within the play of human signs, thereby eliminating any appeal to transcendent entities, originary principles, and, yes, ultimate values.

The sanguine faith in the importance of collapsing metaphysical binaries testifies to a frame of mind, style of consciousness, and psychological pattern that can rightly be called Promethean. From within this psychological pattern, this archetypal disposition, the jubilant effacement of the tyrannical oppositions of an aged and obsolete metaphysics represents a fundamental imperative, one that cannot be questioned. From a less titanic perspective, you and I might ask whether or not a certain danger exists in collapsing such binaries if, in fact, this leads us to adopt a conception of human immortality that appears to hasten our collective demise rather than prolong it. We might question whether, in the struggle to overcome the gods—not least of them Thanatos, the personification of death itself—there is not, perhaps, a blind invocation of their fury.

Complexes and archetypal possession

Appreciating the mythic dimensions of semiological reductionism is a way of "attending to the images in the ideas, the fantasies in the facts, the dreams in the reasons, the myths in the meanings, the archetypes in the arguments, and the complexes in the concepts" (Romanyshyn, 2007, p. 12). It is an application of depth psychological hermeneutics. If theories that purport a language unable to speak to any reality other than the linguistic are the symptomatic expressions of an alienation, and if this, in turn, can be understood in terms of a psychological complex, then giving a mythological reading of these theories is a way of getting at their archetypal core. Addressing the Promethean aspects of the linguistic turn is a way of tending to an archetype concealed within this turn. It is also the cultivation of an understanding that seeks to move, in a sense, beyond this core. Put differently, it is an attempt to not be entirely beholden to the style of consciousness or psychological pattern that is Prometheanism. Placing the linguistic turn within the realm of psyche, and specifically the *archetypal* psyche is an acknowledgment that "metaphysical ideas are hardly independent of their complex roots; so ideas can be foci of sickness, part of an archetypal syndrome" (Hillman & Slater, 2005, p. 120). From within this particular archetypal syndrome, seen through the eyes of the illness, philosophic universals, and inherited understandings of intrinsic and innate characteristics belonging to human beings, appear to be mere *nomina* without substance, little more than the hangover from a history to be overcome. Yet when such ideas are returned to their psychic, archetypal ground, their symptomatic and symbolic content can be engaged because their more fully human provenance has been acknowledged. Returning ideas to their complex, archetypal roots allows for a revisioning of the primary tenets of a deconstructive postmodernism that casts them in a radically different light. They are attitudes, dispositions, styles of consciousness, and psychological patterns intrinsic to human beings. They are archetypal, that is to say, both *archaic* and *typical*.

An archetype, in the sense that Jung used the word, is an a priori structure that precedes any conscious experience (Jung, 1972). It is an inherited mode of psychic functioning analogous to the instinctual behavior of a bird building its nest or an eel swimming in the ocean (Jacobi, 1959). Archetypes are the way in which the psyche arranges itself into associative, affective clusters. They have the ability to organize images and ideas (Jung, 1983). Unlike Plato, Jung conceived the archetypes as possessing a certain dynamism and energy (Jung, 1972) that led him to often describe them as autonomous in relation to the conscious ego. Unlike Kant's a priori ideas, to which Jung (1953) frequently compared them, archetypes possess a *numinous* quality (1983) which, according to Rudolf Otto (1958), who coined the term, is the essential element of religious experience. Numinosity, or the numinous, is present in the experience of the *mysterium tremendum* that "may burst in sudden eruption up from the depths of the soul with spasms and convulsions, or lead to the strangest excitements, to intoxicated frenzy, to transport and to ecstasy" (pp. 12–13). The numinous thus has an irrational and ineffable quality to it that inspires awe, much like the holy, or the sacred, though it does not necessarily carry the connotations of moral goodness that often affix themselves to these latter terms.

Jung (1953) described the archetype as a purely formal and empty *facultas praeformandi* with which humans are born. Although it cannot be represented in and of itself, it allows for the possibility of representation. Thus, he compared it to the latent order of the crystalline structure of a liquid that manifests only under certain conditions and has no material existence in and of itself. Archetypes can be alluded to, but never represented or grasped in their entirety. Thus, every archetypal image is but one manifestation of an essentially elusive, ineffable *something* in the human soul. The archetypal image of the mother might manifest as a Kali-like monstrosity at one given moment, in one given culture or individual, or as the placid and boundlessly loving figure of Kwan Yin. Archetypes form the core of Jung's syncretistic approach to comparative religious studies that allows him to postulate a similar psychic substrate or nature underlying the multifarious and divergent expressions of the divine and demonic. He explains this substrate in terms of anatomical and biological similarities between humans, as well as similarities between human beings and other species:

> It must be pointed out that just as the human body shows a common anatomy over and above all racial differences, so, too, the human psyche possesses a common substratum transcending all differences in culture and consciousness. I have called this substratum the collective unconscious. This unconscious psyche, common to all mankind, does not consist merely of contents capable of becoming conscious, but of latent predispositions towards identical reactions. The collective unconscious is simply the psychic expression of the identity of brain structure irrespective of all racial differences. This explains the analogy, sometimes even identity, between various myth motifs and symbols, and the possibility of human communication in general. The various lines of psychic development start from one common stock whose roots reach back into the most distant past. This also accounts for the psychological parallelisms with animals. (Jung, Hull, & De Laszlo, 1991, pp. 340–41)

Our physical, anatomical commonalities imply psychological commonalities. Our predispositions to identical reactions imply experiential similarities. Human infants the world over, irrespective of race or culture, are predisposed to suckle upon their mother's breast, contract and extend their limbs, follow the movement of objects with their eyes, and carry out many of the same fundamental action patterns. Students and teachers of movement know this well. Our physiology requires us to perform certain movements throughout our lives (Hackney, 2002). The development of human infant movement strongly parallels that of the animal kingdom from its subtle beginnings in the fetus to crawling and creeping, walking and running. There are parallels to be found between human movement development and that of primates, and even single-celled animals (Cohen, Nelson & Smith, 2012).

What Jung states above is, at heart, the simple truth that if, by virtue of a common anatomy, such shared physiologically mandated movements exist, then it is reasonable to suppose that similar experiential, psychological commonalties exist as well. The similarities between anatomic bodies suggest similarities between animate, ensouled bodies. This shared physiological/psychological similitude can express itself even in remarkably similar religious symbolism and dream imagery. Because we humans are of a common stock with all other living creatures on the planet, we share lines of psychic development in common.

Jung believed that, in reaching the archetypal core of a complex, one touched the source of its energy and the nub of its meaning, as well as its curative potential. Understood in this way, offering a mythological reading of deconstructive postmodernism is an attempt at healing, as well as a way of understanding it as *more than* the symptomatic expression of an alienation. Sensing the Promethean aspiration of semiological reductionism allows for conceiving it as *both* a dissociation from lived body and lived earth, *and* the expression of an impulse that is instinctual, universal, and potentially healthy. The desire to usurp the gods and transcend nature, the desire for self-definition and control, even self-deification, paradoxically forms part of our very human nature. But when this archetypal attitude, this innate potential, is in full possession of the conscious mind, when it is the unquestioned default position of a collective or individual attitude, or an overriding style of consciousness, human life becomes out of balance, and human beings grow at odds with themselves. Symptoms are not merely the markers of disease or dysfunction, they are also "attempts at a new synthesis of life – unsuccessful attempts, let it be added in the same breath, yet attempts nevertheless, with a core of value and meaning" (Jung, 1983, p. 152).

Health and illness, in Jung's understanding, are a question of living in right relation to the archetypal psyche, one that both pays it homage and allows for a degree of understanding and autonomy in relationship to it. Given that archetypes form the very substrata of our human makeup, there is no question of ridding ourselves of them or finally overcoming their demands. Health resides in a relationship with the archetypal psyche that is neither one of an abject surrender to its imperatives, nor a willful conquest of those imperatives. What is at issue, then, in the present discussion, is what constitutes a healthy relationship to the Promethean impulse, and what the value and place of that impulse is.

Addressing this sense of a core value within the symptom, Edinger (1992) writes that "a symptom can be transformed into a symbol through awareness of its archetypal foundations. Every symptom derives from the image of some archetypal situation" (p. 115). This awareness, which is understood as a movement from symptom to symbol, is also a movement from an unsuccessful attempt at a new synthesis of life and towards a successful attempt. This experience of the true meaning hidden in the core of the complex is metamorphic because recognition of the archetype, which is also a recognition of the symbolic image behind or within the symptom, transforms it. The meaningless suffering of the symptom becomes the meaningful suffering of the symbol.

References

Bernstein, J. S. (2005). *Living in the borderland: The evolution of consciousness and the challenge of healing trauma*. New York, NY: Brunner-Routledge.

Camus, A. (1991). *The rebel: An essay on man in revolt*. New York, NY: Vintage Books.

Cheetham, T. (2005). *Green man, earth angel: The prophetic tradition and the battle for the soul of the world*. Albany, NY: State University of New York Press.

Chomsky, N., & Foucault, M. (2006). *The Chomsky-Foucault debate: On human nature*. New York, NY: New Press.

Cleary, J. N. (1992). Theory in the age of mechanical annihilation. *Textual Practice*, 6(3), 452–76.

Cohen, B. B., Nelson, L., & Smith, N. S. (2012) *Sensing, feeling, and action: The experiential anatomy of body-mind centering*. Northampton, MA: Contact Editions.

Currie, M. (2013) *The invention of deconstruction*. New York, NY: Palgrave Macmillan.

Derrida, J. (1976). *Of grammatology*. Baltimore, MD: Johns Hopkins University Press.
Derrida, J. (1978). *Writing and difference*. Chicago, IL: University of Chicago Press.
Derrida, J. (1982). *Margins of philosophy*. Chicago: University of Chicago Press.
Dillon, M. C. (1995). *Semiological reductionism: A critique of the deconstructionist movement in postmodern thought*. Albany, NY: State University of New York Press.
Dougherty, C. (2006). *Prometheus*. New York, NY: Routledge.
Dreyfus, H. L. (1992). *What computers still can't do: A critique of artificial reason*. Cambridge, MA: MIT Press.
Eagleton, T. (1996). *The illusions of postmodernism*. Oxford, UK: Blackwell Publishers.
Eagleton, T. (2003). *After theory*. New York, NY: Basic Books.
Edinger, E. F. (1992). *Ego and archetype: Individuation and the religious function of the psyche*. Boston, MA: Shambhala.
Fisher, A. (2002). *Radical ecopsychology: Psychology in the service of life*. Albany, NY: State University of New York Press.
Foucault, M., & Gordon, C. (1980). *Power/knowledge: Selected interviews and other writings, 1972–1977*. Brighton, England: Harvester Press.
Garver, N. (1977). Derrida on Rousseau on writing. *The Journal of Philosophy, 74*(11), 663–73.
Gendlin, E. T. (1992). The wider role of bodily sense in thought and language. In M. Sheets-Johnstone (Ed.), *Giving the body its due* (pp. 192–207). Albany, NY: State University of New York Press.
Girard, R. (1965). *Deceit, desire, and the novel: Self and other in literary structure*. Baltimore, MD: Johns Hopkins Press.
Girard, R., & Doran, R. (2008). *Mimesis and theory: Essays on literature and criticism, 1953–2005*. Stanford, CA: Stanford University Press.
Hackney, P. (2002). *Making connections: Total body integration through Bartenieff fundamentals*. New York, NY: Routledge.
Haraway, D. (1991). *Simians, cyborgs, and women*. New York, NY: Routledge.
Hillman, J. (1975). *Re-visioning psychology*. New York, NY: Harper & Row.
Hillman, J., & Slater, G. (2005). *Senex & puer*. Putnam, CT: Spring Publications.
Hyde, L. (1998). *Trickster makes this world: Mischief, myth, and art*. New York, NY: Farrar, Straus and Giroux.
Jacobi, J. (1959). *Complex/archetype/symbol*. Princeton, NJ: Princeton University Press.
Jung, C. G. (1953). Two essays on analytical psychology. In R. F. C. Hull (Trans.), *The collected works of C. G. Jung* (Vol. 7). Princeton, NJ: Princeton-Bollingen.
Jung, C. G. (1959/1969). Aion: Researches into the phenomenology of the self. In R. F. C. Hull (Trans.), *The collected works of C. G. Jung* (Vol. 9). Princeton, NJ: Princeton-Bollingen (original work published 1959).
Jung, C. G. (1972). Four archetypes: Mother, rebirth, spirit, trickster. In R. F. C. Hull (Trans.), *The collected works of C. G. Jung* (Vol. 9) Princeton, NJ: Princeton-Bollingen.
Jung, C. G. (1977). *Mysterium coniunctionis: An inquiry into the separation and synthesis of psychic opposites in alchemy* (2nd edn.). Princeton, NJ: Princeton University Press.
Jung, C. G. (1983). *The essential Jung* (A. Storr Ed.). Princeton, NJ: Princeton University Press.
Jung, C. G. (2002). *Answer to Job* (50th anniversary edn.). Princeton, NJ: Princeton University Press.

Jung, C. G., Hull, R. F. C., & De Laszlo, V. S. (1991). *Psyche and symbol: A selection from the writings of C. G. Jung*. Princeton, NJ: Princeton University Press.

Jung, C. G., & Sabini, M. (2002). *The earth has a soul: The nature writings of C.G. Jung*. Berkeley, CA: North Atlantic Books.

Kerényi, K. (1997). *Prometheus: Archetypal image of human existence*. Princeton, NJ: Princeton University Press.

Kugler, P. (2005). *Raids on the unthinkable: Freudian and Jungian psychoanalyses*. New Orleans, LA: Spring Journal Books.

Lawlor, L. (2002). *Derrida and Husserl: The basic problem of phenomenology*. Bloomington, IN: Indiana University Press.

López-Pedraza, R. (2003). *Hermes and his children*. Einsiedeln, Switzerland: Daimon Verlag.

López-Pedraza, R. (2012). *Cultural anxiety*. Einsiedeln, Switzerland: Daimon Verlag.

Manithottil, P. (2008). *Difference at the origin: Derrida's critique of Heidegger's philosophy of the work of art*. Unpublished thesis, Universität Münster, New Delhi, India.

Marlan, S. (2005). *The black sun: The alchemy and art of darkness*. College Station, TX: Texas A & M University Press.

Orfanos, D. (2006). Mythos and logos. *Psychoanalytic Dialogues, 16*(4), 481–99.

Otto, R. (1958). *The idea of the Holy*. London, England: Oxford University Press.

Radin, P., Kerényi, K., & Jung, C. G. (1969). *The trickster: A study in American Indian mythology*. New York, NY: Greenwood Press.

Romanyshyn, R. (2004). *Technology as symptom and dream*. New York, NY: Brunner-Routledge.

Romanyshyn, R. (2007). *The wounded researcher: Research with soul in mind*. New Orleans, LA: Spring Journal Books.

Rorty, R. (1989). *Contingency, irony, and solidarity*. New York, NY: Cambridge University Press.

Rorty, R. (1998). *Truth and progress*. New York, NY: Cambridge University Press.

Rorty, R. (1999). *Philosophy and social hope*. New York, NY: Penguin Books.

Shearer, A. (2009). Unlocking the Titans: Unravelling a psychological Olympianism? *International Journal of Jungian Studies, 1*(1), 2–11.

Slater, G. (2006). Cyborgian drift: Resistance is not futile. *Spring: A Journal of Archetype and Culture: Psyche and Nature, 75*, 171–95.

Smith, H. (2003). *Beyond the postmodern mind: The place of meaning in a global civilization*. Wheaton, IL: Quest Books.

Tarnas, R. (1995). *Prometheus the awakener: An essay on the archetypal meaning of the planet Uranus*. Woodstock, CT: Spring.

Taylor, V. E., & Winquist, C. E. (2001). *Encyclopedia of postmodernism*. New York, NY: Routledge.

Chapter 5

Promethean purpose as renewal of the gods

Reconceiving the alienation of sign from referent

The suffering of a necessary inflation

Edward Edinger (1992), though thoroughly Jungian in his orientation, offers a reading of Prometheus that differs in tone from that of Jung, presenting a slightly less dire image of the titan. Whereas Jung often emphasizes what is dangerous, distorted, and disastrous in the story of flouted authority and purloined flame, Edinger underlines the potential value, and even necessity, of states of psychic inflation as epitomized in the Promethean tale. The fire acquired through the titan's stealth symbolizes a consciousness that is evolving towards a degree of human autonomy and independence vis-à-vis the gods. As in the book of Genesis, in which Eve savors the forbidden fruit plucked from the tree of knowledge, the Promethean theft is carried out against divine authority. Symbolized in both myths as an illicit act followed by punishment, it is a willful grasping for greater consciousness. The tale of the flame-bearing titan is but one among many that conforms to this basic pattern: Greater consciousness is acquired through a criminal or sinful act that later results in castigation. Prometheus is cursed by his bondage to the Caucasus Mountains and a wound that will not heal, while his brother Epimetheus is likewise cursed by Pandora and the contents of her proverbial box. Such punishments are comparable to the expulsion from the Garden of Eden. The unending Promethean wound, and the ills unleashed from Pandora's box, as well as the expulsion from the Garden of Eden, are analogous to other punishments and wounds inflicted upon those who dare a form of consciousness that is greater than the one they currently possess. The perpetually renewed Promethean wound "symbolizes the consequences of the break in the original unconscious wholeness, the alienation from the original unity. It is the constant thorn in the flesh" (Edinger, 1992, p. 25). This wound of alienation is the result of a truly inflated act, one that both provokes guilt and also runs the risk of perpetuating a fall, as inflation often does.

Edinger is careful to note that the illicit act provoking retribution is illicit only from the perspective of a value system that is being transcended. The theft is criminal in the eyes of Zeus, the ruling patriarch, whose authority has been undermined. The crime is, in fact, a *necessary* element in the act of moving towards a greater state of awareness. There is always something criminal in the acquisition of greater consciousness, which is a hubristic act against the reigning powers, yet such a criminal acquisition is also necessary; it leads to a needed estrangement from a state of unconscious wholeness. Edinger articulates this dynamic of alienation within a Jungian framework in which consciousness-qua-ego *must* oppose the unconscious out of which it arose, *must* claim its autonomy through an inflated act. Consciousness is, as Jung (1960/1969) was fond of referring to it, a Promethean conquest, a turning away from, and opposition to, the unconscious. It carries with it a degree of *hubris*, or *hybris*, an exaggerated belief in its own self-importance and powers of discernment. As such, it attempts to transcend what previously had been considered proper human limits. Consciousness itself carries with it a certain Promethean arrogance that wishes to appropriate for itself what belongs to divine powers. Inflation is a state in which the ego commandeers for itself qualities that more properly belong to a greater whole, and through this process comes to exceed its proper human dimensions. When you or I are inflated, we abrogate and live out the attributes of deities. The attribute of deity that is lived out in present-day Prometheanism involves believing that all nature and all essence are the sole fabrications of human language.

Edinger's articulation of the hubris of consciousness is subtle, complex, and underscores time and again the ambiguous nature of inflation: It is necessary; inevitable; even to a certain degree, desired; dangerous; seemingly criminal; and laden with suffering. Sometimes this inflation is simply too great. It results in disaster. Like Icarus, who disobeys his father Daedalus, and soars too near the sun, melting his wings, one falls fatally to the sea, disappearing into unconsciousness. But Edinger (1992) offers another possibility, the possibility of an inflated, hubristic, disobedience that, though punished, also results in the acquired boon of greater consciousness. This disobedience, on the deepest level, "is a crime against the universal powers, the powers of nature, or God" (p. 25). Any step, in fact, in the process of individuation is experienced as a Promethean theft, a revolt against previously unquestioned and unquestionable authorities, authorities that may be parental, institutional, or religious. It is a heroic triumph over received ideas, over givens, an overcoming of the inertia inherent in a passive acceptance of inherited truths, of what has heretofore been considered natural, or endowed by God. From the perspective of the authorities being challenged, this is a dubious, reprehensible affair, yet, "what is a crime at one stage of psychological development is lawful at another and one cannot reach a new stage of psychological development without daring to challenge the code of the old stage" (Edinger, 1992, p. 21). What Edinger's reading draws our attention to is the fact that to progress is always to transgress. All movement forward, however that may be defined, is also a movement beyond the boundary or limit of where one currently is. Progression is transgression, a breach or violation of a boundary or limit. There is no *pro*, no forward, no through, without *trans*, without across, over, or beyond.

The inverse proposition, however, is not always true. Some transgression does not represent progress. It is merely a movement beyond a present state.

With Edinger's framing in mind of *a necessary alienation from the natural unconscious state of wholeness*, I would like to return your attention to the closing image of Chapter 3. Imagine our planet once more, floating in the infinite abyss of space. Allow this image to beckon meanings given to it throughout these pages: the earth as place of origin, birth, and home, the earth as what is essential and inherent, primordial and intuitively given. Let this circular, spherical object summon a sense of wholeness, as *mandalas*—magical circles, are said to do (Jung & Von Franz, 1964). Let this image allude to the natural unconscious state of wholeness to which Edinger refers, and remind yourself that the astronautic viewpoint that makes such an image possible is precisely one that has become alienated. What the image suggests is that the entire process which I have described, an alienation from both lived body and lived earth, has been a necessary and even purposeful one. What it implies is that the astronautic, Promethean theories of linguistic reference, those dreams of distance that have allowed us to leave the earth might also have the purpose of letting us land upon it anew. Edinger's framing suggests that the drama of distance may be, potentially, *a movement from an unconscious state of wholeness to a conscious one*. It is only in this distance that "the possibility of remembering home takes place, the possibility of taking up in a new way what was, the possibility of recovering as a destiny what was heretofore a heritage" (Romanyshyn, 2004, p. 203). On this reading, the interpretive strategies that seek to dismantle any sense of nature, essence, truth, reality, and inherency have provided the possibility of taking up these very same issues newly, but with greater awareness. They offer the opportunity to re-member what has been dis-membered. They speak to not merely the death of the gods, but their potential renewal. As Jung says, "our Gods want to be overcome, since they require renewal" (Jung & Shamdasani, 2012, p. 162). The radical alienation of sign from referent is an opportunity to confront the natural and the given, no longer as an unquestioned and unquestionable heritage (a state of unconscious wholeness), but now as a consciously acknowledged destiny (a state of conscious wholeness).

The difference between an unquestionable heritage and a consciously acknowledged destiny involves, among other things, an ability to challenge one's unconscious identity with representatives of collective authority, whether they are ones of family, party, church, nation, or culture. One way in which Promethean postmodernism does this is by continually pointing out the ways in which social or cultural facts are "naturalized" so as to appear permanent, inevitable, and beyond question, in short, authoritative and given. In this way, it takes flame from nature and the gods and places it in the hands of humans. It points to the historical and cultural elements in what we take to be eternal and unchanging. In other words, it ceaselessly questions heritage, inherited presuppositions; it relentlessly queries the given by asking *given by whom? When? For what purpose? With what interest in mind?* Contemporary Prometheanism asks, *who is it that is defining what is natural, and by what authority?* In its focus on mediation (at the expense of what is being mediated), it has called into question the naïve stance that there is an objective reality that exists independently of us that we can know. The key words here are *independent of us.* Promethean postmodernism points out that there is nothing *independent of us* that we can speak of, because the speaking itself is a creative act that, in some sense, constructs the very object under discussion. Any presumption to objectivity, any presumption to speak of things as they are *in themselves* is necessarily mediated by a linguistically, culturally conditioned subject. We each actively construe our sense of what is objectively real, with the help of our own set of biases and foreknowledge. We do not merely passively receive this sense. Rediscovering Nietzsche's understanding of language as an army of metaphors, the linguistic turn, has focused upon our "construction" of the world so that it is now difficult, if not impossible, to maintain a position of naïve realism (Reason and Bradbury, 2006). Humans do not simply perceive the world as is, in a straightforward and unproblematic sort of way, as naïve realism would have it. The metaphors of a given language determine, in part, what is to be perceived. Furthermore, we are engaged, albeit perhaps not consciously, in choosing which metaphors to employ; we actively interpret our world, and in so doing, to some degree, create what appears to be given, form what appears to be already formed.

Naïve realism is an apt moniker for the value system, the powers-that-be, the unquestioned and unquestionable heritage that the postmodern Promethean acquisition of consciousness (through its acknowledgment of the underestimated role of language), allows us to move beyond. *Naïve objectivity* or *naïve objectivism* is another apt name for the Zeus from which contemporary titanism has stolen flame. Such an objectivity was ignorant of, could not include in its understanding, the contingent subject saturated in history, language, and culture. "Objectivism" is another name for metaphysical realism, the doctrine that an objectively existing world exists independent of us and, furthermore, has a determinate nature or knowable essence (Bernstein, 1983). The Promethean acquisition of consciousness of deconstructive postmodernism involves undermining this metaphysical realism by focusing upon the linguistic mediation that takes place in the articulation of what is "out there." In the case of a thinker like Derrida, this "out there" is so heavily mediated that there appears to be little possibility of accurately describing or representing it. The "it" is always deferred. The transcendental signifier is never reached. The "it" is also not independent of us, but is even, in some sense, a creation of the language we use, which has led some to describe deconstruction as a form of linguistic solipsism (Kugler, 2005). Solipsism is derived from *solus ipse*, myself alone. The solipsist sees everything as derivative of, and related to, the individual ego (Edinger, 1992). Solipsism is a form of apotheotic myth, a deification of the *I*, a belief in the ego as demiurge.

Nevertheless, in its critique of objectivity and relentless focus on the subject's linguistic mediation, or even construction, of the object, deconstructive postmodernism has opened up the possibility of a more integral approach that might take into account both subject and object. (The Promethean theft of fire—even if it is based on philosophical trickery, or results in linguistic solipsism—calls into question Zeus' absolute authority.) This possibility of a more integral approach can be seen, for example, in a thinker like Habermas (Habermas & Fultner, 2003) who has embraced the linguistic turn, to a degree, and steered a "middle course between the Scylla and Charybdis of much contemporary thought shaped by the linguistic turn . . . that gives up all claims to objective knowledge and a reductive objectivism that fails to do justice to the participant perspective" (p. xi). In its emphasis on the creative, productive capacity of language over its reflective capacities, deconstructive postmodernism has helped make way for approaches that conceive human knowledge as a co-creative act that ultimately transcends subject-object distinctions (Tarnas, 1991). It has brought *interpretation* to the foreground as a fundamental, ever-present human activity (Wilber, 2001), and in doing so has helped dispel the pretension of an overweening objectivism. In its focus on the signifier over the signified-referent, it has explicitly pointed to the culturally, linguistically imbued subject as an integral part of the equation of reality. It has drawn out the subject behind all statements about the object. In doing so, it has opened up the possibility of conceiving of the given as something that is given by *both* the linguistically mediated, historically contingent subject *and* the object whose qualities are in question, or, put differently, the given is always given through relationship.

Having undermined the reigning authority of a naïve objectivity, ignorant of its own linguistic presuppositions, Promethean postmodernism has also cleared the ground upon which a new authority, a new paradigm might establish itself. Tarnas (1995) sees Prometheus at work in

> the decisive emergence of "postmodernity" itself in our era, bringing the radical dissolution and deconstruction of so many long-established structures and boundaries, roles and hierarchies, so many once firm certainties and beliefs and limiting assumptions. The cultural consciousness has experienced a shift into a state that is fundamentally between paradigms – unprecedentedly flexible, free-floating, uncertain, disoriented, epistemologically and metaphysically confused, and open to possibilities and realities not even permitted within the arena of sensible discourse in an earlier generation. (p. 88)

What Tarnas describes here—the shift towards a state between paradigms that has allowed for *new* possibilities within sensible discourse—might be understood as the hidden Promethean purpose of semiological reductionism. Like modern art, it dissolves traditions of symbolism, meaning, and representation because they no longer speak to contemporary experience (Rowland, 2010). When the cultural, linguistic forms that the gods inhabit become obsolete, they are in need of deconstruction, and the perennial Promethean urge to undermine their authority manifests itself. Prometheus, who is, by his very nature, the epitome of radical change, transgression of limits, rebellion against structure, and a yearning for absolute freedom, is also a harbinger of the new. As his name, which means foresight or forethought, suggests, his story speaks of a forward movement in time, a progression that involves overcoming what is antiquated and aged in service of what is novel and unprecedented.

It is important to acknowledge multiple possible readings of the Promethean tale. The nature of mythic image demands it. The Promethean and titanic legacy is more mixed than the present text, or any text, could ever portray. When we render this tale solely as an admonition against the excess of human arrogance in relation to divine authority, we side with the Olympians. Too frequently, as Ann Shearer (2009) has pointed out, depth psychologists have uncritically allied themselves against this usurper of divine authority. Yet if we conceive of Promethean purpose in his titanic attitude, we acknowledge something of the truth that "we are inescapably and for all time both Titan and Olympian" (p. 5). As titans, we desire to undermine divine authority, to rebel against fate, to irreverently defy nature's laws, and the cultures that have given them their specific form. In our postmodern Prometheanism, we aspire to deconstruct any god-term that, in our eyes, no longer merits our unthinking reverence. Acknowledging this fact need not dull the cutting edge of the present critique. It may even, in some sense, strengthen it. If the negative, dangerous aspects of the Promethean attitude are given all emphasis at the expense of what is of positive value, then the titan becomes a shadow figure of sorts, an evil other, and a bête noire. The negative aspects of the archetype are sure to "redouble their negativity if they are dismissed, repressed or demonized as 'the enemy', rather than engaged within an attempt at understanding" (p. 5).

To better appreciate how semiological reductionism, as symptom, can reflect alienation and fragmentation while simultaneously forming part of a progressive, necessary, and valuable acquisition of consciousness, the following words of Edinger (1992) may be of use:

> Psychological development is characterized by two processes occurring simultaneously, namely, progressive ego-Self separation and also increasing emergence of the ego-Self axis into consciousness. If this is a correct representation of the facts, it means that ego-Self separation and growing consciousness of the ego as dependent on the Self are actually two aspects of a single emergent process continuous from birth to death. (p. 6)

As the astronautic intelligence gradually separates itself from the earth, the whole from which it arose, the essential nature of which it forms a part, it also, at least potentially, becomes increasingly aware of its dependence on this whole from which it arose. This takes place in a single emergent process by which the alienated intelligence that has left both body and nature behind grows aware of its dependence upon this very body and nature. This progressive alienation forms part of a stage of psychological development that is as innate as the movements of a newborn babe. For both Edinger and Jung, the polarization of opposites, the tension between consciousness and the unconscious is necessary and unavoidable, as are duality, dissociation, and repression. As Edinger notes, they "have been born in the human psyche simultaneously with the birth of consciousness. This means simply that consciousness in order to exist in its own right must, initially at least, be antagonistic to the unconscious" (p. 20). To be antagonistic, as the etymology of the word suggests, involves a pushing against. The astronaut's rocket, to gain altitude, must push violently *against* this earth. Without this pushing against, without this antagonism, no journey of departure and return, no journey from unconscious wholeness to conscious wholeness, is possible. Duality, dissociation, and repression have their purpose and form part of a natural, organic process.

Tarnas (1991) expresses a kindred insight, though one concerned less with individual psychic development than a collective one, when he reflects that the trajectory of the modern mind's alienation "has not been simply an error, an unfortunate human aberration, a mere manifestation of human blindness, but has rather reflected a much deeper archetypal process impelled by forces beyond the merely human" (p. 435). What is alienated and astronautic, what is split off and dissociated is not merely aberrant, a regrettable circumstance to be remedied. There is purpose, there is *telos* involved. The autonomous and alienated intellect is itself the expression of a natural unfolding. It is the very vehicle through which nature's truth emerges. This truth is not objective, independent of human cognition. Nor is it purely phenomenal. It is birthed through the human mind and in this very birthing nature becomes intelligible to itself. Such an understanding forms part of what he calls a *participatory epistemology*, which, he notes, is not to be understood as a regression to a naïve participation mystique, but as the product of a slow development from primordial unconsciousness towards dualistic alienation, a development that incorporates postmodern (deconstructive) approaches and moves beyond them. This incorporation involves the acknowledgment of the linguistically mediated mind's contribution to structuring our seemingly objective knowledge of the world. It recognizes that the idea that human beings simply produce concepts that directly and seamlessly correspond to an objective reality is problematic insofar as it leaves out the question of human mediation. Yet a participatory epistemology also rejects the notion that human beings simply impose their own order on the world. The contribution of the linguistically mediated mind is brought forth by the *telos* of the universe itself for its own self-revelation. The interpenetrating and omnipresent relationship of humans and nature is acknowledged simultaneously with the constructive character of human thought, which allows for epistemological alienation to be overcome.

Bernstein (2005), in his idea of *co-evolutionary partnership*, offers a notion that shares much in common with participatory epistemology, and like Tarnas he sees purpose and value behind the consciousness that has alienated itself from its natural ground. He believes, also, that collectively we may be involved in overcoming this alienation. His reading of the inflated Western ego is consonant with the understanding of Prometheanism that I have put forth here. For Bernstein, however, the touchstone myth of our time is Genesis, a myth, it should be noted, that Edinger (1972) often mentions in the same breath as that of Prometheus in his exposition of the necessary dangers of inflation. The archetypal thrust of Genesis is perhaps best encapsulated in this verse from the Jerusalem Bible: "Be fruitful, multiply, fill the earth and conquer it. Be masters of the fish of the sea, the birds of heaven and all living animals on the earth" (Bernstein, 2005, pp. 20–21). This mandate, given by Yahweh and carried out in service to him, has seemingly gone awry, or morphed, so that it is no longer carried out in service to a Biblical God. Now the mandate is carried out by an ego that has deified itself and serves only itself. Displacing Yahweh as creator, this ego believes in its own auto-genesis, its own self-creation. Bernstein sees in this process of self-deification both danger and purpose. The danger of the Western ego enthralled by its own sense of omniscience and omnipotence is that it threatens not only our collective survival, but also that of other species. It is an ego built upon a split with nature, a split that is one of dominator and dominated, in which the ego views nature in a utilitarian and often adversarial manner. This is the split that I have described through the Promethean myth and a tale of alienation from animate body and animate earth.

Yet there is purpose, too, in this seemingly perverse inflation and self-deification. The underlying goal of this inflationary dynamic is not mere domination, but rather a certain *type* of ego, one that is self-contained, and "based on logic and the *logos* principle. *This* ego, unlike the ego merged-with-nature that preceded it, would elevate logic and left-brained thinking to the exclusion of the a-rational, the irrational, and the transrational" (Bernstein, 2005, p. 21). This is also an ego that holds "logic and rational process as superior and more real than feeling and intuition. It would consider any reality other than rationality as being inferior and less real" (p. 21). An ego based on logos is an ego based in the word, and in rational processes articulated through the word. It could, perhaps, even be an ego that subsumes the phenomenal, experiential, intuitive, and sensual under the auspice of linguistic play and signification. Such an ego, with its exclusion of the a-rational, the irrational, and the transrational might even seek to disenfranchise perception as an origin of sense. It might deny an extralinguistic space within human experience, or any *opening* beyond linguistic construction, and thereby disallow any retrievable domain of primordial experience. This ego based in the word might conceive reality itself as derivative of the production of signs and understand even differentiated objects in the phenomenal world as being the result of semiosis. It might, furthermore, have little sense of how *meaning* cannot be reduced to the intralinguistic play of signs, but rather, also derives itself from such things as feeling, intuition, and sensation. Such an ego might even see these latter functions as merely semiological placeholders, terms that signify, surely, but not terms that allude to some fundamental aspect of human experience.

Ever mindful of the hubris of consciousness, Bernstein does not claim to know what the essential aim behind the formation of this boundaried and contained ego has been. But he does believe that we can discern at least something of its purpose, which, on his reading is a state in which the ego and the Self learn to function as co-evolutionary partners. The challenge for the Western ego at this point in history is to surrender something of its power drive so as to work with a greater whole, "*with* the Self as a co-evolutionary participant in the evolution of a new psychic paradigm and a new, transcendent, consciousness" (p. 61). The boundaried ego, to do this, to work with the greater whole, must learn the limits of its capacities and comprehend that logos, the rationality of the word, is but one faculty among many. To have even made such a relationship of co-evolutionary participation possible, first, a separation, a movement beyond the state of the ego merged-with-nature, was needed. Without this, its potential could not be realized. First a participation mystique had to be overcome.

This state of participation mystique, for Edinger, is represented in the Prometheus myth by humans and gods eating at the same table. Here, there is an ego-Self identity. The human "I" is not differentiated from the greater whole. Differentiation begins with the dividing of meat between humans and gods: "[T]he ego, to establish itself as an autonomous entity, must appropriate the food (energy) for itself" (Edinger, 1992, p. 24). The process is furthered by the titanic trickery of replacing lean meat with fat and bones. And it is furthered still by the eventual theft of fire. Each event marks a progressive differentiation between the human "I" and the whole from which it arose, a progressive differentiation accompanied by a sense of empowerment, self-determination, and autonomy. The theft of fire in the Promethean myth is paralleled by the savoring of fruit in the Garden of Eden. Each crime against the deity brings a corresponding differentiation and sense of independence; after the eating from the tree of knowledge, humans no longer walk side by side with Yahweh, nor do they commingle peaceably with other animals. Through transgression they have become different, differentiated.

What is striking in both Bernstein's and Edinger's account of this dynamic of ego-differentiation and inflation is the simultaneous appreciation of this process as being both necessary and purposeful on the one hand, and potentially catastrophic, even apocalyptic on the other. For both writers, a deflation of human grandiosity is needed and a simultaneous embrace of the mysterious *telos* of the greater whole, the Self. Bernstein (2005) puts it thus:

> We explored the threat to the survival of species *Homo sapiens* by an overspecialized western ego too inflated with its own power complex to contain its grandiosity and competition with God. It is important to note before moving on that although I have placed necessary emphasis on this threat to our survival, *all* dimensions of experience have both a negative and a positive pole. Thus, that western ego that I have described as so menacing to our survival, is also an indispensable instrument for our potential salvation. What the *final cause*, in the Aristotelian sense, might be remains yet a mystery. And, by definition, mysteries are never fully known. The ultimate challenge is whether we can take advantage of our new consciousness so as to be able to participate as an aware coevolutionary partner in reining in our own self-destructive nature. Doing so holds the prospect for crossing a threshold into a broader and deeper relationship with all of life, and for embracing the intriguing mystery of the greater fullness of who we are and who we are intended to become – not merely who we choose to be. (p. 121)

In consonance with Bernstein's thinking here, one can say, likewise, that the titanic will to deconstruct all god-terms has both a negative and a positive pole. Insofar as it undermines *any* conception of the essential, the intrinsic, the innate, and the inherent, as well as subverting *any* sense of humans as beings subject to forces not of their own creation, it is negative, delusional. Insofar as it provides the possibility for conceiving of these things anew and the conscious acceptance of our roles as active co-creators, or co-evolutionary partners, it is positive, a potential boon. There is no final, absolute, definitive abandonment of ground, or of nature, or of human nature. But there is a creative reconfiguring of our representations of the human and the natural that the Promethean suspension of reference makes possible.

Questions, then, that might be asked are: In what ways might we take advantage of a new consciousness of ourselves as linguistic beings, creators of seemingly demiurgic dimensions, while simultaneously acknowledging that we are finite, vulnerable, feeling animals? In what ways might we incorporate what has been learned by postmodern Prometheanism and thereby move beyond both a slavish obedience to the latter-day Zeus of a naïve objectivism, and an equally blind rebellion to it? In what ways might we understand ourselves as co-creators, as co-emergent, co-evolutionary partners with (and within) a greater whole, be it called Nature, or Self, or by any other name? In addressing these issues, and the complex philosophical knots that come with them, it is not so much important to me to find absolute theoretical clarity, or establish some coherent set of ideas that brook no contradiction. In fact, I confess to a certain humility in addressing such complex abstractions. What concerns me more is a sense of psychological balance. In what ways might we humans conceive of things like language, reference, essences, nature, objectivity, gods, and god-terms that are emotionally healthy and conducive to greater vitality? How might we understand our own autonomy and will to self-determination so as to encourage planetary well-being? In what ways might we conceive all of these complex philosophical issues that *feel* congruent with our deepest *intuitions* and *perceptions*?

Myths of the given: re-imagining Pandora

Zeus, having unchained Prometheus after several thousand years of the rebel's daily evisceration, in a gesture of seeming benevolence, offers the titan an entrancing and enticing female figure of irresistible beauty and delicacy. Her name is Pandora, the first woman. Created by the gods, she reflects their grandeur. Prometheus, scarred and tormented by Zeus, skeptical and suspicious of his generosity, refuses the gift. But his brother, Epimetheus, the namesake of hindsight, the titan, therefore, who is also a figure of reflective awareness (Thomas, 2009), falls in love. Mesmerized, and with the blessing of the divine patriarch, he decides to marry this enthralling feminine figure. In honor of their betrothal, the almighty Olympian bestows upon Pandora a *pithos*, meaning jar, though this term has been mistranslated as "box." The excited groom eagerly uncorks the pithos. What follows has become the source of legend and, to this day, remains a haunting presence in the imagery of popular speech. The proverbial Pandora's box was opened, and "violence, terror, pain, greed, depression, poisons, loneliness, malice, dissociation, hubris, rejection, hunger, envy, narcissism, pride, and disease screeched over the land" (Orfanos, 2006, p. 482). The gods and goddesses, angered by the Promethean theft, had fashioned in the figure of Pandora a ruse, one that would bring every variety of misfortune to human kind. Yes, a ruse, for unbeknownst to the mortals, the woman was the goddess *Ge*, Earth Wisdom (Thomas, 2009).

Gail Thomas (2009), in her eminently readable work of scholarly imagination, *Healing Pandora: The Restoration of Hope and Abundance*, creatively illuminates this ruse. How can this Grecian Eve, this maiden renowned for the unleashing of every form of petulance and plague, in actuality be a goddess? This bringer of banes, this source of all evils and ills, all death and disease is in fact *Ge*, whose divinity resounds to this day in our words geology, geometry, and geographic. Pandora is the mythic incarnation of the great earth mother, for this maligned feminine figure has a prior divine identity that pre-dates the story of her proverbial box. The Pandora that has come to be known to contemporary readers is largely the work of Hesiod, whose story tells of her creation by the Olympians as a mortal woman, in retribution for the theft of fire. Yet sources that speak of another Pandora, pre-dating Hesiod, gathered from the images of ancient vase paintings and papyrus, tell another story. It is the story of a goddess rising out of the earth, arms extended in endless bounty and infinite embrace, a mother of *all* gods, a source of *all* creation. This prior, or perhaps merely veiled, identity can be found in the etymology of her name. *Pan* means *all*, and *dor* signifies *gift* (Dougherty, 2006). Thus, she is the giver of all, and not merely the bestower of blights. She is all that gives, and not merely a gift. To acknowledge this earlier understanding of the goddess that pre-dates her expulsion from the Greek pantheon is to witness a radical transformation of perspective. Her figure is not merely diminished or demoted from divine to mortal. The crafter of all has become the crafted. The giver of all has become the giver of only what is evil, repugnant, and reviled. What was once the image of a divine and ubiquitous feminine presence, a container from which all deities had sprung, is now merely the carrier of a tiny jar, filled with only vile things. And in this very shift, "she who was mother of men and gods is now replaced by he who is father of men and gods" (Thomas, 2009, p. 56).

This replacement "sets the stage for two thousand years for a cultural milieu that has quickened the imagination of the Western world to accept the inferiority of the feminine principle" (Thomas, 2009, p. 6). The fact that Pandora is held responsible for all the ills of existence is indicative of a mindset that devalues the feminine. This devaluation, as I envision it, is double-edged: The imagined evil unleashed from Pandora's pithos reflects the vilification and scapegoating of the feminine. It is the projection of patriarchy. At the same time, these evils are real, the actual consequence of the feminine's vilification, ills that arise when the feminine is unduly contained, restricted, and devalued. Pandora's box is the tragic consequence of the feminine boxed in, constrained, confined, imprisoned like a genie in a bottle for thousands of years. Another name that Thomas gives to what Pandora represents is *soul*. Soul, as has been noted throughout this inquiry, has also gone by the name of anima, the anima of animated bodies and animated earth.

The radical transformation of perspective, the metamorphosis of Pandora from container to contained, from an infinite and immortal all, to a mere finite mortal, constitutes a shift in perception that may feel familiar to the reader. There has been something analogous to this shift at work over the trajectory of the present story of the alienation of language. A comparable transformation has threaded its way through these pages, in which I have played upon two fundamentally different perceptions of the earth. One consists of the earth experienced as the coarse ground that supports our steps, a living, breathing biosphere that sustains every moment of our lives. On this earth, the wind pours past our ears, and flows through our hair. We are always already in contact with it because we have an immediate experience of living enfolded within it. We are of it. The earth, on this understanding, is not 'in' space but, rather, provides it. It is not merely one celestial body among many others. This earth is a sentient one. Humans can speak to, and with, its inhabitants. It could be called, perhaps, a pre-Hesiod, Pandoran earth, insofar as it bespeaks the ethos of an animistic mother earth mythology.

The other fundamental sense of earth we have explored has been that of a blue and dappled-white sphere as seen in photos taken from a distance made possible only within the last several decades. This is an earth perceived from the outside, one that comes into view by having escaped the pull of terrestrial gravity. It is the product of a perspective that sees our home as, first and foremost, the third planet from the sun, an orb floating in vacuity. This astronautic perspective also understands nature itself to be a mere construct, an epistemological indicator designating certain types of discourse. On this view, human nature is not as close to us as human skin, or as essential to us as the air we breathe but, rather, something more analogous to the earth observed from afar. It is a neutralized nature, existing within language, a mortal Pandora safely confined within a post-Hesiod order.

The demotion of the goddess, from all-embracing deity to lowly creature created by Olympians, parallels another—the demotion of the earth as all-embracing biosphere, a living, sentient being, to the earth as image, as mere representation, or conversely, as mere object. Her relegation to a minor figure within the patriarchal Olympian order parallels the relegation of an all-giving mother nature to the status of "mother nature": a linguistic trope of dubious validity, a prejudice to be deconstructed. I imagine the scare quotes in the previous passage as a contemporary version of the Pandoran pithos; they contain, confine, reduce, and limit the primordial goddess and all the gods that she has created, but only for a while. Once her jar is opened, all ills are loosed upon the world. Gods and ills are unleashed alike, for "the gods have become our diseases" (Jung, as cited by Thomas, 2009, p. 157). But, once the contemporary pithos is opened, and "nature" thus becomes nature, then, once more, she can be understood as a mighty force to be reckoned with, an all-embracing source from which all intrinsic order, innate characteristic, and inherent attribute arises.

Pandora's containment within the patriarchal order has multiple dimensions, perhaps infinitely so. As mythic image of the earth, she alludes to all that is primordial, natural, and given. As such, she is diminished by any conception that might reconfigure the intrinsic and inherent as being derivative rather than primary. And this is, in a sense, exactly what happens to her within the Promethean tale. Her image as the primary, primal, original, and originary divinity from which all forms are born is reconceived as being secondary, something constructed within the context of a power struggle between two male deities. Her pure primordial presence is reconstituted and understood as being both derivative and merely mortal.

The movement from pre-Hesiod to post-Hesiod versions of Pandora constitutes a radical shift of perspective much like the shift from animate body to anatomical body. In this book we have been chronicling a vision that sees body, earth, and language from the outside, as astronomical and anatomical objects. With this in mind, Thomas's (2009) understanding of Pandora as soul image, as anima, takes on new resonance. On her reading, a loss of Pandoran consciousness means that "we have lost touch with the soul of things and with the soul of body" (p. 159). The loss of Pandoran consciousness, construed in slightly different terms, is an abandonment of the animate body, the animate earth. Robert Sardello (2009), in his introduction to Thomas's work, remarks that she teaches us how to think and live "*with* the things of the world rather than *about* them. Thinking and living with the things of the world requires developing the mythic imagination, the capacity of approaching earth and world as *who* rather than an *it*" (p. xi, original emphasis). This imagination, this Pandoran consciousness, involves a willingness to *speak to* and *with* others and not merely about them. It also involves extending an understanding of *who* it is that speaks, so that it embraces those of other species and an entire living, sensate planet. Thomas warns that living without a Pandoran consciousness "has created a split so severe as to threaten our earth and its people" (Thomas, 2009, p. xxiv). One aspect of acknowledging this split involves recognizing that humans are not merely spectators viewing a world of objects, speaking of them, acquiring an objective knowledge of their behavior. An animate, ensouled world speaks to us and us to her. Human language is born of this world and is not merely an imposition upon it.

Thomas tells her reader that the gifts given by Pandora are "rejected by a Promethean ego-centered attitude but received as a fulfillment by an Epimethean or reflective attitude" (p. 159). Epimetheus, the oft-considered dullard sibling of his rebellious and crafty brother, is enamored of the beautiful woman. Not having been disfigured and tortured by Zeus, he is less reluctant to accept the maiden as gift and, in turn, the gifts of the maiden. Because he is always looking backwards, he is acutely aware of what has been lost. He is attached to the past. He understands that there are things of value there that should not be forsaken. One can read his love of Pandora as a love for what has been lost, the pre-Hesiodic world before the dethronement of the goddess, and the demise of animism. His eager opening of the proverbial pithos, understood as a conscious act, testifies to a willingness to endure all hardship, chaos, disease, hunger, and calamity for the cause of love. In his image is contained the understanding that loving opens one to hurts of all kinds, hurts that might be avoided by a more diffident heart.

The Promethean attitude, in turn, seeks control. It seeks to overcome the unconscious union with both Zeus and the Pandoran (earth mother) naturalness of things. In relation to the latter of these two, Jung states that "fire-making is a preeminently conscious act and therefore 'kills' the dark state of union with the mother" (Jung, cited by Thomas, 2009, p. 57). The titanic illumination by flame seeks to overcome the whims of nature, desires to transcend the life of mere animals. And as Thomas suggests, and has been suggested throughout these pages, such an illumination has its place, its purpose. The Promethean urge leads to a valuable acquisition of consciousness and potentials that cannot be realized while the psyche is in a merged state of participation mystique, a "cultural stage of union with the Mother" (p. 57). The titan's theft thus "initiates the making of the mortal Pandora" (p. 57). This mortal Pandora is one that can be betrothed; she no longer possesses the intimidating dimensions of the great mother, giver of all. She has taken on a more diminutive human form, thereby making marriage possible, a conscious union of masculine and feminine that is not one of mother and son, but of bride and groom as equal partners.

Pandora, as her name suggests, is an image of our changing relationship with the given. The linguistic turn, in its undermining of immediacy and experience as an arbiter of truth has served to combat what philosophers refer to as *the myth of the given*, the belief that reality is in no way constructed by human participation and cognition. Pre-Homeric Pandora, the all-giving goddess, is a fecund image of what it is to live within such a myth, for her image suggests a relationship towards the given that is passive, enthralled by participation mystique, and ignorant of any human agency in human knowing. For a thinker like Rorty, to oppose this myth means accepting that "knowledge is inseparable from a social practice—the practice of justifying one's assertions to one's fellow-humans. It is not presupposed by this practice but comes into being along with it" (Rorty, cited in Kuipers, 2013, p. 74). There is simply no possible knowledge that comes before, or is in any way independent of, the social practices of justification by way of assertions couched in language. On his reasoning, then, there is nothing simply bestowed by experience or the nature of things. This is the Promethean attitude. The Promethean deification of human agency eliminates any appeal to Pandora, to nature, essences, and inherency. Yet the Pandoran myth suggests, perhaps, another possible attitude: that of Epimetheus and his marriage to Pandora. This marriage is the mythic image of the co-creative, participatory epistemology that Tarnas envisions, the co-evolutionary partnership that Bernstein alludes to, and even the transfiguration of a heritage into a destiny, as Romanyshyn conceives it. I believe that it has opened up the possibility of conceiving of the given as something that is given by *both* the linguistically mediated, historically contingent subject *and* the object whose qualities are in question, or, put differently, the given is always given through relationship.

Promethean crucifixion: aporias as call to the earth

> If the hero, instead of submitting to all of the initiatory tests, has, like Prometheus, simply darted to his goal (by violence, quick device, or luck) and plucked the boon for the world that he intended, then the powers that he has unbalanced may react so sharply that he will be blasted from within and without—crucified, like Prometheus, on the rock of his own violated unconscious. (Campbell, 1967, p. 37)

In Chapter 2, we explored a critique of originary principles, or god-terms by way of the idea of semantic indeterminacy—the ostensibly problematic ambiguity of pivotal terms within a conceptual system. Inevitably, such terms have both literal and metaphorical meanings that cannot be separated one from the other. On this view, the simultaneously literal and metaphorical significance of critical concepts is seen as an opportunity for a deconstruction of meaning, a dismantling of authorial intent. Such a deconstruction relies upon the disparity between figurative and literal senses of a term or statement. Pointing out a text's semantic indeterminacy is one technique by which thinkers of a deconstructive or post-structuralist bent undermine the validity of metaphysical universals (Kugler, 2005). In doing so, they point to an aporia, that is to say, an irresolvable internal contradiction or logical disjunction within a text or theory. They assiduously discern within the text the multiple meanings that are at odds with one another, and thereby threaten the text's integrity (Johnson, 1981).

There is another aporia that deconstruction relentlessly sheds light upon, one that is, in fact, at the core of Derrida's critique of a metaphysics of presence. This disjunction or cleavage is understood to exist between the finite and the infinite, the temporal and the eternal, the immanent and the transcendent. Just as *différance* places an unbridgeable abyss between text and referent, it also posits an abyssal rupture between the aforementioned oppositional pairings. And in positing this abyss, it affirms the impossibility of true statements; for Derrida, truth requires the concurrence between two incommensurables—the temporal and the eternal, finite consciousness and absolute consciousness (Dillon, 1995). That is to say that my consciousness, as an individual, historically contingent human being, located in time and space, must concur with something truly incomparable—the eternal. Yet this concurrence, so the argument goes, is impossible "because the finite time of unfolding, succession, and synthesis is incommensurate with the absolute time of reality cognized aperspectively, that is, atemporally" (p. 18). The time that I live as a unique, inimitable, mortal human being, living one moment followed by another, to be followed by another, cannot correspond to the atemporal time of eternity, the perspectiveless perspective of absolute reality. In this sense, human speaking must correspond to divine speaking in order to be true, though this is exactly what it cannot do. Truth requires that one's perception be comparable to god's, comparable to that of (an) eternal being. Yet, one is finite, and as such, incapable of such perception:

> To claim that a statement is true is to assert a coincidence between what is known to a given intellect and what is independent of that intellect. Deconstruction contends that this coincidence is necessary for the assertion of a truth, but is also an impossibility: The impossibility of a finite, circumscribed, human mind coinciding in its knowledge with what *is* absolutely. (Dillon, 1995, p. 17)

Derrida establishes conditions for truth that can never be met, by virtue of a seemingly insurmountable disjunction between the temporal and the eternal, the finite and the infinite, the human and the divine. By pointing to the existence of a construct within historical time, and within culture, he vitiates the sense in which it may also allude to something given, as it were, by the eternal nature of things. What is given, rather, is given by authorities that "have not dropped from the sky; they are contingent formations, constituted products" (Caputo, 1987, p. 145).

Within a text, the need for a concurrence between the finite and the infinite, the temporal and the eternal manifests in an attempt to ground interpretation in explanatory principles such as *reality*, *Self*, *archetype*, and *truth*, which all attempt to allude to some ultimate presence or ground that serves to justify all other elements in a text. Yet, those absolutes must transcend the system of signs they attempt to explain in order to carry out their interpretive function (Kugler, 2005). The human word, product of a finite intelligence, a limited intellect temporally circumscribed, must posit terms that transcend the very system of thought they attempt to underwrite and elucidate. Terms like *sexuality*, *self*, *wholeness*, and so on, must concur with, coincide with, a transcendent something independent of, or beyond, those terms. Yet this transcendence, it is argued, is as impossible as it is indispensable. If these terms are to function as a ground, "they cannot be implicated in the very system of thought and language they are being used to explain" (Kugler, 2005, p. 33). Yet it is also the case that they cannot "have the same semantic status as the other meanings within the system. Their semantic status must be 'the meaning of meaning' or the 'metaphor of metaphors'" (pp. 33–4). The god-terms, the metaphysical universals, the originary principles must do what they cannot do. Their implication in a human system of signs precludes their capacity for grounding the system.

As was addressed earlier in Marlan's (2005) reading of Derrida, terms such as Self, Being, and God cannot, it is believed, be given privileged status outside the matrix of language from which they are derived. Any attempt to do so ends in tautological formulation: the meaning of meaning, the metaphor of metaphor, the reality of the real, the trueness of truth. This line of thinking bears a significant resemblance to Rorty's skepticism, reviewed in Chapter 2, as regards theories of linguistic reference. For this self-proclaimed pragmatist, any theory that would link language and world arises from the very theoretical milieu that it attempts to stand outside of and explain. It is thereby implicated in the very system of thought that it must remain independent of in order to have any validity. This lack of independence creates the questionable situation of using a portion of one's present theory to support the remainder of it. For Rorty, the search for an adequate theory of reference requires the impossible—a transcendental standpoint outside the language system from which we can examine the relationship between our representations and what they purport to represent.

There is a certain validity to these insights that should not be ignored; conceptual systems, on their own, cannot underwrite themselves. They cannot serve as their own support. Language cannot provide its own ground. No term, or set of terms, can act as a foundation to support an entire theory. Terms are implicated in the very system of thought and language they are being used to explain.

Semiological reductionism reveals aporias, internal contradictions, that are real. Yet the internal contradictions that it reveals are contradictory because internal; the aporias result from the very premises that distance sign systems from an outside to which they might relate, whether this outside is conceived of as Being, or referents, or anything that might be considered extralinguistic. Semiological reductionism first radically dissevers language from the ground, then claims as insight the groundlessness of language. Yet this is what it *must do* to the extent that it construes all meaning as being the result of intralinguistic relations. Having its eyes so myopically focused upon the text, semiological reductionism looks for the ground *within* language, and then bemoans or celebrates what it has not found. The problematic fissures within texts that this reductionism tirelessly reveals are products of a prior fissure—between language and the land, between sign systems and animated, human bodies. It is only language previously dissociated from the earth that suffers from a lack of ground. The aporias that semiological reductionism points to are the fruit of a prior disjunction: that of text and its other.

Here, as in Chapter 2, with its focus on semantic indeterminacy, I invite you to see the seeming flaws (of internal textual contradictions) as potential boons. A creative re-envisioning of these internal incongruities might imagine them as a call from the ground, a call to the earth, a beckoning to the immediate, an opportunity for seduction by the other of language, by conviction born of human sensing, intuiting, feeling, by a knowing that is not erased by the play of signs but that, rather, *always already* informs this play. If the semantic status of our god-terms, our explanatory principles, must lead to such tautological formulations as the 'reality of the real' or the 'metaphor of metaphors,' perhaps it is time to see this state of affairs as being testament to the existence of a meaning outside of language, or at least not completely reducible to it. It may be time to acknowledge that not all meaning has been prefigured by a play of signs embedded in culture and history (Dillon, 1995). Such an acknowledgment understands the mind's perplexity as the body's and the earth's opportunity, for where are we to go when language collapses, but the immediacy of the body and the supporting ground of the earth itself? With this in mind, our god-terms, like the gods and goddesses that preceded them, testify to our dependence, and the dependence of language, on an "other" that is greater, more substantial, primary. The paradox of the god-terms is less of an irresolvable internal contradiction than an opportunity to acknowledge our dependence upon an ensouled, animate world, an opportunity to acknowledge *anima mundi*.

I imagine such reflections taking place as a form of Promethean crucifixion, a dismemberment upon the earth. Having filched the fire of the gods, and put the combustive blaze of creation squarely in the hands of mere mortals, Prometheus is condemned to suffer upon stone, to bleed upon rock. He is chained, bound, submitted. The sacrificial subterfuge of placing bones and fat in lieu of meat is now paid for by the ritual sacrifice of Prometheus himself. The personification of humanity's titanic will to transcend all limitation, breach all restraint, and transgress all frontiers finds himself limited, restrained, confined. This is the moment when the heroic attitude of conquest and transcendence is called back by the spirit of the depths and is prevented from further ascent, the moment when incapacity and failure beckons (Jung & Shamdasani, 2012). Prometheus has stolen the flame from the reigning patriarch whose present-day name is multiple: metaphysics, essentialism, objectivism, regimes of truth, power/knowledge, the myth of the given. Thus, humans now know a heretofore unknown creative power, the creative power of the word that illuminates and constructs, "the essences, ideas, or concepts [that] have retreated from the nature of things into the rules of language" (Habermas & Fultner, 2003, p. 157). A linguistically constituted lifeworld has, under the patronage of this latest incarnation of the titan, taken over the legacy of metaphysical realism (Habermas & Fultner, 2003). Human beings can now conceive of their own demiurgic quality; they are producers of signs, and with signs worlds are created. The titan's necessary rebellion has shed an almost blinding light upon the role of human agency in human knowing; we actively construct our understandings, we need not be merely the recipients of truths given from on high. Yet the price of this heroic accomplishment is the death of the hero himself, the most absolute manifestation of his utter limitation.

The titan, too, has liberated humans from Gaia, from great mother earth. Nature, having been nominalistically eviscerated, has been rendered mute, or so it seems, for the Promethean victory is ambiguous and polyvalent; having undermined all authority, this rival to divine power has also, it would seem, undermined his own—the negation of linguistic reference allows for the rejection of *all* authorities at *all* times (Girard & Doran, 2008). This negation is, thus, only as potent as it is impotent, for the very force that deconstructs the god-terms, must disempower itself and suffer its own deconstruction. The hero must die. The impulse that liberated humans from the despotic rule of obedient sacrifice must become the sacrificial victim, for what can the semiological reduction affirm that its own revelations will not cast a skeptical light upon? What values can it posit that will not exist forever and always under erasure? If the interpretive freedom this latter-day Prometheus has bestowed upon us is itself a mere construct floating, somehow, independent of all living corporeity, of what value can it be? What is this freedom if it does not touch upon animate flesh, if such a freedom is itself a hollow husk with no living germ within?

In the world of mythic imagination, punishments always befit the crime. Without fail, the metaphoric logic of myth renders a poetic justice. Each offense against a cosmic order is coupled with a punishment that, in its very character, emotional tenor, and associative possibilities is ironically appropriate. The torture fits the sin. Often the punishment alludes to, and even seeks to compensate, a lack in the illicit psychological attitude of the guilty party. Thus, the justice rendered is not merely punitive, but potentially restorative and redemptive. It is with an attunement to the resonance between castigation and transgression that we must view the Promethean bondage. It is the perfect cure for this particular ill, for Prometheanism suffers precisely from a lack of ground, from a failure to acknowledge what is bedrock, from a denial of the sustaining earth. It may even be that this titanic torment upon the land represents the very goal at work in this mythic tale; the archetype appears to act "with seeming foreknowledge, or as if it were already in possession of a goal" (Jung, 1960/1969, p. 209 [*CW* 8 pt. 3 para. 411]). Regardless, the healing lies near the wound, and the titan who severed signs from the ground from which they arose must return to the ground to heal the severance. The image of the titan's *corporeal suffering*, his figure contorted in *visceral grief* while bound tight to the earth aptly depicts precisely what is needed to heal contemporary Prometheanism. It might also serve as an image of what Jung termed *legitimate suffering*, the suffering that one must endure in order to heal the *illegitimate* suffering of neurosis (Jacobi, 1968).

Upon the crags of the Caucasus, the titan is obliged to learn the perplexity, paradox, and partiality of his victory over such metaphysical universals and originary principles as *truth*, *self*, *center*, *unity*, *origin*, and *archetype*. As he writhes upon the rock, his pain compels him to acknowledge the reality of the experiential, perceptual, sensual, and phenomenal. Pain can be very convincing. He is forced to learn of hunger, attraction, repulsion, satiation, and death—the perennial constants of all embodied beings, all animate bodies. He is learning what it is to be incarnate. To be embodied means to suffer (Ryley, 1998). So he suffers the elements. When he is thirsty, the now-helpless titan waits for rain to moisten his parched lips and tongue, mouth and throat. To the sun exposed, he burns and blisters upon an ever-warming planet. He lives his own creaturely vulnerability, and in so doing, he remembers, but "to remember the body which one is, to recover beneath the 'official' body of anatomy the lived pantomimic body of daily life, is not . . . an easy task" (Romanyshyn, 2004, p. 112). Yet this is what must happen, for the anatomical body, and language qua corpus, can only truly have meaning, and be more than mere schemata, through a recovery of the lived, experiential body. The Promethean ability to stand seemingly outside this animate body, outside animate language, and view them as objects of dissection, to be split into smaller and smaller atoms, must be paid for. True Promethean purpose can only be achieved by a return to the immediacy of flesh. Like all symbols, the image of Prometheus unites the opposites (Jung, 1977); it contains within itself both the ambition to transcend earthly limitation, and the inability to do so, the desire to avoid suffering, and the inevitable confrontation with it, the will to power, and the defeat of this will, the flight from flesh and a return to it.

I imagine the contemporary Prometheus bound, to boulder fettered, flightless and pinned to the earth that he is natal to and nascent from, forced to learn of his consanguinity with all those that are of soil. He is *humbled*, and as the roots of this word testify, humbling is a bringing down to earth, an encounter with *humus*, a return to what is most human. He is forced to acquiesce to suffering, defeat, and failure. Shackled to stone, the titan learns something of mortality and pain, weakness and frailty, and in doing so, he learns what is bedrock, what is foundational. Where he once saw only absurd tautological formulations, he now hears an echo, an echo that is difficult to articulate without sounding hopelessly self-referential: *the "meaning" of meaning*. He has hit rock bottom. No act of guile, no interpretive slight of hand can save him now. Denial is no longer possible. There is no intellectual trickery to avoid his suffering. No bargain can be made. Even the infinite play of signs cannot immune him from his finitude as flesh. Even the infinite play of signs must rest upon a ground, as human and animal bodies do.

Regardless of how one construes postmodern Promethean purpose—as the overcoming of a naïve realism, the advent of a co-evolutionary partnership or participatory epistemology, the movement from unconscious wholeness to conscious wholeness, the transfiguration of a heritage into a destiny, or a renewal of the gods—the trajectory of Prometheanism leads to grief. In this regard, Marlan (2005) is right to associate it with the alchemical *nigredo* phase, the torturous decomposition and rotting that is an eclipse of ego consciousness. Hubristic, inflated acts, are always followed by compensatory, deflationary humblings, if not humiliations (Edinger, 1992; Jung, 1953). Pride, as is so often said, comes before the fall. And Prometheus is proud, and does fall. He soars above the earth, bursts the bonds of mere instinctuality, and flouts divine authority, acting out his irreverence and fierce desire for autonomy. Yet by the inexorable law of enantiodromia—nature's dictate that everything must turn into its opposite, that the sun must begin its descent precisely at the apex of its climb—Prometheus must return to the earth that bore him.

If deconstructive postmodernism is antithetical to the values espoused by more geocentric and ecocentric disciplines, it is relevant to note here that "the bearing of pain and suffering [is] a central principle of ecopsychological work" (Fisher, 2002, p. 189). An acceptance of grief, and with it an acknowledgment of human limits, is essential to remedy present-day Prometheanism. This grieving process includes an acknowledgment of the limits on our ability to manipulate and control our environment through technology—a thoroughly Promethean ability. Fisher (2002) also rightly recognizes that "our technologized and economized society does not encourage the creation of . . . cultural frameworks for bearing pain and suffering—only for avoiding and trying to kill it" (p. 190). Postmodern Prometheanism shares much in common with this attitude of avoidance. Its lack of grounding in the body, and conceptual denial of nature, facilitates an evasion of the human (and therefore animal) experience of vulnerability.

Grief, depression, mourning, suffering, pain, all speak to a deflation of grandiosity and a rooting to both body and earth. They are the shadow of a titanic longing for mastery, ascent, and autonomy. Dillon (1995) describes this return to earth that is the psychological necessity of having flouted, indeed even murdered, divine authority, with the following metaphor:

> Derrida leaves us, self-consciously pounding nails in the coffin of the dying god, facing the abyss resolutely, with our desire for transcendence foreclosed by the bar that separates us from the transcendental signified, that is, with nothing left to love save the diacriticality that generates the bar, that is, with nothing left to love: no embodied selves we can reach or touch, only mirrored representations we can read.
>
> There is another way to contend with the death of the god, and that is to return to the birthplace of the god, the earth forsaken and despised. In the same breath with which he announced the death of god, Nietzsche cautioned us to be true to the earth. (p. 174)

When there is no embodied, animate self, all that is left are the spectral fragments of representation. But this is not an inevitability. The abyss left by the dying gods and goddesses is also a call to earth, a call to their place of birth, and the intimation of their possible renewal.

References

Bernstein, J. S. (2005). *Living in the borderland: The evolution of consciousness and the challenge of healing trauma*. New York, NY: Brunner-Routledge.

Bernstein, R. J. (1983). *Beyond objectivism and relativism: Science, hermeneutics, and praxis*. Oxford, England: Blackwell.

Campbell, J. (1967). *The hero with a thousand faces*. New York, NY: Meridian Books.

Caputo, J. D. (1987). *Radical hermeneutics: Repetition, deconstruction, and the hermeneutic project*. Bloomington, IN: Indiana University Press.

Dillon, M. C. (1995). *Semiological reductionism: A critique of the deconstructionist movement in postmodern thought*. Albany, NY: State University of New York Press.

Dougherty, C. (2006). *Prometheus*. New York, NY: Routledge.

Edinger, E. F. (1992). *Ego and archetype: Individuation and the religious function of the psyche*. Boston, MA: Shambhala.

Fisher, A. (2002). *Radical ecopsychology: Psychology in the service of life*. Albany, NY: State University of New York Press.

Girard, R., & Doran, R. (2008). *Mimesis and theory: Essays on literature and criticism, 1953–2005*. Stanford, CA: Stanford University Press.

Habermas, J., & Fultner, B. (2003). *Truth and justification*. Cambridge, MA: MIT Press.

Jacobi, J. (1968). *The psychology of C. G. Jung: An introduction with illustrations* (7th edn.). London: Routledge.

Johnson, B. (1981). Introduction. In J. Derrida, *Dissemination* (pp. vii–xxxiii). Chicago, IL: University Press.

Jung, C. G. (1953). Two essays on analytical psychology. In R. F. C. Hull (Trans.), *The collected works of C. G. Jung* (Vol. 7). Princeton, NJ: Princeton-Bollingen.

Jung, C. G. (1960/1969). *The structure and dynamics of the psyche* (2nd edn.). Princeton, NJ: Princeton University Press (original work published 1960).

Jung, C. G. (1977). *Mysterium coniunctionis: An inquiry into the separation and synthesis of psychic opposites in alchemy* (2nd edn.). Princeton, NJ: Princeton University Press.

Jung, C. G., & Shamdasani, S. (2012). *The red book: A reader's edition*. New York, NY: W. W. Norton & Co.
Jung, C. G., & Von Franz, M.-L. (1964). *Man and his symbols*. Garden City, NY: Doubleday.
Kugler, P. (2005). *Raids on the unthinkable: Freudian and Jungian psychoanalyses*. New Orleans, LA: Spring Journal Books.
Kuipers, R. A. (2013). *Richard Rorty*. New York, NY: Bloomsbury Publishing.
Marlan, S. (2005). *The black sun: The alchemy and art of darkness*. College Station, TX: Texas A & M University Press.
Orfanos, D. (2006). Mythos and logos. *Psychoanalytic Dialogues, 16*(4), 481–99.
Reason, P., & Bradbury, H. (Eds.). (2006). *Handbook of action research: Concise paperback edition*. Thousand Oaks, CA: Sage.
Romanyshyn, R. (2004). *Technology as symptom and dream*. New York, NY: Brunner-Routledge.
Rowland, S. (2010). *C. G. Jung in the humanities: Taking the soul's path*. New Orleans, LA: Spring Journal Books.
Ryley, N. (1998). *The forsaken garden: Four conversations on the deep meaning of environmental illness*. Wheaton, IL: Quest Books.
Sardello, R. (2009). Foreword. In G. Thomas, *Healing Pandora: The restoration of hope and abundance* (pp. xi–xix). Berkeley, CA: North Atlantic Books.
Shearer, A. (2009). Unlocking the Titans: Unravelling a psychological Olympianism? *International Journal of Jungian Studies, 1*(1), 2–11.
Tarnas, R. (1991). *The passion of the Western mind: Understanding the ideas that have shaped our world view*. New York, NY: Harmony Books.
Tarnas, R. (1995). *Prometheus the awakener: An essay on the archetypal meaning of the planet Uranus*. Woodstock, CT: Spring.
Thomas, G. (2009). *Healing Pandora: The restoration of hope and abundance*. Berkeley, CA: North Atlantic Books.
Wilber, K. (2001). *The marriage of sense and soul: Integrating science and religion*. Dublin: Gateway.

Conclusion

Imagine once more that young Flemish anatomist of the Renaissance with which we began this tale, Andreas Vesalius. He gently slices into a female cadaver, a lifeless body. This is the body as object, a body made all the more objective by its de-animation. This is *körper*, corpse. Imagine the blue and white dappled sphere that is the third planet from the sun, the image as seen from satellites of the celestial body known as earth. Both bodies are made possible by a particular style of vision. Both bodies are seen by way of a geometric grid, established through vanishing points and horizon lines, the drawing of squares to be divided and subdivided, and the determination of a fixed vantage point, creating a plane that is measurable and quantifiable. Through this vision both anatomical and astronomical bodies are conceived, as spectacles *out there*. Witness these Cartesian and Copernican bodies. But also witness these words, these objects within your vision, signifiers that play one off of another in infinite variation. Among them appears the signifier *man*. Perhaps it impresses itself upon the lifeless female body we have invoked, inscribing itself like a tattoo. What does it mean, there, stenciled upon this anatomical mass?

As you read these words, feel the smooth, dry, granular surface of the pages, their lithe pliability as they are palmed and fingered, absorbing the oily perspiration of sustained attention. Or, perhaps, sense your vision focused upon the dark iridescent letters in sequence upon a screen until their meaning, it would seem, requires a turning of your head, a diffuse stare open to the peripheral. Notice the subtle, slow ebb of inhalation and exhalation that has continued beneath your awareness, sustaining it, making it possible. The inherited wisdom of many languages understands this breath as spirit or soul, anima and animus, the force that enlivens (Barnhart, 1995). This breathing somebody that you are is *leib*, the body as experiential locus and center of subjectivity. But are not these two bodies, the anatomical and animate, in actuality one? Yes, in a certain sense they certainly are.

Some consider the words you are reading, these words here, as being capable of producing meaning *only* by way of their play upon one another. But imagine that this simple word *play* has value for you not only by way of a highly developed, complex, and nuanced interaction of utterances written, read, spoken, heard, and thought. Imagine that your very embodiment, your existence as *leib*, holds all the experiences of your childhood play within it, in fact all the experiences of being a child in motion that inform your understanding of words like *play*, *movement*, and *dance*. Your infant body is still with you. Your somatic memory knows of the bouncy, tentative, awkward steps taken by you years ago and, perhaps, the presence of a responsive hand guiding you from behind, pushing you gently along (Rothschild, 2000). You know what it means to be pushed along *too hard*, *not enough*, and *just enough* because you have fallen, as I have, backwards and forwards, to one side or the other. You know this in the same way that mammal babies know to seek certain sensations and experiences and avoid others (Levine, 2010). You know how it feels to take a tumble, to roll, to stride forward, or to be caught off balance. There is memory of such experiences within you, and although each tumble, role, stride, or state of disequilibrium is unique to your person, and the particular place, moment, and situation in which it occurred, it is also, simultaneously, an experience shared by others; tumbling, rolling, striding, and teetering simply form part of our collective, human experience as embodied beings. Because this is so, reference to these experiences, in languages the world over, form the basis of metaphorical expressions that, in their very ubiquity, speak to a sense of meaning that cannot be reduced to the workings of arbitrary social constructs (Lakoff and Johnson 1999, 2003).

Körper, the body as object, is the image with which we began our tale, an initial association given to the primary symbol in a dream, a dream of multiple iterations and various guises: words do not refer to things; language is completely self-referential; the transcendental signified is absent. In attempting to elucidate something of the meaning in such affirmations and understand them as statements by and about psyche, a tale of radical alienation has unfolded: not only an alienation of words from things and signs from referents, but also of animate body and earth from anatomical body and earth. If previously we articulated this alienation as a loss of the immediacy of perception (among other losses), perhaps now it is time to find terms that speak to the recovery of this immediacy.

Husserl's student, Merleau-Ponty (Merleau-Ponty & Lefort, 1968) knew of such a recovery, and knew of the works of Saussure, Heidegger, and Wittgenstein, those nascent murmurings of what would later become, after his death, a postmodern era fascinated by semiotics. Although his work, like that of Derrida, took issue with Husserl's phenomenology, unlike Derrida, he did not shy from speaking of a perception not so exceedingly mediated by the workings of language as to prevent the most intimate of contact. He did not inveigh against the possibility of reaching *the thing itself*, or a *transcendental signified*. He did not place the other of language at an unreachable distance. Contact with a phenomenal, sensual, intuited world was not, for him, forever differed: "One can say that we perceive the things themselves, that we are the world that thinks itself-or that the world is at the heart of our flesh" (p. 136).

Flesh is the term developed by this pioneer of phenomenology to speak of the kindred nature, the consanguinity of human beings and the world we inhabit. Flesh is "the reciprocal presence of the sentient in the sensible and of the sensible in the sentient" (p. 67). It is, in this sense, not merely the body, as a material thing (an anatomical body), nor even the body as a condition of perception (an animate body). It can be sensed in the movement between the two, a movement that has pervaded the present work, a tacking back and forth between bodies that see and perceive and bodies that are seen and perceived. Flesh is not something proper to only living beings. The term speaks to the quality of reversibility: The touching hand is touchable. The viewing eye is visible. The sensate body is sensible. The tangible world is perceived by an equally tangible perceiver. Every object I touch also touches me. Because this is so, there is an element of affinity in all perception. I am akin to all that I see, touch, taste, smell, and hear insofar as I can be seen, touched, tasted, smelled, and heard. I am kindred to the world I inhabit. As seer, I am not foreign to the world that I see. In the act of seeing, vision is doubled "with another vision: myself seen from without, such as another would see me, installed in the midst of the visible, occupied in considering it from a certain spot" (Merleau-Ponty & Lefort, 1968, p. 134). There is for the French phenomenologist always an identity between the seer and the seen. This identity is not absolute; it does not preclude difference. The identity to which he refers is one in which the person "who sees cannot possess the visible unless he is possessed by it, unless he *is of it*" (pp. 134–5, original emphasis). There is always a connaturality at work between perceiver and perceived.

Though this specific understanding of flesh as reversibility does not appear in Merleau-Ponty's work until the unfinished, posthumously published *The Visible and the Invisible* (Merleau-Ponty & Lefort, 1968), one can sense its precursor in the notion of a *carnal generality* in another unfinished, posthumously published work *The Prose of the World* (1973). There, in a footnote reflecting on the relationship of speaker and spoken-to, he writes that language

> is founded on the phenomena of the mirror, ego-alter ego, or of the echo, in other words, of a carnal generality: what warms me, warms him; it is founded on the magical action of like upon like (the warm sun makes me warm), on the fusion of me embodied—and the world. This foundation does not prevent language from coming back dialectically over what preceded it and transforming the purely carnal and vital coexistence with the world and bodies into a coexistence of language. (p. 20 *n*)

What warms me warms you. We are kindred. I am "fused," as it were, with the world, and likewise are you. Our words can act as mirrors with which we reflect to ourselves, and to one another, this world of which we form a part. They echo, and are integral to, the carnal generality, the flesh, to which you and I also belong. Language is of the flesh, in the sense that it too, participates in this fundamental reversibility, not only because it can come back dialectically over what preceded it, but because "in every instance language resembles the objects and ideas expressed in it. Language is the double of being" (Merleau-Ponty, 1973, pp. 5–6). Through resemblance, through doubling, words participate in this carnal generality, this flesh that is the fundamental identity between, and reciprocal constitution of, perceiver and perceived, self and other—for, in speaking, "I point to a world around me which already speaks, just as I point my finger toward an object already in the visual field of others" (pp. 6–7). With this understanding of a carnal generality, "we now regard language as the reverberation of my relations with myself and with others" (p. 20). Because all phenomena intertwine or mirror one another as a common flesh our words intertwine and mirror as well.

Language, understood in this way, is not always already deferring presence, à la Derrida, as much as it is always already informed by it. It does not vitiate the immediacy of perception. It is not, as in an astronautic dream of distance, on one side of an impassable abyss. Not everything begins by way of representation. The primordial, the experiential, the perceptual, the sensual, the phenomenal, and the intuitive are not produced via semiosis. In this regard, Merleau-Ponty's understanding of language participating in a carnal generality challenges a general tendency within the linguistic turn, and all fields within the wake of this turn. This tendency undermines the presumed immediacy of perception, even the most seemingly immediate and indubitable perceptions of sense impressions, so that they can no longer serve as a court of appeal.

Flesh, or a carnal generality, might serve as a philosophical expression of Prometheus grounded, insofar as it speaks to the dialectical return of language over what preceded it, allowing for its vital coexistence with the world and bodies that inhabit it. This dialectical return is, metaphorically speaking, the moment when astronautic language touches the earth, or when souls inhabit linguistic bodies.

There are many ways to conceive of a return to the immediacy of experience, an overcoming of the abyss left by the death of the gods, many ways to envision a return to earth made necessary by an alienation of language from its other. One vision, other than Merleau-Ponty's, that might serve our own contemporary Promethean grounding is the semiotics of novelist-essayist Walker Percy. At the core of Percy's understanding of language is the notion of coupling. To use language is to couple, and this coupling forms a part of our natural genius as human beings. One aspect of this coupling is the "linking of semological elements (forms of experience) with phonological elements (forms of sound)" (Percy, 1975, p. 308). Through this activity, humans acquire semological-phonological complexes that Percy calls "semophones." This linking takes place in the very ontogenesis of language. As a child acquires more and more semophones, he or she is able to combine them to form increasingly complex sentences. The child has "a sudden inkling that the thing ball 'is' the sound ball" (p. 308)—that the semological element is the phonological element—and this is the "progenitor not only of all future sentences about balls but also of his grasp of metaphor, art, and music" (p. 308).

This essential linking of experience and sound is but one type of coupling. Placing both subject and predicate in a sentence is another. The formation of metaphor is yet another. When I say that DNA is a blueprint or that there is a fire in my belly, I have coupled by way of metaphor; I have linked two distinct elements by way of the verb *is*. I have thereby established an identity. Although the statements *DNA is a blueprint* and *This is a pencil* may seem quite different in the sense that one is metaphorical while the other may be a statement of fact (depending on what the *this* refers to), they are not so different as they appear. Both establish an identity between disparate elements. The identity of disparate elements in the sentence *This is a pencil* involves our letting the word *pencil* stand in for, or be, an actual pencil. It is as if there is always a fundamental analogical or metaphorical assumption at work in language that says *language is like the other of language* or *language = not language*. So the object I write with is a *pencil*. Or as Percy says, "*Yellow* becomes yellow" (p. 317).

This fundamental coupling of experience with sound, or, to use Percy's terminology, semological elements with phonological elements, has not been widely recognized in the triumphant traditions of modern linguistics. A wide variety of dominant theoretical approaches all share an important trait in common—they approach their subject matter

> through a formal analysis of the corpora of languages, an analysis which abstracts both from the people who speak the language and the things they talk about. Semantics or the relation between words and things . . . is treated by and large like a bastard at a family reunion . . . "experience" is stuck onto an otherwise neat hierarchy of phonemes, morphemes, and such, somewhat like a sore thumb. (p. 299)

Yet even within the field of semantics, Percy tells us, the imputed identity between word and thing is deplored as a calamity because it leads to reifying meanings and "word magic" (p. 260). This "word magic" goes by the name of *logocentrism* or *a metaphysics of presence* in Derrida's thought and *différance* is the conceptual undermining of the imputed identity of which Percy speaks; it is a forceful subordination of identity to difference, the establishment of the logical priority of the latter over the former (Dews, 1994). Percy's attitude towards the identity between word and thing, sign and referent, signifier and signified is not to render it suspect or problematic. Rather, he simply allows for a fundamental analogical or metaphorical assumption at work in language. He replaces a hermeneutics of suspicion and radical differences with one of trust in an identity between language and its other.

Percy's semiotics, with its ample berth given to both extralinguistic experience and the mooring of this experience to language by way of semophones, harbors within itself a potentially scandalous conclusion for those (with Promethean fervor) who might see the study of signs as a final escape from the tyranny of metaphysics: Semiotics, rather than being "the *coup de grace* of metaphysics . . . validates a classical metaphysical relation" (p. 245). Or, more precisely, it validates two relations, the first of which is the relation of identity by which "a 'formal sign,' comes to contain within itself *in alio esse* the thing signified" (p. 246). The second metaphysical relation it reveals is the relation of intersubjectivity without which no talk of language and meaning would be possible. Indeed, for Percy, semiotics is a unique opportunity that, rather than negating the possibility of a philosophy of being, an onto-theology in Derridean terms, actually provides the opportunity for the renewal of such a philosophy.

References

Barnhart, R. K. (1995). *The Barnhart concise dictionary of etymology*. New York, NY: HarperCollins.

Dews, P. (1994). Adorno, poststructuralism, and the critique of identity. In S. Žižek (Ed.), *Mapping ideology*. (pp. 46–64). New York, NY: Verso.

Lakoff, G., & Johnson, M. (1999). *Philosophy in the flesh: The embodied mind and its challenge to Western thought*. New York, NY: Basic Books.

Lakoff, G., & Johnson, M. (2003). *Metaphors we live by*. Chicago, IL: University of Chicago Press.

Levine, P. A. (2010). *In an unspoken voice: How the body releases trauma and restores goodness*. Berkeley, CA: North Atlantic Books.

Merleau-Ponty, M. (1973). *The prose of the world*. Evanston, IL: Northwestern University Press.

Merleau-Ponty, M., & Lefort, C. (1968). *The visible and the invisible: Followed by working notes*. Evanston, IL: Northwestern University Press.

Percy, W. (1975). *The message in the bottle: How queer man is, how queer language is, and what one has to do with the other*. New York, NY: Farrar, Straus and Giroux.

Rothschild, B. (2000). *The body remembers: The psychophysiology of trauma and trauma treatment*. New York, NY: Norton.

Index

Made in the USA
Monee, IL
13 September 2026

62977544R00092